Becoming a Nation

Americana from the Diplomatic Reception Rooms
U.S. Department of State

Jonathan L. Fairbanks,
Guest Curator
Gerald W. R. Ward, Editor

Becoming a Nation

Americana from the Diplomatic Reception Rooms
U.S. Department of State

RIZZOLI
NEW YORK

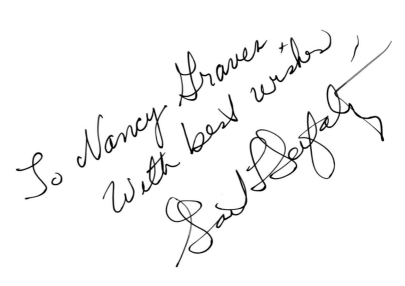

Cover: Entrance Hall, Diplomatic Reception Rooms, 1979, designed by Edward Vason Jones

Half-title: Detail, Fitz Hugh Lane, View of Boston Harbor (see pages 180-81)

Title page: Benjamin Franklin State Dining Room, set for formal entertaining, designed by John Blatteau, 1985

Contents: Plaster ceiling medallion, Benjamin Franklin State Dining Room

Acknowledgments: Treaty Room, 1986, designed by Allan Greenberg

Secretary's Message: Office of the Secretary of State, 1984, designed by Allan Greenberg

The Catalogue: Detail, Newport tall-case clock

ISBN (hardcover edition): 0-8478-2528-0
ISBN (paperback edition): 0-8478-2584-1

Library of Congress Cataloging-in-Publication Data available upon request

2003 2004 2005 2006/10 9 8 7 6 5 4 3 2 1

PHOTOGRAPHY CREDITS

All entries in the catalogue photographed by Will Brown. Views of the Diplomatic Reception Rooms before renovation, courtesy of the U.S. Department of State. Views of the Diplomatic Reception Rooms after renovation by Richard Cheek except for the following which are by Breger and Associates, Inc.: Entrance Hall, cover; Elevator Hall, page 19; John Quincy Adams State Drawing Room, page 30; Entrance Hall, page 41; and The Gallery, page 175.

All images shown in detail also appear in their entirety elsewhere in the catalogue.

Designed by Abigail Sturges

Printed in Belgium

Exhibition Itinerary

Portland Art Museum
Portland, Oregon
April 11–June 8, 2003

Georgia Museum of Art
Athens, Georgia
July 3–August 31, 2003

Fresno Metropolitan Museum
Fresno, California
September 26–December 14, 2003

Society of the Four Arts
Palm Beach, Florida
January 2–February 8, 2004

Cincinnati Art Museum
Cincinnati, Ohio
February 27–April 25, 2004

Huntsville Museum of Art
Huntsville, Alabama
May 21–July 18, 2004

Sioux City Art Center
Sioux City, Iowa
August 13–October 10, 2004

Portland Museum of Art
Portland, Maine
November 4, 2004–January 2, 2005

**THIS CATALOGUE WAS MADE POSSIBLE
THROUGH THE GENEROSITY OF**

The Americana Foundation
in honor of Clement E. Conger

Anonymous Donors

The Bobolink Foundation
in memory of Henry M. Paulson

Mr. and Mrs. Carlyle C. Eubank II and family

Mrs. O. Ray Moore

Arnold and Marie Schwartz Fund
for Education and Health Research

Betty R. Wright

Contents

Acknowledgments / 9

Message from the Secretary of State / 10

Preface / 12

Introduction: Becoming a Nation / 22

The Catalogue / 37

Charting the New World:
Views and Visions of America / 38

The Look of Colonial America:
Commerce and Crafts, Artisans and Patrons / 58

The Road to Independence:
Statesmen and Diplomats / 98

A Nation United:
Neoclassicism in the Federal Era / 126

The Nation Expands Westward:
Discovery, Bounty, and Beauty / 168

Notes / 215

Contributors / 225

Bibliography / 226

Index / 230

Acknowledgments

The idea for *Becoming a Nation* germinated over a long period of time. Finally, in January 2000, Gail Serfaty, Director of the Diplomatic Reception Rooms, decided that the time was just right. The time, that is, to share with Americans throughout our country, glorious examples of furniture, paintings, porcelains and silver from the Reception Rooms that vividly and dramatically document the founding of our Nation. And thus, a beautiful and historically significant exhibition began to take form.

Founding fathers and America's first diplomats George Washington, Thomas Jefferson, James Monroe, James Madison, and John Quincy Adams come to life for us through portraits by the great painters of America's colonial and Federal periods: Gilbert Stuart, Charles Willson Peale, Thomas Sully, Charles Bird King, and John Singleton Copley. America's finest craftsmen reveal for us the truly magnificent furniture and silver that in sophistication equaled anything produced in England at the time. The exhibition is replete with works by renowned artisans, including Goddard and Townsend, Benjamin Frothingham, Joseph Delaveau, and Paul Revere. In fact, these treasures sumptuously displayed on the eighth floor of the U. S. Department of State—and assembled in elegant surroundings to entertain thousands of distinguished foreign visitors each year—actually belong to the American people, few of whom have the opportunity to see them in situ.

The Trust for Museum Exhibitions (TME) is honored that it was invited to assist the Diplomatic Reception Rooms of the Department of State in organizing and touring this unequalled collection, and we would like to express our gratitude to Secretary of State Colin Powell and to Gail Serfaty and her staff (Patricia Heflin and Lynn Turner) for making the State Department holdings available for this exhibition. Gail, in turn, would like to recognize Under Secretary Bonnie R. Cohen and Under Secretary Grant Green for enthusiastically supporting the exhibition during its inception and organization.

We were fortunate to have the talents of Jonathan Fairbanks and Gerry Ward in the writing and editing of this catalogue as well as the many other scholars who wrote the catalogue entries and Marilyn Mazer who assisted with the preface. We are also indebted to Isabel Venero, our editor at Rizzoli, for her dedication to this project, to Abigail Sturges, our designer, and to Val Lewton and Clifford La Fontaine for the design expertise they brought to the exhibition presentation.

We would like to acknowledge Rick Yamada and the staff at Ely Inc. for providing the finest crates for decorative arts and furniture for the exhibition tour and Jack Ring at Ramar (United) Moving Systems, Inc., for providing specialized fine arts shipping from venue to venue. To ready the State Department's beautiful objects for a long, trans-continental tour we are indebted to the following extraordinary conservators: William B. Adair, Thom Gentle, Victoria Jeffries, Robert Mussey, and Christine Thompson.

Most importantly, we should recognize that the preparations for this exhibition have revolved around TME's Exhibitions Office and realized through the superb performance of Diane Salisbury, Director of Exhibitions. We would also like to recognize our Chief Registrar, Christopher Whittington, for his tireless work in organizing the packing, shipping, and conditioning of the exhibition works, which he could not have completed without the direct involvement of Lynn Turner, State Department Registrar. Both Diane and Christopher have benefited greatly from the assistance of TME's staff and volunteers: Lewis Townsend, Ginger Crockett, Cynthia Spain, Cindy Salyards, Jerry Saltzman, Alice Rowen, and Gill Heyert.

Finally, we herald the generosity of the participating museums that have brought such enthusiasm to this project.

Ann Van Devanter Townsend
Chairman, Trust for Museum Exhibitions

The Diplomatic Reception Rooms of the Department of State are not only cultural treasures, they are invaluable diplomatic assets for our country. Appointed with fine and decorative arts of the 18th and 19th centuries, they serve as the setting for hundreds of official events every year.

The Heads of State and Government, Foreign Ministers and other distinguished visitors I host in these beautiful surroundings cannot help but come away with a better appreciation of America's early history and the richness of our cultural heritage. Guests also come away with a better appreciation of the extent to which democratic ideas have infused all aspects of our national life -- and not least American arts -- from our nation's very beginning.

Those of us who have the privilege of entertaining in the Reception Rooms on behalf of the American people do so with great pride. I am delighted that *Becoming a Nation* now gives the public a chance to enjoy 170 pieces from this outstanding collection of Americana as it travels to eight cities across our country.

Colin L. Powell

Preface

GAIL F. SERFATY
Director, Diplomatic Reception Rooms

The Diplomatic Reception Rooms of the Department of State are a genuine American success story. They fulfill a vision first articulated a mere forty years ago: to provide United States secretaries of state with an environment of rare beauty and civility in which to host official diplomatic events. Today, those responsible for carrying out America's foreign policy proudly preside over formal dinners and ceremonies, casual meetings and quiet conversations in rooms of classical balance and dignity. Their guests—kings and presidents, diplomats and foreign ministers—readily sense the American spirit in these spaces. This book and the exhibition it accompanies offer a glimpse into this elegant yet home-like, very American milieu. We hope you will be proud of what you see.

The objects gathered here are the cream of the Collection of the Diplomatic Reception Rooms. Each work is a superb example of American design—redolent with

Previous pages: James Monroe Reception Room, 1960;
James Monroe Room Reception Room, 1983, designed
by Walter M. Macomber

Left: The Gallery, 1960

Opposite: The Gallery, 1969, designed by Edward Vason Jones

important historic or diplomatic associations. Each has been acquired by the State Department in a unique, American way, entirely through the generosity of patriotic donors.

The Americana collection formed so recently and in such public-spirited fashion is now considered one of the three finest in the country. Its purpose, though, sets it apart from the great collections at the Winterthur Museum and the Metropolitan Museum of Art. These supreme examples of the American craftsmanship of the eighteenth and early nineteenth centuries are in daily use at the State Department. Probably nowhere in the United States, not even in the White House, is entertaining done more often for so many amid such a fine collection. One hundred thousand guests are hosted here annually, and public tours that are worked in among these engagements draw an additional sixty thousand visitors a year.

For all their importance, these objects are part of an accessible, democratic environment. Now, for the first time ever, we are proud to make them accessible outside Washington, D.C., sending them to museums in regions across the country that do not have their own major decorative arts collections. As traveling ambassadors, we hope they will also bring Americans an enhanced understanding of the work of the State Department.

While many of the most important pieces are traveling, others have been redistributed so that the rooms remain elegant. Where a particularly fine piece was too fragile to travel, another was substituted. We excluded some objects because their unique associations with our history make them absolutely irreplaceable.

I could think of no one better able to put all the treasures in the exhibition in the context of the history of this country than Jonathan Fairbanks, guest curator. I knew he would draw not only on his enormous curatorial expertise and familiarity with the Collection but also on his love of

American history and his interest in all the fine and decorative arts. Indeed, Jonathan contributed his expertise to the first book devoted to this collection. *Treasures of State*, published in 1991 and edited by Clement E. Conger and Alexandra W. Rollins, was a key step in bringing the Collection to the attention of a wide audience and in getting much of the Collection conserved and photographed. The current exhibition is a logical outgrowth of that project and goes beyond by sharing not only the printed word with the general public but a significant selection of the actual objects from the Collection as well. The theme Jonathan selected for this new book, *Becoming a Nation,* skillfully weaves the objects into the stages of our early history—discovery, colonial growth, revolutionary change, federal consolidation, and westward expansion.

As I reflect upon it, the development of the Diplomatic Reception Rooms in modern times somewhat echoes these stages. Like our republic, the collection began with a brilliant, implausible idea, then quickly grew from small beginnings to great things. As Jonathan Fairbanks writes in his Introduction, when the State Department headquarters were built in 1961, the eighth floor suite allotted for official diplomatic entertaining was devoid of dignity. Clement Conger, who later became the legendary first curator of the rooms, looked at these vast, sparsely furnished rooms and envisioned civilized spaces for civilized discourse. He believed that if furnished with the finest examples of American artistic ingenuity the eighth-floor would provide an optimum environment for advancing foreign policy.

Clem was then special assistant to the director and secretary of the Arms Control and Disarmament Agency, but he volunteered to form a Fine Arts Committee. I was straight out of college with a full-time job in another section at the State Department. For a number of years, Clem, my colleague Pat Heflin, and I, propelled by optimism, naiveté, hard work, and resourcefulness born of utter lack of money, carried out the work of the Fine Arts Committee on the weekends.

Through Clem's extraordinary vision, courage, and enthusiasm, and with the support of both the Fine Arts Committee and the Diplomatic Rooms Endowment Fund, the Diplomatic Reception Rooms did gradually become, like our nation, self-sustaining, independent, sure of their mission, successful, and solvent—a strong federal entity. Though the project moved along in sometimes halt-

ing stages of acquisition and refinement, it grew to encompass 42 rooms with 5,000 objects worth over $100 million. The first of their kind in the country, the Diplomatic Reception Rooms are now among the most beautiful public spaces in America.

At the outset, we chose to seek out citizens' support rather than government funding. Foreign visitors to the Diplomatic Reception Rooms are surprised to learn that private donors, corporations, and foundations have contributed every object, or the funds to acquire it. While this is a new idea to those who come from systems where such largess would only be government-initiated, in the United States it is an old idea for private citizens to donate time and resources to public projects. It has been common practice since patriotic colonists like Bostonian Ebenezer Storer, whose chest of drawers is presented here, helped to underwrite the American Revolution. We each make our own decisions about charitable giving, and our government gives us a subsidy for doing so in the form of a tax deduction. In this way, citizens define where support will be extended, and this, I believe is uniquely American and democratic.

It was truly amazing to witness the degree to which Americans immediately defined this project as worthy of their funds, their treasures, and their counsel. The very fact that it was to be a public space propelled their generosity. Donors took patriotic pleasure in the idea that their gifts would be in the public domain, not in a private collection or a small museum that might be visited infrequently. They were proud that these objects would be in our nation's capital, available not only for world leaders to enjoy, but also for the public, unlike in many foreign ministries.

With such a large area to fill, the first task was simply to try to furnish unpromising spaces. This gathering of resources was, I suppose, our colonial phase, and we did not realize quite where it would lead us. We needed sideboards for the dining room and chairs for the drawing room. Mostly, we needed donors willing to take a leap of faith, and we found them. Mark Bortman was one of them. He was an elderly gentleman, a wonderful collector of New England silver, who would arrive at the State Department, very often with just a paper or cloth bag in hand. Out of it would come a

Paul Revere pot or a bowl, or a piece done by Myer Myers, the eighteenth-century silversmith. He brought an Indian peace medal in a paper bag and said, "This is yours." It was always like Christmas when he came. His enthusiasm was just catching. A sauceboat, a tankard, a coffeepot, and a peace medal described in these pages were all gifts from his family in his memory.

Dealers, collectors, and scholars shared their knowledge in an enormously supportive way, and their gifts flowed into the State Department. Collecting and studying American decorative arts only began in earnest in the twentieth century, and it is still a young field. Its devotees have proved uniquely generous. They often alerted us to appropriate items and their whereabouts. When we did not own much and we were dependent on loans to give the rooms a slightly furnished look, Benjamin Ginsburg was the very first dealer to help us out. Harold Sack of Israel Sack, Inc., was a great mentor to all of us, and to me, in particular. No one was as generous as Richard Dietrich, a Fine Arts Committee member, who lent more than a hundred pieces of porcelain, silver, paintings, and furniture from the Dietrich Americana Foundation.

As Clem used to say, "Nothing succeeds like success," and once people saw how the rooms were developing even more joined in. Gifts came in from people in all walks of life.

Some were great collectors like Lansdell Christie, who donated a high chest and low chest. Alice Harrison Warwick took great interest in the Collection and came by from time to time, having driven across country from California with her elderly dog. She brought us treasures of silver, including a wonderful rococo teapot and a silver coffeepot, which appear in these pages.

Family pride emerged as a strong impetus to giving. We received an extraordinary gift of silver by Elias Pelletreau, a well-known eighteenth-century silversmith of Long Island. The silver was donated by his descendants, Mr. and Mrs. Robert H. Pelletreau, in honor of their son, Robert H. Pelletreau, Jr., a career Foreign Service officer who had served as ambassador to Tunisia and Egypt and Assistant Secretary of State for the Middle East. We were very moved by this wonderful gift that had been in the family for so many years. They even included the weights that Pelletreau used to weigh out his silver.

The important portraits of John Quincy Adams and his wife, Louisa Catherine Johnson Adams, included here, were the gift of three Adams descendants. The three of them found themselves in possession of the two portraits, which could not be divided up, and gave them in memory of their father, Robert Homans. We have also purchased many objects directly from families. Most commonly, though, we have acquired objects from dealers or at auction, often with funds that were donated by small family foundations.

After almost ten years of Collection-building, the mahogany furniture, fine clocks, Chinese export porcelain, and the images of our founding generation acutely needed an appropriate setting. In 1969, we launched our Revolutionary phase and began to replace the motel environment of the rooms through major architectural improvements. One by one, the rooms began to blossom architecturally in a somewhat haphazard pattern until the last one was complete in 1985. They were an astonishing success, and Jonathan Fairbanks describes their development in the Introduction.

Beginning with Dean Rusk in 1961, all secretaries of state have actively involved themselves in the Americana project to furnish the rooms. They are, after all, responsible for more official entertaining than any other public figures in the United States. Several, including Secretaries Rogers, Kissinger, Shultz, Vance, and Baker have supported the rooms financially with personal gifts. Secretary Rusk secured the loan of Houdon's bust of Benjamin Franklin, and kept it

prominently displayed on his desk so that he might solicit funds for its purchase from among any likely visitors inclined to help. It is now in the Thomas Jefferson State Reception Room.

Secretary Rusk also had the idea to name each room after a secretary of state who went on to become president. He made one exception, though—Benjamin Franklin. Franklin was neither secretary nor president but he was one of the most beloved ambassadors to serve our country. Considered the father of American diplomacy, he was also one of Secretary Rusk's favorite statesmen. Thus we have the Benjamin Franklin State Dining Room. The period of great founding statesmen—among them Adams, Jefferson, Monroe, and Madison—fortuitously coincides with the golden age of American cabinetmaking, which is the period from which the objects for the rooms were selected.

In 1984, after the great success of the Diplomatic Reception Rooms on the eighth floor, the full panoply of dramatic enhancements moved on to the seventh floor offices of the secretary of state, the deputy secretary, and the Treaty Room area. Secretary George P. Shultz moved out of

his office suite, claiming no other secretary of state would be willing to do so, and gave us exactly six months to complete the renovations. We met his deadline to the day.

I particularly enjoyed the opportunity to work with Secretary Shultz. Having worked for the architect/engineering firm Bechtel, he understood blueprints and design. I met with him on numerous occasions to go over everything from space flow issues (his particular interest) to the colors of rooms.

Secretary William P. Rogers also took a particular interest in the architectural changes, though all the secretaries were inclined to stop and scrutinize the extraordinary skill of the master craftsmen working in their midst. Secretary Henry A. Kissinger, who used to tease that we were making everything eighteenth century, including his office, chose wonderful modern art for his walls.

Initially the secretaries used the gradually evolving reception areas only for formal state occasions. As the rooms became increasingly handsome, more and more people wanted to entertain in them, and the variety of official events grew into the lively, varied, and unending mix it is today.

Now, between five and twenty-five times a week, the secretary of state, assistant secretaries, the vice president, and members of the Cabinet use the rooms to host dinners, receptions, press conferences, and ceremonies that are international in nature.

Happily, Secretary Rusk and his successors also discovered that the gleaming, historic ambiance of the rooms proved highly conducive not only to entertaining but also to harmonious diplomatic discussion. Many secretaries have told me that meeting in the comfort and ease of the rooms, rather than in formal conference-table environments, has actually facilitated negotiations.

Of all the secretaries of state, none has been a more active champion of the rooms than Secretary of State Colin Powell. He has been photographed here probably more than any other secretary. He has chosen whenever possible to officiate at functions, personally swearing in almost every American ambassador going abroad and all incoming classes of Foreign Service personnel—occasions normally presided over by the deputy secretary or another member of the State Department. He has always used these occasions to talk about the rooms, and ask for donor support for acquisitions and maintenance.

Secretary Powell tells me that when things get very sticky in meetings in his office, he'll say, "Well, let's take a break and visit the eighth floor," and then he will give his guests his own personal tour. In fact he unhesitatingly gives tours to students and world leaders alike. I have, on many occasions, come out of a room and unexpectedly found him giving forty-five schoolchildren a tour, walking backwards

as he speaks about the artists. The children are mesmerized. His favorite object in the rooms is the desk that Thomas Jefferson commissioned during the Continental Congress.

With the rooms now humming with diplomatic activity, the original mission had been fulfilled. We had arrived at our Federal period. Our identity was established. We had achieved an ambiance suitable for American statesmen to promote and create American foreign policy.

Large-scale diplomatic entertaining, American-style, is in place, and on any given evening, there might be an example of it underway. The gathering might typically be an equal mix of foreign dignitaries and heads of state and their counterparts in the United States. Guests arrive, then traverse the State Department's clinically modern Diplomatic Lobby. They are whisked up to the eighth floor in an elevator, and step out into a splendid, thirteen-foot-high room with pilasters and cornices, and paneling inspired by the drawing room at a great colonial house in Virginia called Marmion. This moment of surprise and delight for newcomers is one that I still experience myself. Each time I get off the elevator, it is as if it were for the first time.

Guests move through the Entrance Hall, lined with some of the finest examples of colonial furniture made in Boston, Newport, and Philadelphia. There are greetings, a receiving line, cocktails, perhaps a stroll on the balcony to view the monuments, and then dinner. After dinner, guests are free to visit all the rooms. Paintings on view extend beyond the era of colonial portraiture in order to include the great American landscapes of the nineteenth century. The furniture, silver, and porcelain date from 1740 to 1825. It is fortuitous that foreign leaders are entertained first at the Department of State by the secretary of state, and then go to the White House to be entertained by the president and first lady, where they can then view the subsequent era of nineteenth-century American furniture.

Every object in the rooms is intrinsically interesting and approachable. What guests see are the taste, optimism, self-reliance, and self-confidence of both the twentieth-century Americans who generously donated these objects and our immigrant forebears who crafted and commissioned them.

So much dignity, beauty, and sophistication comes as a surprise to foreign visitors, who may not have imagined that such craftsmanship was possible when we were still such a young country. For them the rooms are a sudden and grati-

Below: Treaty Room, 1960

Opposite: Treaty Room, 1986,
designed by Allan Greenberg

fying immersion in eighteenth-century American decorative arts. Though they may come to Washington frequently, they tend to stay only briefly, and time constraints prevent them from visiting museums and historic sites. Often they leave without having experienced America's history or cultural achievements.

We want guests to feel as if they are visiting a fine eighteenth-century American home, though we do not mean to suggest that any American family in the eighteenth century ever actually lived with such a quantity of high-style furniture, chandeliers, and fine rugs. Our color palette is strong enough to enhance even these large spaces, and simple enough to convey warmth. The furniture is pleasantly scaled, sturdy, tall, and boldly designed. Though wonderfully crafted, it is not overly ornamented, elaborately painted, or highly gilded. Richness is expressed in the gloss and figure of mahogany, in the liveliness of crisp carving. The form and utility of a piece is always clearly expressed. The case pieces were intended to hold clothing or books or papers. These large formal rooms feel comforting, natural, and even organic.

By the time the evening's dinner guests leave, they should feel that they have been graciously entertained, they have enhanced their knowledge of American history, and the

Department of State has represented itself in a style appropriate to a great republic.

Now that the rooms are quite furnished, and the last of the architectural changes have been made, our primary mandate has become to maintain the Collection in the finest state of conservation and preservation, and build an endowment fund to keep it that way for centuries to come. Yet, there remains a need to raise funds for great acquisitions—particularly of pieces that relate to early United States diplomatic history or that are unique to America. For example, early scenes of American cities, portraits of Dolley Madison and Elizabeth Monroe, and a Boston japanned high chest are sought to complete the Collection.

Recent acquisitions include a plate from a dinner service purchased by Dolley and James Madison when he was secretary of state and subsequently brought to the White House, and a classical New York card table attributed to Duncan Phyfe. The table is documented as having been owned by Henry Clay when he was secretary of state under John Quincy Adams. Both of these objects are included here.

Fortunately, the idea has remained constant among donors, from the earliest to the most recent; that the Department of State should show the best there is of America's cultural heritage. Donations continue to come from Americans from all walks of life. Since the inception of the Americana project, 1,165 donors have contributed funds or donated objects to the Collection.

With this exhibition, the Collection enters a westward expansion phase that may in time extend to international outreach. Wherever the Collection may travel, we hope visitors will come away with an appreciation for the objects and a better understanding of how they fit into American diplomatic history.

The exhibition will certainly succeed if it provides the impetus for many people to visit the State Department so that they may see that the objects look even more beautiful when they are all together. As wonderful as these objects are in the Diplomatic Rooms setting, they are never as beautiful or as right as when the rooms are full of people. That is the way the Collection was meant to be seen. We believe that everyone who experiences the Collection, whether at an event or on a tour, will take away the same enormous pride that we all have in working here and in having been a small part of putting the Collection together.

Becoming a Nation

Jonathan L. Fairbanks

*A*merica has undergone so many changes that it is difficult to comprehend what civilization and the "polite arts" were like during this country's formative years between 1730 and 1840. However, the objects in this volume, and the exhibition it accompanies, open a window to this era. Made for and owned by Americans in the years that led to nationhood, they are grouped into five thematic sections. The sections move chronologically from the early years of the eighteenth century through the 1840s, the era when the nation began its expansion across the continent.

All of the works presented here are drawn from the Collection of the Diplomatic Reception Rooms of the United States Department of State in Washington, D.C. The Collection was brilliantly assembled in order to provide the Department of State and the nation with beautiful and suitable surroundings for the benefit of American statesmanship. No other collection in America has been created with such a singular mandate.

The Collection was formed by Clement E. Conger, its founding curator, and his staff, with the invaluable assistance of individuals and family donors—of both specific objects and of acquisition funds. Every one of these precious objects was collected at no expense to the citizen-taxpayers of this country. This Collection represents, therefore, both enormous generosity on the part of the donors and a singular comprehension of the past as envisioned by Clement Conger. He chose works having both extraordinary aesthetics and meaning. They possess great beauty and craftsmanship but also serve as important documents, shedding light on our history and the growth of the nation.

The Confluence of History and Design in Colonial and Federal America

Mute objects from the past offer visitors few clues about the intellectual and political ferment that generated their design and production. Yet few citizens today who appreciate how this nation came into being are unaware of the lasting achievements of the Founding Fathers. Very real connections exist between these extraordinary works of art and the underlying principles that shaped the views of the time when the people of the British colonies of North America chose a common destiny. They joined the colonies together under the banner of liberty to form the United States.

When the pre-Revolutionary objects in this volume were made, many Anglo-American colonials had learned from the great thinkers abroad about new and enlightened concepts concerning natural order in the universe. These had been expressed a century earlier by Francis Bacon, the French rationalist René Descartes, the physicist Isaac Newton, and the philosopher John Locke, whose influential *Essay Concerning Human Understanding* was published in 1690, just three years after *Newton's Philosophiae Naturalis Principia Mathematica*. By 1700 the printing presses of western nations had saturated the reading public with information about the "natural world." For British colonials in North America during the Enlightenment of the eighteenth century, the word "natural" meant "good" or pleasing. Order was good; disorder was bad. Things believed unnatural, such as poverty or pain, were the result of disorder.[1]

New knowledge was acquired through direct observation and analysis; beauty was judged by sensory experience. In 1753 the great British painter and satirical printmaker William Hogarth (1697–1764) published his *Analysis of Beauty*, in which he claimed that the slim S line was the fundamental source of beautiful design, as it activates the eye and leads it on a "merry chase." Hogarth's works were well known in this country, for his prints were widely circulated.

The search for principles that governed beauty was but one aspect of the Enlightenment. Rational analysis by British colonials in North America also led thoughtful leaders to assert natural rights for representative government. One can view this as a bold experiment with the social order or as the logical conclusion to their understanding of natural laws first articulated by philosophers abroad and, after thorough study and debate, applied to New World circumstances.

Art developed in similar ways through analysis, collective efforts, and applied skills, and also through a proliferation of printed images and opinions of writers who advocated new stylistic adaptations to old, classicist models from abroad. New and old inspirational sources shaped the material world of architecture, furniture, silver, and other arts as similar sources influenced the logic of order in law, commerce, and government. Although it may be difficult to reveal visible and literal connections between the abstract principles governing the development of a new nation, and the progress in the history of the three-dimensional arts, the very founders who shaped the nation would have sensed many relationships between both activities. Cohesiveness resulted from their adopting and adapting the best that they knew from British law and from the arts of design from the mother country.

Like other British subjects, Americans also studied sixteenth-century Italian sources, such as the works of architect Andrea Palladio (1508–1580). Editions of Renaissance books and British illustrated books were consulted in order to understand early artistic canons. The ancient past also inspired colonials, who turned to the Republic of Rome for inspirational models for art and government. Rational balance of power for proper representation of the people was at the heart of the new government. Likewise, geometrical balance was a pervasive theme in the arts of design.

Stitched throughout this accumulated appreciation of arts and wisdom from the classical world was another strand—a fascination with the Far East that expressed itself with imported tea, silk, spices, and ceramic wares from China. Although trade between Europe and China began as early as 1517, British provincials in North America participated in a later "mania" for things Asian that can be well documented to the 1720s, when furniture decorated with simulated lacquer-work known as japanning began to be produced in urban shops, primarily in Boston. Colonials imported Chinese porcelain from Holland, England, and the Continent, where tin-glazed earthenware was also produced and exported to supply the consumer's need for objects produced in the Chinese taste. This vogue for consumer goods made by or inspired by Asian civilizations is now called *chinoiserie*. It provided imaginative freedom from the formal order of patterns of the classical world—inviting asymmetry and exoticism to coexist and to adapt with changing styles as trade expanded and knowledge of ancient worlds, both classical and Asian, flourished. The form of many objects pro-

duced in early America—tea tables, chairs, teapots, bowls, and others—was profoundly influenced by shapes perfected by Far Eastern artisans many generations before. For example, Paul Revere's silver bowl of about 1795 made for Boston merchant Moses Michael Hays probably derived its form from a Dutch delft bowl, which, in turn, imitated a Chinese porcelain punch bowl (cat. no. 85).

The most famous piece of Chinese export porcelain in this exhibition was purchased for George Washington by Colonel Henry Lee in 1789 as part of a dinner service of 302 pieces (cat. no. 50). Today, pieces from this set are among the rarest and most sought-after China-trade porcelain. The Collection's piece displays a "Fitzhugh" border in underglaze blue and in its center features an angel of fame trumpeting and holding the badge of the Society of the Cincinnati.[2]

Such themes of classicism, Asian influence, and patriotism run throughout the State Department's Collection. During the past forty years, these works were assembled and displayed not only to provide handsome appointments for great ceremonial rooms but also to dispel misguided notions

the buyer shared precepts about what constituted good design, workmanship, and government.

No controlling guilds governed craft production in early America, but apprenticeship systems did. Some seven years earnestly spent with a mentor "at the bench" in a workshop, studio, or office was and still is an effective way for a craftsman/artist/designer/merchant to learn the "art and mystery" of a trade. Not all masters fulfilled their promise to adequately clothe, house, and instruct. Not all apprentices performed their agreed-upon duties faithfully. Yet those who kept their promise helped complex ideas, attitudes, and skills concerning design and workmanship transfer from one generation to another.

Under this system, tradition was far more important than innovation.[3] Both clients and master craftsmen were familiar with imported trade books for ordering such useful things as tools and manufactured parts such as furniture brasses. Also, illustrated design books, filled with engraved plates of designs in the newest fashion from the mother country, were essential for a craftsman to keep stylistically current and competitive with imported furniture, silver, or other crafted work. Such books were almost always prefaced with a discussion of *symmetry*. This usually was explained and illustrated with the classical orders of architecture followed by an analysis of many complex proportional divisions or systems of measurement inherent in all designs either made by mankind, reflective of the human body, or found in nature. The British cabinetmaker Thomas Sheraton (1751–1806) opened his influential work *The Cabinet-Maker and Upholsterer's Drawing-Book* (London, 1791)—a surviving copy of which, now at the Museum of Fine Arts, Boston, was owned and used by Boston's master cabinetmaker Thomas Seymour (1771–1848)—with the following statement: "Time alters fashions and frequently obliterates the works of art and ingenuity; but that which is founded on Geometry & real Science, will remain unalterable."

Craftsman and client both appreciated and understood in differing degrees what was meant by these words. Sheraton's statement was not unique. Thomas Chippendale (1718–1779), an even more famous British cabinetmaker who published his folio-size *Gentleman and Cabinet-Maker's Director* in London in 1754, was also an author whose publications were well known by cabinetmakers in most port towns of British North America. As did Sheraton's, his work emphasized the importance of basing designs on the classical architectural orders. This, of course, involved the study of parts, proportions, and

that this country was born of an unlearned or rude populace that possessed neither a civilized culture nor a developed taste. The Collection formed by Mr. Conger eloquently testifies to early American imagination, taste, art, and skill. This book offers the reader a chance to take pride in the achievements of the artists, craftsmen, patrons, and others who not only shaped the notion of a new nation but also filled it with superb works of art.

While this book, and the accompanying exhibition, does not feature the story of the common man, his presence is real and implied. Many of the decorative arts displayed were made by unnamed craftsmen and were marketed by anonymous tradesmen to a wealthy clientele. The works reflect a dynamic mercantile and craft economy, participants in which were conversant with fashions from abroad. Merchants, craftsmen, and tradesmen all provided for the well-to-do of colonial and Federal society. If prosperous, craftsmen and tradesmen sometimes became gentlemen. It was at this upper level of society where sophisticated taste and learning came about through education, travel, and reading. Since most Americans aspired to better themselves, both the maker and

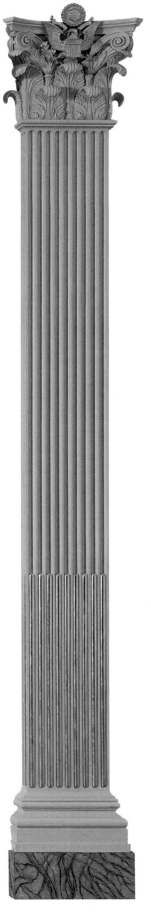

perspective (or how to represent a three-dimensional object on a two-dimensional surface).

The study of symmetry was central to all aesthetic systems of eighteenth-century art. It persisted through much of the nineteenth century as well. It was believed that the five classical orders—Tuscan, Doric, Ionic, Corinthian, and Composite—and their proportional geometry were fundamental for the creation of successful art. By applying classical proportions to furniture design, forms of silver, ceramics, and painting, the artist/craftsman both acknowledged the authority of the ancient past and illuminated his contemporary search for universal principles of symmetry and proportion.

The "true" measure of all things also involved a study of the proportions of the ideal human figure as articulated by Marcus Vitruvius Pollio, the celebrated Roman architect who served under Julius Caesar in 46 B.C. and thereafter under Augustus. It is hard for many persons today to find merit in the search for rules of order in the design of architecture, furniture, sculpture, portraits, and all the arts. However, in our country's early years, such was the belief in the classical past that it generated a creative search for universal principles or rules of order with compelling force and presence.

This applied not just to the material artifacts but also to rules of civility or public and personal behavior, dress, and posture by which George Washington, among others, patterned their lives. Inspiration from the classics also related to those precepts of fundamental human rights that logically led to the American Revolution. The writings of the aforementioned Vitruvius, articulated in his ten-volume work *De architectura*, were known to colonials through eighteenth-century publications. They understood that what Vitruvius recommended as an ideal human body of ten face-lengths was not, in fact, a common reality. But the ideal was appealing, and when applied to sculpture or painting, it made an impressive appearance. A ten-face-length figure was also related to proportions of classical columns.

Even as early as 1670 such artistic principles as these were being read in Boston by the minister Increase Mather (1639–1723). He owned and marked in his own hand a small illustrated book written by John Bate titled *The Mysteries of Nature and Art* (second edition, London: Ralph Mabb, 1635). In it Bate had plagiarized the work of a translation made into English by Richard Haydocke in 1578 of Italian author Giovanni Paolo Lomazzo's *Trattato, or Tract Containing the Artes of Curious Painting* (1571); Lamazzo, in turn, cited Vitruvius as the source of the ten-face-length human-body ideal. While this rule-seeking stretching back into classical times may seem pedantic today, it was important to craftsmen and statesmen in early Boston. Members of civilized society in colonial America earnestly engaged in the study of the remote past so that they would not lose connections with wisdom from abroad.

Leaders endeavored to discover and embrace the universal principles that they believed could or would help to create an ordered and cultivated society in the New World. It is no accident, therefore, that the architectural settings in which the objects in these pages are normally displayed within the Diplomatic Reception Rooms (although new creations) are visually harmonious with the antique furniture and furnishings. This architecture represents a living legacy of classical traditions that have survived in this country in the hands of a few gifted architects. They worked with Clement Conger not only to provide functionally effective rooms for affairs of state but also beautifully organized and richly ornamented chambers. These rooms would have met with the approval of George Washington, Thomas Jefferson, James Madison, or any other American statesman, past or present, who was or is concerned with refinement, civility, and balanced government as expressed by early American architectural and furnishing styles.

Below: Utilitarian, architecturally uninspired
example of the International Style,
James Madison State Dining Room, 1960

The Diplomatic Reception Rooms

The Diplomatic Reception Rooms became totally transformed from the drab institutional look of a late-modern structure, completed in 1961, into a vibrant, coherent, and architecturally appropriate setting for American antiques under the direction of Clement E. Conger. The government's emphasis upon utilitarianism and its requirements for obtaining the maximum square footage of space from the lowest bidder meant that the State Department building, like so many other government office buildings of similar vintage, was architecturally uninspired. Stylistically it reflected a late manifestation of what, in the 1930s, came to be known as the International Style.

By the 1960s this style had lost its vigor, but was still adapted by architects as a solution for generic office buildings. In order to emphasize horizontal planes of floors and ceilings, the walls of such International Style buildings tended to be visually eliminated through the use of large spans of glass. This was the case in the State Department rooms, which were boringly modern. Ornament was severely limited to the natural figure of the finish materials on broad surfaces, rather than being expressed through more traditional enrichments of carving, gilding, and painting. These features of modern design in the State Department building were echoed in the large-scale spaces for the Diplomatic Reception Rooms, which had proportions completely unsympathetic to early American furnishings.

Despite pervasive modernism, there persists in the public memory and therefore in actual design practice a deep affection for traditional design. Indeed, it will surprise many to discover that in the twentieth century what may variously be called traditional, early American, or colonial has been the most consistent and popular artistic movement, whether through historic preservation or via new designs in architecture and all the arts of design. Traditional design simply does not attract the widespread publicity or promotion that is gained by modern and postmodern design. Certainly a good part of the reason for this popular survival can be explained by the high level of comfort provided by its humanistic scale.

As a Virginian, Clem Conger had grown up in the presence of Georgian architecture and was therefore fully aware of its popularity and of the power of traditional design to serve the needs of state. In 1961 he was introduced to interior designer and architect Edward Vason Jones (1909–1980) by the prominent New York antiques dealer Benjamin Ginsburg, who also agreed to lend a "roomful of furniture" to help start the project. Eight years after accepting the State Department project, Clem was asked by President Richard Nixon also to become the curator of the White House. In this dual position, Clem began to make important Collection additions while developing artistic coherence for historic rooms in that distinguished historic building. Again, he called upon Edward Jones for assistance.

Through a lifetime of study of historic architecture, Jones had mastered the vocabulary of traditional classical taste, in part by making measured drawings of historic architecture in Savannah, Georgia. Jones also came to understand early design practices in the same way that gentlemen architects of the eighteenth century mastered their discipline— through the ownership and study of richly illustrated period design books.

Jones was a natural choice for the work. The first room at the State Department designed and rebuilt by Jones was a long gallery in the Diplomatic Reception Rooms. It was completed in 1969. This gallery contains a triumphal procession of superb mid-eighteenth-century chests and chairs over which hang extraordinary paintings. Most notable among the chests is one of the finest made in Boston, fashioned in a bombé and serpentine shape, which was originally owned by

Right: Rococo plaster ceiling ornaments taken from molds made from the ceiling of a 1765 Philadelphia house, Entrance Hall

the merchant Ebenezer Storer (cat. no. 21). Decorating the spaces between chests is a set of arguably the finest chairs made between the years 1730 and 1760, during Philadelphia's golden age of cabinetmaking (cat. no. 32), and a superb Newport three-shell dressing table (cat. no. 18). On the walls are resplendent portraits of elegant women painted by John Singleton Copley, including the elegant profile portrait of Mrs. John Montresor (cat. no. 48). Gilbert Stuart's portrait of George Washington (cat. no. 6), normally graces a long wall of this gallery. Jones designed the architectural appointments of this hall by dividing the long space with fluted Doric pilasters that rest on bases on the top of the chair rail. The deeply profiled entablature, pedimented doorways, and large Palladian windows of this hall enclose and unite these strong works of art within a bold framework.

A decade after finishing the gallery, Jones and the talented craftsmen who worked with him completed the elevator and entrance halls. The elevator hallway is framed with an abundance of architectural details. These include fluted pilasters supporting a heavily profiled entablature, all of which are painted to simulate a roseate and veined marble. The walls are made of fielded panels painted a light putty or stone color. A polished, dark, King of Prussia marble floor serves as the composition's base. Here Jones triumphs over the sterility of a formerly steel-faced and linoleum lobby by demonstrating how a modern elevator entry can function as a waiting space and at the same time impress the viewer with the authority of traditionally crafted architecture.

While the elevator hall displays few Collection objects, the adjacent Entrance Hall to the Diplomatic Reception Rooms is abundantly furnished. Prominently featured in this room is an astonishing and historically important example of Boston-area cabinetmaking, a magnificent bombé desk and bookcase made and signed by Benjamin Frothingham of Charlestown, Massachusetts, and dated 1753 (cat. no. 10). Clem was brilliant to place this work right at the beginning of the entrance to the galleries, as the desk is a masterpiece. The architectural setting also provides for focus on a rare French bisque porcelain statuette that depicts Benjamin Franklin in the presence of Louis XVI, made about 1780–85 at the Niderville factory in France (cat. no. 46). The words "Liberté Des Mers" (Freedom of the seas) on the scroll in the hand of Louis XVI refer to two treaties obtained in 1778, whereby France and America pledged mutual defense against British interference in maritime trade. Franklin was a member of that treaty delegation. Contrasts between the dress of the two figures and their body language suggest more than words could express with regard to courtly manners.

In the room selected for the display of this precious figural group, Jones combines architectural features that were inspired by houses in Virginia, Georgia, and Pennsylvania. The abundant floral plasterwork of the ceiling was taken from molds made from the ceiling of an upstairs parlor from Philadelphia's Powell House (1765), now installed as a period room at the Philadelphia Museum of Art. He also added features to the rococo ornament of the ceiling from the Andrew Low house in Savannah, which he had restored. The raised panel walls, Greek fret entablatures, and doorway pediments had precedent in great Virginia houses. While such creative borrowings and adaptation of architectural features to solve new problems may be disparaged by many critics today, such practice is exactly how eighteenth-century designer/builders approached their client's needs. The acclaimed classical architect Allan Greenberg wrote that Jones "managed to think of design problems in exactly the same manner as the original architects and artisans. It is precisely this quality of being able to enter into the mind and

Left: Palladian style architecture featuring a richly carved fireplace and tabernacle frame overmantel, John Quincy Adams State Drawing Room

almost become the hand of an eighteenth- or early nineteenth-century architect that makes Jones's work so special."[4]

Greenberg analyzed all of the rooms designed by Jones, including his masterful Adams State Drawing Room, completed in 1972. This room reflects the Palladian style of architecture current in Philadelphia at the time of the meeting of the Continental Congress. Its richly carved fireplace, replete with a tabernacle frame overmantel and flanked by powerful fluted pilasters with Ionic capitals, was inspired by the upper front parlor of the Powell House in Philadelphia. While Jones took inspiration from this source, he had his master carver, Herbert Millard, incorporate details that differ from those found in the original woodwork. The richness of sculptural effect revealed by the somber, putty-colored walls is astonishing. Gold and scarlet upholstery form a triadic harmony with the deep blue of the carpet that is in perfect keeping with the period of the room's furniture and furnishings.

This room contains the greatest concentration in the State Department of objects made on the eve of the Revolution. It is truly a repository of treasures, as it also contains furniture, paintings, documents, memorabilia, and china associated with Jefferson and Washington, as well as dramatic life-size portraits of John Quincy Adams and his wife, Louisa Catherine Johnson Adams, painted in 1816 by Charles Robert Leslie, an English artist who studied under the American painter Washington Allston (cat. nos. 108, 109). Perhaps the most delicate and rare piece of furniture from the Adams Drawing Room is a tea table (the period term used by Chippendale was "China Table") with finely cut gallery

fretwork made in Portsmouth, New Hampshire (cat. no. 19). Contrasting with the delicacy of the table is a powerful side chair (cat. no. 40)—one of a set of six made in Philadelphia about 1755–75—which has a back splat festooned with carving of tassel, ruffle, and leafage. Among many silver treasures displayed in an arched cupboard in the Drawing Room is an early silver tankard (cat. no. 22) made in about 1740 by Jacob Hurd, Boston's best silversmith at the time.

Jones's most spectacular achievement, the Thomas Jefferson State Reception Room, was completed in 1974. It measures 35-by-48 feet with a ceiling 19 feet high, much larger than any room Jefferson ever designed. Over doorways at one end of the room, Jones designed circular blind niches like those used by Jefferson at Monticello. Carved foliate brackets beneath these porthole niches provide support for sculptural portraits of John Paul Jones and George Washington, both of which were made after models by the French sculptor Jean-Antoine Houdon. The room's architrave, with its metopes of ox skulls alternating with rosettes, echoes similar designs used by Jefferson at the University of Virginia. A large architectural niche in one wall of this room presents a life-size marble sculpture of Thomas Jefferson represented with quill pen and holding the Declaration of Independence. This sculpture was made especially for this room by Arthur Bruce Hoheb after a bronze (now in the United States Capitol) made in 1833 by the French sculptor Pierre-Jean David d'Angers (1788–1856). The color of the marble sculpture, niches, and handsomely figured Carrara marble mantelpiece established the off-white marble color of the room's entablature, cove cornice, and ceiling with its delicate Adamesque patera in the center. All were painted an off-white color. Walls and draperies are a soft neoclassical blue like that used on ceramic jasperware by Wedgwood. The dark polished wood of the floor with its geometric inlaid stripes anchors the floor to the solid mahogany furniture. From ceiling to floor, in a sweeping view, the composition consists of white, blue, gold (of window cornice frames, carpet, and upholstery) and the rich mahogany-color of furniture and floor. Jones seemed to give his all to this masterpiece of design. He wrote, "I tried to do something I thought Jefferson might have done, appreciated, given his approval to. . . . I just did the room . . . using all of the original design books in my library. I think I have nearly every book Jefferson had in his library. This is the way all the early architects got their design inspiration."[5]

The Thomas Jefferson State Reception Room houses the Jefferson portrait included here (cat. no. 45), attributed to the artist Charles Willson Peale, Jefferson's friend. Other objects include an armchair (cat. no. 41) made in Philadelphia between 1760 and 1770 for members of the Vincent Loockerman family of Dover, Delaware. This is part of the largest and most elaborately carved set of chairs in the Chippendale style to have survived together to the present day. From this room also comes a resplendent tall-case clock (cat. no. 17) having a gilded and fretted bonnet and with an elaborate brass arch above the face that bears the signature of the clockmaker William Claggett of Newport, Rhode Island. The clock's case, with its handsome carved shell, undoubtedly was made by a gifted craftsman of the justly famous Newport cabinetmaking families of Goddard and Townsend about 1750. Among the gaming tables displayed in the Jefferson Room, a distinguished example (cat. no. 27) in this book was made in New York City of dense mahogany. It descended in the Varick family and is related to others made for members of the prominent Beekman family of New York.

Two additional rooms were begun by Jones before he passed away in 1980. These were the Dolley Madison Powder Room and the Martha Washington Ladies' Lounge. The former contains a collection of furniture made in New York City by Duncan Phyfe and others working in a similar style. The Phyfe suite in this exhibition (cat. nos. 105-7) represents the highest order of workmanship in the so-called English Regency style in the United States. In the latter room is concentrated a collection of the finest Queen Anne–style furniture. From that gathering a handsome spice chest (cat. no. 13) from Philadelphia is included here, as well as one of the most artfully conceived tea tables (cat. no. 15) made in the colonies. While Jones did not live to see these two rooms finished, the team of craftsmen who had worked for him for some thirty-six years carried out their completion. The late David Byers, designer, and Odolph Blaylock, master carpenter/building tradesman, oversaw the work on

these two rooms. The aforementioned Allan Greenberg, an architect who completed designs for and oversaw work on the most impressive architectural achievements for the State Department, praised Jones with the following generous words: "It has been a rare privilege for me to sit at the feet of this great master and to learn from the example of his work. I regret not having known him, and wish that he could have lived long enough to see the rising tide of interest in traditional American architecture."[6]

Following Jones's death, Walter M. Macomber was engaged to design and reinstall spaces now identified as the James Monroe State Reception Room, the James Madison State Dining Room, and a suite of rooms that includes the Henry Clay Dining Room and the Martin Van Buren, Daniel Webster, James Buchanan, and Robert Livingston Executive Dining Rooms. Smaller than the Jones rooms, these spaces provided for more intimate, domestic-scale functions. Antique furnishings in them look remarkably comfortable in scale, as if in a home. A linen press (cat. no. 115) made between 1800 and 1810 by Michael Allison of New York City, comes to this book and exhibition from the Monroe State Reception Room. It displays the bold geom-

Left: Allan Greenberg's geometry of sequenced vestibules, vaulting and deep, rich cornice profiles, George C. Marshall Reception Room

Below: Overdoor entablature, George C. Marshall Reception Room

etry of string inlay on brilliantly figured mahogany that is characteristic of New York design of the first decade of the nineteenth century. It also features splendid pictorial inlays, two of which represent facing American eagles with shields on their breasts. These inlays at once reference patriotism and call to mind the Great Seal of the United States, kept by the Department of State for use on official documents.

By contrast, the next project, the Benjamin Franklin State Dining Room, is the largest of the remodeled spaces in the Department of State. This room was completed in 1985 after designs by the architect John Blatteau of Philadelphia. It consists of a colossal chamber with a coffered cove and deep entablature supported by engaged Corinthian-style fluted columns painted to simulate French marble. The central medallion of the ceiling features the Great Seal of the United States.[7] This room might be described as a processional space, suitable for large gatherings. Antiques and works of art are judiciously arranged among columns against the walls, including a handsome painting of fruit and flowers by Severin Roesen (cat. no. 125) that evokes a sense of abundance enjoyed by many Americans in the mid nineteenth century. New World abundance is one facet of the expansive and confident America of the age of steam, coal, iron, and transcontinental travel. Another was the celebration of the American landscape and its astonishing wonders as represented by Thomas Moran's *The Cliffs of Green River Wyoming* (cat. no. 133), painted in 1900. This painting, which also comes from the Benjamin Franklin State Dining Room, was based on sketches made by Moran in the 1870s. A patriotic note is struck by another work from this chamber: the extremely popular painting *The Spirit of '76*, which was painted in 1875 by Archibald Willard (cat. no. 11). After the Civil War, this image spoke to Americans who searched their historic past for inspiration and a sense of national unity. The central figure of a drummer must have recalled, for many, the symbolic American figure of Brother Jonathan who, by the Civil War, had become transformed into Uncle Sam—the resourceful and lean Yankee type used to personify America to this day.

The last rooms remodeled by means of Clem Conger's incomparable fundraising and management abilities involved the outstanding classical architect Allan Greenberg of New Haven, Connecticut, whose appreciation of Edward Vason Jones's work was discussed earlier. Art historian George L. Hersey noted how Greenberg's classicism represents a deep

erudition, encompassing knowledge reaching back seventy generations, in strong contrast to architectural practice today, which typically reaches back only one or two generations.[8] Greenberg's rooms in the Department of State were built in the mid- to late 1980s. They include the John Jay Reception Room, the Marshall Reception Room, the offices of the secretary of state and the deputy secretary of state, and the sculpturally muscular Treaty Room with its impressive adjacent elevator hall.

Greenberg's works are masterly examples of "processional architecture." His rooms gain their authority and momentum through the geometry of sequenced vestibules, vaulting, and deep, rich cornice profiles. Greenberg is an architectural humanist who believes that his art, derived from classical sources, is parallel with and reflective of democratic values. For Greenberg, the task of designing rooms for diplomacy is to relate the architecture to the human body—or to the measure of mankind. It is further the task of his compositions, Greenberg notes, simply to give pleasure.[9]

This principle of pleasure or delight, which was so thoroughly understood in colonial and Federal America, is important to all the arts, as it is to architecture. Happily, visitors who take the tour commonly report that it is indeed a great pleasure—and an inspiration—merely to pass through the Diplomatic Reception Rooms of the United States

Department of State. The rooms designed by Greenberg are, in large measure, ceremonial and not furnished with antiques. However, from the office of the deputy secretary of state there comes to this book and exhibition a painting of Niagara Falls by Ferdinand Richardt (cat. no. 8) and a five-piece garniture of Chinese export porcelain (cat. nos. 65-69).

Becoming a Nation

The pleasure principle is certainly a unifying theme shared by all objects in the exhibition. Surely a search for beauty—that ineffable quality so hard to define—was central to the pleasure principle. But what makes a crafted work that is based on British design formulae identifiably American? Connoisseurs of Americana do readily differentiate comparable works made in this country from their British counterparts. In general, American furniture and silver is relatively spare in ornament and, in the main, displays a greater aesthetic reliance on broad, bold surfaces than their comparable British forms.

Each generation in this country, consciously or unconsciously, shifted tastes as consumers and craftsmen understood newly imported styles—sometimes imperceptibly groping toward the ideal as new fashions arrived across the Atlantic Ocean either through imported goods, fashion guides, design books, or by way of skillful artists and artisans who were seeking a new market for their work in the New World. Although newly arrived craftsmen in America carried with them the same tools and "language" of craftsmanship they employed abroad, the colonial experience brought about change. Through time, imported craft practices and stylistic patterns mutated, and various blends or dialects of preferences developed as New World craftsmen passed on their knowledge and skills to and through their apprentices. Recognizable regional "schools" of craftsmen centered around dominant shops in urban colonial settlements—most of which were harbor towns. Following apprenticeship, skilled artisans left their master's shop to become a journeyman—or one who jobbed his work by travel from shop to shop—thus enhancing the congress of ideas until he found a place conducive to settlement, where he could set up as master of his own shop. By this process a phenomenon called "cultural drift" took place. No one who was born and trained in America could be expected to make a work iden-

tical to a similar piece made abroad unless the patron provided an imported example for the craftsman to copy. Slavish copying was not the general practice in eighteenth-century American craftsmanship. The idea was to emulate the stylistic ideal and to use a vocabulary of form and ornament that was accepted by society. For the wealthy elite elaborate ornament was to be expected, as station in society was judged not just by manners, dress, and housing but also by the obvious expense lavished on possessions.

While rich appearance suggested wealth and elevated social station, there were also those who lived beyond their means and affected signs of wealth that they did not possess. Sumptuary laws passed in seventeenth-century America in an effort to prevent the commoner from obtaining expensive possessions were ineffective in maintaining social differentiation. Generations later, in the spirit of the Enlightenment, one of the favorite mottoes of the Masonic Order was "Follow Reason." Benjamin Franklin found this an agreeable concept as he observed: "So convenient a thing it is to be a reasonable Creature, since it enables one to find or make a Reason for every thing one has a mind to do."[10] For those who followed the Quaker way of avowed simplicity, William Penn left the door open to prized possessions. In his little book, *Fruits of a Father's Love*, he advised (but did not dictate): "Be plain in clothes, furniture and food, but clean, and then the coarser the better, the rest is folly and a snare. Therefore next to sin, avoid daintiness and choiceness about your person and houses. For if it be not an evil in itself, it is a temptation to it; and may be accounted a nest for sin to brood in."[11]

Penn's recommendation for plainness in furniture seems hard to square with what many Quakers actually possessed. Certainly the magnificent furniture in Stenton, James Logan's home in Germantown, is far from being "plain" by today's standards. Logan (1674–1751) was a member of the Society of Friends who, in 1699, accompanied William Penn to Philadelphia as his secretary. A master of the French, Greek, Latin, and German languages and a published author, Logan amassed some three thousand volumes for his personal library. He was appointed secretary of the province in 1701, became Pennsylvania Supreme Court chief justice in 1731, and president of the Governor's Council from 1736 to 1738.[12]

Surely, the plenitude of ornament found on furniture from Philadelphia displayed in these pages does not necessarily argue against much of it having been made for and owned by well-to-do Quakers. Indeed, by 1724, a Germantown

Left: English looking glass with carved gilt ornament favored by eighteenth-century aristocrats

Below: American knife box of solid, well-wrought design (see page 102 for inside detail)

be what provincial Americans meant in their use of the word "plain." Compared with some of the more extravagantly ornamented goods that were imported by officers of the Crown for ostentatious display and assertion of power or authority, that which colonials produced at home, however well wrought, was relatively plain. Also, Quakers were not the only inhabitants of Philadelphia. Penn's great town was open to people from all nations, languages, and beliefs. Hector St. Jean de Crèvecoeur (1735–1813), a Frenchman who immigrated to America in 1754 and settled in a farm in New York, was utterly dazzled with the diversity of peoples in the middle colonies. In his *Letters from an American Farmer* (1782) he writes: "[W]hence came all these people? They are a mixture of English, Scotch, Irish, French, Dutch, Germans, and Swedes. From this promiscuous breed, that race, now called Americans have arisen."

clockmaker and printer observed that "according to appearances, plainness is vanishing pretty much."[13] The term "plain" seems to not have had the same meaning for design in the eighteenth century as it has today.

In the eighteenth century, in mansions occupied by royal governors, there was an aristocratic level of decorative arts. Extraordinarily rich objects of carved gilt, cut velvet, silk, and silver plate were imported to and displayed in this country. Some of these pretensions were, inevitably, imitated by well-to-do colonials. But the mercantile class that made up most of the wealthy colonials comprised a fairly conservative, practical lot. They liked their luxuries to be solid—to be well wrought, to endure. Even the best object made in this country must have seemed "plain" compared to that imported by royal officials. Pennsylvania Quakers were pleased to acquire works of "the best sort but plain"—works wrought of the finest, richest material, but only accented, not covered, with fashionable London-style ornament. In long and eloquent sermons New England ministers claimed that their words were plain and unadorned with rhetorical flourishes.

Clarity and directness of design and manners, with emphasis upon sound form and solid construction of parts, seems to

The Catalogue

Americana from the Diplomatic Reception Rooms
U.S. Department of State

Charting the New World

VIEWS AND VISIONS OF AMERICA

$\mathcal{E}$very object in *Becoming a Nation* has a story to tell, often one that relates to its special role in American history. Each object, when examined in its social, historical, and artistic context, becomes a window to the past and a testament to the beauty of workmanship achieved by artists and craftsmen working in America or producing objects for the American market.

A small cluster of works of art are gathered together at the beginning of this exhibition, primarily maps and paintings, to suggest changes in the literal views and symbolic vision of America from the seventeenth to the nineteenth century.

The discovery of the New World by explorers and adventurers in the fifteenth century was a wonder to those who lived in the Old. At first, the American continent was imagined as a hostile, uncivilized, wilderness—uncharted, accidentally discovered, and not wanted. Mariners hoped to find a way around it in their search for Cathay. Jacques Cartier, who encountered Labrador's coast in 1534, regarded this land "as the one God gave to Cain." Not until Spanish settlement in Peru, including the discovery of the silver mines of Potosí in 1545 and the consequent profit to the Crown, did attitudes toward the New World radically change.

Tales of vast resources in the Americas spread throughout Great Britain. Sir Walter Raleigh was among those who first brought reports of the great wealth that Spain was gathering from Peru. The vision of America was transformed: The New World was now seen as a land of opportunity for colonization, trade, and exploitation. This new view prompted competition among Spain, France, Holland, and Great Britain, as well as other nations, to stake claims to the new territory.

Maps that illustrate the discovery of America represent visions of the new land as depicted abroad in the sixteenth and seventeenth centuries. The earliest map—and the oldest object altogether—in the Department of State's collection

dates to 1590 (cat. no. 1). It was published by Theodore DeBry in Frankfurt am Main, Germany, after drawings made by John White, who in 1584 accompanied an expedition to establish a colony on Roanoke Island. The colony (including much of North America) was named Virginia, after Elizabeth I, the virgin queen of England, and the fate of the original colonists remains a mystery to this day. DeBry's text, which fills ten illustrated volumes, is taken from Girolamo Benzoni's *Historia del mondo nuovo*, published in 1565. The text tells in lurid detail of Spanish imperialism and cruelty to the natives.[1] The map is oriented as if the viewer were sailing from England, in the east, at the bottom of the chart; westward across the Atlantic Ocean, toward its top, are Pamlico Sound and the Outer Banks. Cape Hatteras (known to mariners as the "graveyard of ships") is on the left side; the Chesapeake Bay is on the right.

One hundred and twenty-five years later, Herman Moll, a German in London, produced a map (cat. no. 3) that pictured in surprising detail what was known of the entire North American continent, including California and parts of Canada. Greenland and a northern section of South America are also shown. This map is oriented north to south from top to bottom, respectively, as maps are today, and, although California is represented as an island, much of the rest of the continent is depicted with remarkable accuracy. A mere century before, it was believed that New England was a large island—like those that form the British Isles. In the 1630s a visitor to New England, John Josselyn, speculated that the River Canada (the St. Lawrence) and the Hudson River were conjoined at an imagined great south sea and hence embraced a great island (like that of England) that formed New England. Significantly, the Moll map shows British boundaries west of the Appalachian Mountains, in direct contest with French claims. Yet French sources were used to place the Mississippi River on its correct meridian. Ten inset harbor scenes offer detailed information useful for maritime commerce.

Even as maps offer clues to public perceptions, so also do paintings. Perhaps the best-known American portrait is that of

George Washington painted by Gilbert Stuart in 1796. Stuart made many versions of this image, including the Collection version, completed ca. 1803–1805 (cat. no. 6). The original, for which the president sat, is known as the Athenaeum portrait. This is the portrait recapitulated in an engraved image on the U.S. dollar bill. It is now owned by both the National Portrait Gallery and the Museum of Fine Arts, Boston (along with its companion portrait depicting Martha Washington; the paintings shuttle every five years between Washington, D.C., and Boston). The most famous image of the most famous American president, the portrait has become an American icon.

As early as 1803 a merchant prince of Salem, Massachusetts, hired an Italian immigrant, Michele Felice Corné, to celebrate the history of the new nation with a painting representing the landing of the Pilgrims at Plymouth Rock in 1620 (cat. no. 4). It is clear that the artist had not a clue as to the appearance of Plymouth harbor, the clothing that the Pilgrims wore, or the kind of vessel in which they sailed to the New World. Yet the painting remains an important and early attempt to celebrate the past of this country at a time shortly after the Revolution when patriotic fervor drenched the imagination of citizens of the new nation.

Another icon that helps define an American self-vision is a nineteenth-century copy of Benjamin West's 1771–72 painting *William Penn's Treaty with the Indians.* West, born into a Quaker family in Springfield, Pennsylvania, and largely self-taught, was the first American-born artist to study in Italy. In his 1760 sojourn, he assimilated the lessons to be learned from works by Raphael, Poussin, the Carracci family, and the artist Anton Raphael Mengs, West's contemporary. In London by 1763, he soon became that city's leading history painter. He painted large and compositionally complex religious subjects, as well as events from ancient history, in a heroic, neoclassical style. In 1772, a year after exhibiting his dramatic *Death of General Wolfe,* West was appointed "Historical Painter to the King."

In the same year, West painted his history lesson about Quaker kindness and its benefits to colonization in a society

Right: Bombé desk and bookcase signed by cabinetmaker Benjamin Frothingham, Jr. (see pages 54–55), chair owned by Francis Scott Key (see page 92), and painting of Penn's Treaty with the Indians *(see pages 51–52), Entrance Hall*

open to all, including Native Americans. (The original is now in the collection of the Pennsylvania Academy of the Fine Arts.) *William Penn's Treaty with the Indians*, of course, depicts an event that West could not have witnessed. Like moviemaking today, history painting in West's time was a way of creating larger-than-life myths about the past. Such images of American history served the people of a new nation who were eager to imagine themselves as players in an important historical time. The charming later copy of that work in the Collection, by an unidentified artist, illustrates that retrospective image-making is not likely to yield historically accurate facts. But the picture does reflect what Americans wished to believe about themselves and the origins of their nation, while affirming an ideal moral condition.[2]

Portraits and history paintings remained popular as the nineteenth century progressed, even as a tremendous interest in Nature—especially the extraordinary American terrain—led to a flowering in the genre of landscape painting. The power of nature to impress is captured in the Collection's painting of Niagara Falls by Ferdinand Richardt (cat. no. 8). Viewers were meant to be overwhelmed by the splendor and drama of God's sublime handiwork, which graced the American landscape. Natural wonder paintings of this type almost always depict the human figure as an extremely small detail. This may be simply a necessity in order to convey the vastness of the prospect in question. But this pictorial convention is also expressive of the sublime. By the mid-nineteenth century, the vast territory of the continent, from Niagara Falls to the Grand Canyon and beyond, seemed to be complete under the sovereign wings of the bald eagle (cat. no. 9).

Surveys, portraits, and history paintings all help to map the collective image of the United States. This exhibition also includes includes a rich collection of three-dimensional objects of the other "polite arts," as they were called—"bespoke," or individually ordered, furniture, silver, china, and other furnishings enjoyed by well-bred colonists and, later, citizens of the new nation.

A stunning piece of furniture in this section is a celebrated desk and bookcase (cat. no. 10) made by Benjamin Frothingham, Jr., of Charlestown, Massachusetts, signed and dated 1753. The magnificent pattern of its mahogany and its splendid architectural detail and proportions elevate this work to masterpiece level. It is the earliest dated bombé-based furniture made in this country. Its workmanship and design are within the mainstream of Anglo-American taste,

and it is comparable to London-made furniture of the best sort. Some authorities have identified its style as Chippendale, but as there is little that is rococo in its detail, and as it is dated a year before Chippendale's *Director* was published, a better term for its style would simply be Georgian or late baroque.

From the moment of initial settlement British subjects in North America were part of an extensive, international trade network. Although independence brought the ability to trade freely with other countries, particularly France, whose blockade of Chesapeake Bay led to the defeat of Lord Cornwallis at Yorktown, United States citizens still favored styles in the arts of design originating in England rather than elsewhere and still relied on English imports for many luxury goods.

Nothing speaks to this phenomenon more eloquently than objects ordered and owned by George Washington. For example, Washington turned to England for many fused-plate (or Sheffield plate) objects in the late 1780s, including a wine cooler (cat. no. 5). In 1795, as president, Washington appointed Timothy Pickering of Salem, Massachusetts, his secretary of state. When he left office, Washington presented the double-bottle cooler to Pickering as a memento. This cooler, therefore, resonates with special meaning in the State Department Collection. The Collection also includes Pickering's Society of the Cincinnati medal (cat. no. 49)—the eagle on the face of this medal is also to be seen on the Great Seal of the United States—and other objects related to the society (cat. nos. 50, 51).

—*Jonathan L. Fairbanks*

Cat. 1

Drafted by John White (working 1585–1593);
engraved and published by Theodore DeBry
(1528–1598)

Americae pars, Nunc Virginia dicta.

1590

Engraving on laid paper, 12 x 16 ⅛ (plate mark) in.
Gift of Mr. Sandy M. Pringle (1984.0052)

In 1584 Elizabeth I allowed Sir Walter
Raleigh to send Philip Amadas and Arthur
Barlow to North America to establish a
colony. The expedition landed on Roanoke
Island and named the colony Virginia. At
that time maps were drafted by the expedition's artist and cartographer, John White,
who was to return as governor in 1591.
It is thought that White worked with John
Hariot, a mathematician who wrote a narrative of the discoveries in the land that
today comprises Virginia and the Carolinas.
The narrative, accompanied by White's
map, was published by Theodore DeBry
in Frankfurt am Main, Germany. In an age
of astounding Renaissance discoveries,
this publication must have been one of
the most exciting.

William P. Cumming describes this map
as "the most careful delineation made in the
sixteenth century of any considerable part
of the North American coastline."[1] The
geographic delineations are primitive but
show firsthand knowledge of the rivers
flowing into Pamlico Sound and the outlets
through the Outer Banks into the Atlantic
Ocean. Such details have provided scholars
with information on the ever-changing
configurations of the coast from Cape
Hatteras to the Chesapeake Bay. To the right
is a very early depiction of the mouth of
the Chesapeake Bay, reflecting little specific
information but indicating the
presence of a mighty body of water.

Artistically, this map is a superb example
of Renaissance decoration applied to
cartography. Exquisite strapwork ornamentation enhances the title, the scale of miles,
the credits, and the entire ensemble.
The ocean contains numerous sailing ships,
a sea monster, and an intricate compass
rose. In the sound and on the land are
minute figures of American Indians taken
from John White's watercolors.[2] The map
is oriented to the west so that a reader can
conceive how one approaches the coast
of the New World.

—*Donald H. Cresswell*

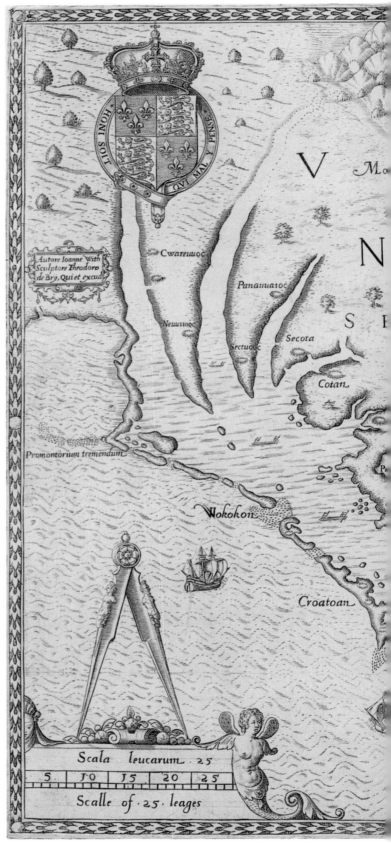

Cat. 2

Drafted by Captain John Smith (1580–1631);
engraved by William Hole (working 1600–1646)

Virginia

1612–24

Engraving on laid paper, 12 ⅝ x 16 ⅛ (plate mark) in.
Funds donated by Mrs. Alexander O. Vietor (1982.0009)

Jamestown, founded in 1607, was the first permanent English settlement in North America, and its success can be credited largely to Captain John Smith. He is famous for his strict disciplining of cavaliers at Jamestown and, thanks to Henry Wadsworth Longfellow, for his lack of wooing prowess at Plymouth, but it is less known that Smith was an able and intrepid cartographer. He drew the first map to have any semblance of accuracy of the Chesapeake Bay, a work considered an excellent rendering in Smith's day. This map was widely disseminated and often copied by Dutch and other British cartographers throughout most of the seventeenth century.[1]

With the demise of the Roanoke colony,

the settled part of "Virginia" was limited to the western shore of the Chesapeake. Smith's map charts the huge bay and its many tributaries; the settlements it shows are almost exclusively adjacent to the navigable waters, with well-marked European plantations and Indian villages. Some topography is described in stylized renderings of molehill-like mountains, which is exceptional information for the time. In a fascinating innovation, Maltese crosses mark the points in the rivers where Smith's actual surveys ended and information gleaned from Indian descriptions began.

The decorative elements—a compass rose, ship, and sea monster—are often found on the best Renaissance maps. The large

standing figure of the Indian was taken from John White's earlier drawing, engraved in Theodore DeBry's *Major Voyages* (first published in 1590), and the rendering of Powhatan's lodge is the earliest picture of an Indian dwelling to appear on any map. The first printings of Smith's *Virginia* were issued separately in London; they also appear in his pamphlet titled *A True Relation of . . . Virginia* (London, 1612) and in numerous editions of his *General History of Virginia*, published from 1624 through 1632.[2] This state of the map, number 10 of 12 states, has also been recorded in early editions of Purchas's *Pilgrimage* (1625). The first "I" in the title is a restoration.

—*Donald H. Cresswell*

Cat. 3

Drafted and published by Herman Moll (d. 1732)

Map of North America

ca. 1715

Engraving on laid paper; outline hand-colored, 23 x 38 ¼ (plate mark) in.
Funds donated by Mrs. Alexander O. Vietor (1990.0001)

Herman Moll was a German who established a map-publishing house in London about the year 1700. He was a proponent of the exploration and development of foreign lands for British investment and created maps to advance these goals. A picture on the left side of this map shows a codfish factory prospering in the north country. Above it, a lovely baroque cartouche is flanked by images of noble natives, with sugarcane, gold, textiles, tobacco, and furs, all under a prominent British coat of arms. The map refutes French claims to North America by showing the British boundaries west of the Appalachian Mountains.[1]

The geography is based primarily on the best French sources of the time. The sinusoidal projection is taken from Nicolas Sanson's earlier experiments at showing the midregions of continents to best advantage. Information on the Mississippi River system is obviously derived from Guillaume Delisle's famous maps of New France, which first placed that river on its proper meridian in 1703. The map is one of the more prominent works to show California as an island, a misconception that persisted for more than a hundred years.[2] In the Gulf of Mexico a dotted line traces the route of the Spanish galleons from Vera Cruz to Havana and from Havana to Spain. The ten inset plans of harbors in the lower left corner attest to the many fine and thriving harbors in North America and the West Indies in the early eighteenth century.

—*Donald H. Cresswell*

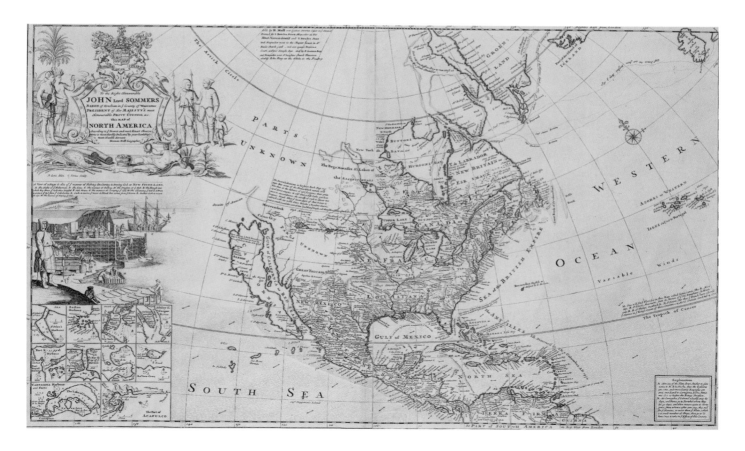

Cat. 4

Michele Felice Corné (1752–1845)

The Landing of the Pilgrims

1803

Oil on canvas, 36 x 56 in.
Funds donated by the National Art Association of Los Angeles (1971.0146)

Corné was one in the uncountable cavalcade of artists who came to America to escape political upheaval or oppression and to further their fortunes. Born on Elba, he was probably trained as a decorative painter in Naples, a fertile source of artist-craftsmen in the eighteenth century. We know that Corné was serving in the Neapolitan army, which futilely resisted the French invasion at the outset of 1799.

The Napoleonic army held Naples until Admiral Horatio Nelson's fleet drove them out in June. To escape the ensuing turmoil, Corné managed to gain passage on an American merchant ship, the *Mount Vernon*, whose master was Elias Hasket Derby, Jr., of Salem, Massachusetts.[1] Sailing from Naples on November 8, the vessel reached Salem on July 7, 1800. Corné apparently secured his passage in exchange for paintings of the *Mount Vernon* either in the Bay of Naples or engaged in sea battles. Thus began his American career.[2]

In Salem, Corné painted portraits of people and ships, seascapes, and landscapes, first for the Derbys and then for other leading families. Many commissions probably came from Corné's frequent association with Samuel McIntire, the city's leading carver and architect.[3] Sometime in 1807 the painter moved to Boston, and in 1822, at the age of seventy, he moved to Newport, Rhode Island, where he died in 1845.[4]

Corné painted perhaps as many as five versions of *The Landing of the Pilgrims*. His inspiration, for composition as well as subject, was apparently an engraving by Samuel Hill, which may have existed independently as a mezzotint, but served as the invitation to the first meeting (December 22, 1800) of a group of Bostonians, the Sons of the Pilgrims. The Hill engraving was also the source for several Chinese reverse paintings on glass created for the export trade, but since Corné's representation in the Collection is dated 1803, it almost certainly is based directly upon the Hill engraving and not upon one of the (later) Chinese versions. Because none of Corné's other versions is dated, this can be considered his earliest known painting of the subject. It was probably executed for his first patron, Derby, since it seems to have descended in the family.[5]

Corné (following Hill) portrayed a fanciful Plymouth: the marshes of reality are exchanged for rugged rocks, the landing party wears British uniforms (and some sport French hats of the Napoleonic era), the Union Jack flies from the ship at anchor, and a scattering of Indians awaits the pilgrims on shore, though none was in fact encountered. Still, the site is identifiable if not exactly recognizable: Plymouth, with its fabled rock on which a sailor stands; Long Beach, off which the ship is moored; and Clark's Island in the distance. The commemorative nature of the painting is clear from the inscription on Plymouth Rock, "Dec. 22/1620."

—*William Kloss*

Wine cooler

Sheffield, England, ca. 1789

Fused plate, 8 1/16 x 11 x 6 7/8 in.
Funds donated by Mrs. Frank L. Wright in memory of her husband (1994.0014)

Shortly after his election as first president of the United States, George Washington began to acquire silver and fused-plate objects that would allow him to entertain in a manner befitting his new office. In October 1789 he asked Gouverneur Morris to procure for him, in London or Paris, "Plated Coolers, Mirrers, and Table ornaments."[1] Washington had the services of a French confectioner who was able to create the sugar ornaments displayed on mirrored plateaus, and he was anxious to have one like those owned by "Mr. Morris & Mr. Bingham . . . and the French and Spanish Ministers."[2] Along with the plateau Washington ordered several wine coolers of specific designs:

> Of plated ware may be made I conceive handsome and useful Coolers for wine at and after dinner. Those I am in need of

viz. eight double ones (for Madeira and claret the wines usually drank at dinner) each of the apertures to be sufficient to contain a pint decanter, with an allowance in the depth of it for ice at bottom so as to raise the neck of the decanter above the cooler; between the apertures a handle is to be placed by which these double coolers may with convenience be removed from one part of the table to the other. For the wine after dinner four quadruple coolers will be necessary. . . . The reason why I prefer an aperture for every decanter or bottle to coolers that would contain two and four is that whether full or empty the bottles will always stand upright and never be at variance with each other.[3]

In addition to these private purchases, a much larger quantity of plate and plated

ware was furnished by the government for his use. When he left Philadelphia, the president left a large portion of his private "table furniture" behind. On August 14, 1797, Washington wrote to Secretary James McHenry and mentioned the double wine coolers, requesting, "Not for the value of the thing, but as a token of my friendship and as a remembrancer of it, I ask you, Colonel Pickering, and Mr. Wolcott to accept, each one of the two bottle Coolers; I think there are three of them."[4]

The coolers thus became valued gifts. This example is inscribed "Presented by Washington at the expiration of his presidency to T. Pickering, Secretary of State of the U.S." (See also cat. no. 49.)

—*Barbara McLean Ward*

Cat. 6
Gilbert Stuart (1755–1828)

George Washington

ca. 1803–05

Oil on canvas, 30 x 25 in.
Gift of Mrs. Robert G. Stone (1981.0068)

There is an understandable tendency to generalize when discussing one of Gilbert Stuart's numerous replicas of his life portrait of President Washington, and to speak of it as essentially indistinguishable from its comrades. To have seen a dozen or so casually leaves such an impression. But when one has the opportunity to study several such pictures attentively it soon becomes clear that there are many differences, and that they are significant in terms of both expressiveness and of quality.

We refer, of course, to the so-called "Athenaeum" type of Washington portrait in which the head and torso turn to the sitter's right, showing the proper left side of his face. This is the second likeness Stuart made of the president, and the one which has become canonical. After painting this portrait (it was completed in April 1796), Stuart retained it for the rest of his life despite the fact that it was apparently promised to Martha Washington. He used it as the model for perhaps seventy replicas over the next three decades, a ready source of income for an artist who habitually lived beyond his means. Indeed, Stuart had returned to America in 1793 from a successful career in Ireland and England precisely in order to "make a fortune by Washington," as he told an Irish artist before his departure.[2] Despite the strong demand on the artist to multiply replicas of the most famous American, Stuart's genius apparently would not permit him to literally repeat himself but led him to make numerous changes from one canvas to the next—of emphasis, mood, modeling, color, and costume.

Perhaps the first impression of the State Department's replica is that the nose seems very prominent, indeed almost massive. As if keyed by the nose, the eye sockets, mouth, and jaw are also strongly described with modeling that imbues this version with an uncommon degree of structure. The brushwork is very evident, free and confident. The strongest effect is produced by the pedestal-like neck wrapped in its white neckcloth, and by the skillful, shadowed transition to the head. Although the color is not as "high" as in some replicas—

less pink, with less emphatic silverish highlights on the forehead—there are expressive touches such as the highlight on the tip of the nose and the rose-pink stroke high on the chin.

Stuart had barely sketched the costume in the life portrait, and so was free to paint it as he wished in the many replicas. Here the shirt ruffle is thinly painted, giving a translucent effect. The dashing, improvisational brushwork in the ruffle and in the neckcloth is sufficient evidence of the artist's skill. A detail most likely unfamiliar to the present-day viewer is the curved, serrated black shape seen over the president's shoulder. It is a hair bag, described

thus by one who saw Washington address the Congress in Philadelphia: "His hair [was] profusely powdered, fully dressed, so as to project at the sides, and gathered behind in a silk bag, ornamented with a large rose of black riband."[3]

The dating of the replicas is usually dependent either upon knowledge of the first owner or upon stylistic comparisons with datable replicas or other portraits by Stuart. In this case, it is proposed that similarities with the so-called "Pennington" Washington, of about 1803–1805 (United States Senate), make that a likely date for the State Department portrait as well.

—*William Kloss*

Cat. 7

Unidentified artist, after Benjamin West (1738–1820)

Penn's Treaty with the Indians

Date unknown

Oil on canvas, 25 x 29 ½ in.
Funds donated by Mrs. Benjamin C. Russell
in memory of Benjamin Commander Russell (1975.0042)

The subject of Benjamin West's famous painting (1771–72; Pennsylvania Academy of the Fine Arts) is the oft-told story of William Penn meeting with the Delaware (Lenape) Indians in 1682 and compensating them with manufactured goods for the land "granted" him by the king of England. Until then, it was said, no European colonist had thought it necessary to trade *legally* with Native Americans to secure a common peace. The story was widely known. Indeed, in 1733 Voltaire is said to have singled out Penn's agreement with the Delaware as the only never-broken treaty between Christians and Native Americans.[1]

In the scene as imagined by West, Penn's treaty with the Indians is linked with the actual foundation of the colony of Pennsylvania through the buildings under construction in the background. In the original painting, commissioned from West by Penn's son John, the founding date of 1682 is inscribed on the gable of the house behind Penn, but in the State Department copy this detail does not survive. Indeed, the buildings are much less prominent in the copy, which was made not from the original painting but from an engraving of it. It was engraved in 1776 by William Wollett and published by the dealer John Boydell. In the eighteenth century the print was second in popularity only to the engraving of West's *Death of General Wolfe* with which it was paired, and together they made Boydell rich.[2] The engraving was in its turn copied by many painters whose copies are instantly recognizable because, like the engraving, they reproduce the original composition in mirror image reversal.[3]

The large number of engraved and painted copies affirmed and furthered the fame of West's painting, and of the legend it depicted. But it is a legend, one that reflects a widespread belief in Penn's pacific Quaker character. No treaty exists, and the popular assumption that it does exist must be credited to West's painting. The first written description of the treaty ceremony is found only in 1813, in Thomas Clarkson's *Memoirs of the Private and Public Life of William Penn*, and Clarkson consulted West while writing his book. Clarkson's account of the treaty ceremony is in fact a description of West's painting, which thus becomes the primary document, the authorized standard version of the supposed event. The history painting has "authenticated" the legend.[4]

—*William Kloss*

Cat. 8
Ferdinand Richardt (1819–1895)

View of Niagara Falls and Terrapin Tower from the American Side

ca. 1857–60

Oil on canvas, 36 x 29 ¼ in.
Funds donated by the F. M. Kirby Foundation, Inc. (1989.0014)

Vertical views of Niagara Falls are rather uncommon before midcentury, although one of a pair of such views attributed to John Vanderlyn (ca. 1832; private collection) is similar in composition to this work by Ferdinand Richardt.[1] Vanderlyn used the vertical format to enhance the drama by placing the viewer in the gorge, near the bottom of the cataract.[2] Richardt, in contrast, takes a high viewpoint, which distances us from the falls. This vantage is more artful and picturesque, and Richardt takes advantage of it to display his gifts as a colorist.

The luminosity of the painting is striking. Opalescent billows of spray rise from the brilliant green water. Much of the drama and beauty are found in the sweep of dark gray clouds, with light streaking their tops, and in the transient patches of light playing over the land and water. Some forty diminutive figures, often mere squiggles of paint, are scattered through the landscape. Their presence emphasizes the falls as a tourist attraction, a scenic wonder rather than a terrifying force.

This painting has not been identified as one of the dozens of views of Niagara painted by Richardt between 1855 and 1860 that were exhibited together as the "Great Niagara Gallery," but it is nearly identical in composition to a much larger painting, which has been dated ca. 1860 (private collection).[3] The central formal difference is an arched top in the larger painting, which also dictates a more symmetrical disposition of the clouds.

—*William Kloss*

Cat. 9
Possibly by John Haley Bellamy (1836–1914)

Eagle wall plaque

Portsmouth, N.H., ca. 1860–80

Painted and gilt pine, 23 x 40 ¹/₂ x 5 ⁷/₈ in.
Funds donated by Mr. and Mrs. Ashley H. Priddy (1982.0030)

American wood-carvers of the nineteenth century, from Samuel McIntire of Salem and William Rush of Philadelphia in the early nineteenth century to John Haley Bellamy of Portsmouth, whose career ended a century later, were often called upon to depict the eagle. Both an ancient Roman symbol and the icon of the New Republic, the eagle offered carvers a subject that was at once historic, stylish, and patriotic.[1] Although Benjamin Franklin regarded the eagle as a bad choice to represent the new United States ("He is a bird of bad moral character," Franklin advised. "He is generally very poor, and often very lousy."), the great number of surviving carved eagles indicates that most Americans disagreed.[2] Whatever ornithologists may tell us about its conduct as a bird, as a carved figure the eagle was given many positive attributes that resonated with the American people's view of themselves.

The Collection's eagle may be an early work of the talented and prolific Bellamy, who worked in the Piscataqua River area of New Hampshire and Maine, although it varies considerably from his well-documented and somewhat formulaic later style.[3] The vigorously carved bird, shown with outstretched wings, is accompanied by a pole that carries an American flag with thirty-five applied gilt stars, fluttering in the breeze.[4] The eye of the eagle is a faceted glass bead, blue or purple in color, while the bird of prey's scalloped beak encloses a scarlet tongue. The carver created his work in sections, which were then painted before being assembled into the final composition. Evidence on the back indicates that the eagle was designed to be hung on the wall.

—*Gerald W. R. Ward*

Benjamin Frothingham, Jr. (1734–1809)

Bombé desk and bookcase

Charlestown, Mass., 1753

Mahogany; white pine, eastern red cedar, Spanish cedar,
98 ¹/₄ (without finials) x 44 ¹/₂ x 24 ¹/₄ in.
Gift of Mr. Dana C. Ackerly and Mr. Earle S. Thompson, estate executors, in memory of
Mrs. Bell McKerlie Watts and Mr. Samuel Hughes Watts of Fairfield, Conn. (1970.0094)

Until its gift to the Diplomatic Reception Rooms, this imposing piece had never been considered in a published work of furniture scholarship.[1] An icon of Boston furniture of any period, it is the first documented piece of bombé-shaped furniture made in America.[2] It is perhaps one of the first examples of Chippendale-style furniture made in the colonies, predating the publication of Thomas Chippendale's *Gentleman and Cabinet-Maker's Director* by one year.[3] The desk and bookcase is also the earliest piece documented to Benjamin Frothingham of Charlestown, Massachusetts. It is the only known piece of American furniture of any form with molded architectural feet of this pattern.

The bombé form derived from a shape commonly used for ancient Roman sarcophagi. The form was adopted in the sixteenth century by Italian craftsmen and in succession by Dutch, French, and then English workers, each in characteristic fashion to suit national taste. Boston craftsmen, with their strong loyalty to English design sources, in turn embraced the form as suitable for merchants and citizens of wealth and importance. Judging from the list of Boston owners, display of this costly form must have been almost de rigueur. The style enjoyed popularity well into the 1780s, thirty years after being superseded in England by newer fashions.[4]

Frothingham was twenty years old when he made this piece. His liberal use of engraved labels later in his career has led to voluminous research by furniture historians. But little is known about the owner, Dr. Sprague. He and Frothingham were members of the First Church of Charlestown and were also founding members of the Ancient Fire Society, a private fire-protection group.[5] Both sustained considerable losses when the British burned Charlestown.[6] At his death in 1766, Frothingham's father owed Sprague more than £58, a debt later settled by Benjamin, Jr., as estate administrator.[7]

The desk and bookcase shares a number of characteristics with high-style block-front furniture made in Boston in the late 1740s and 1750s. The waist molding surrounding the midsection of the lower case follows common English practice of the day, a holdover from earlier methods of constructing the desk portion in two separate pieces.[8]

Although Frothingham primarily used a standard Boston design vocabulary, his innovative, unique use of molded architectural feet displays adoption of the latest English details. The exact model he followed is unknown, but another American desk and bookcase, nearly identical in all respects, including molded feet, may have inspired Frothingham's masterpiece.[9]

—*Robert D. Mussey, Jr.*

Cat. 11
Archibald Willard (1836–1918)

The Spirit of '76

1875

Oil on canvas, 24 x 18 in.
Gift of Gerald E. Czulewicz and Sue Huffaker-Czulewicz (1990.0006)

In the Centennial Exhibition mounted in Philadelphia in 1876, a large painting by a little-known Ohio painter appeared. At ten by eight feet, it would have caught the attention of any who chanced to see it in the Art Annex, but its visibility was ensured by the simultaneous publication of a chromolithograph purchased by thousands of visitors and by many thousands more from distributors across the country. The painting, then called *Yankee Doodle*, was the work of Archibald Willard, a one-time painter of wagons in Wellington, Ohio, who had entered into a business relationship with James F. Ryder, a Cleveland daguerreotypist and entrepreneur. Willard drew and painted humorous, anecdotal images, and Ryder sold photomechanical reproductions of them. *Yankee Doodle* also was conceived as a comic image, of a Fourth of July celebration, but Willard decided instead upon a pulsating patriotic image.

For the reproduction of *Yankee Doodle*, Ryder enlisted the services of Clay, Cosack and Company, chromolithographic printers in Buffalo, New York. The printers charged only seventeen cents per print, and Ryder usually retailed the print for only two dollars, which guaranteed a large sales volume and a huge profit, since it was probably the most popular chromo ever produced in America.[1] The small painting now in the State Department Collection is the model for the chromolithograph. Of the same dimensions and colors, it was painted by Willard as an exact guide for the printers. The State Department canvas is the first completed version of a much-replicated painting. Willard later wrote: "The first *Yankee Doodle* canvas was the regulation chromo size." It was, he added, "a small one which was reproduced in chromo."[2] The first large painting was only finished a short time before the Centennial; that work is usually identified as the painting now at Abbot Hall, Marblehead, Massachusetts. Willard painted the perfervid old drummer in the scene from a photograph of his late father, the Reverend Samuel Willard, taken by Ryder. The artist's sentimental patriotism was clearly stirred by this image, which he

combined with photographed heads of Hugh Mosher, a friend and fifer, and Henry Devereux, a cadet at Cleveland's Brooks School.[3] The three generations movingly evoked are saluted by the dying soldier with a doffing of his cap. The flag seen through the smoke of battle behind them echoes the imagery of the national anthem.

This picture was born at the precise moment it was most needed. The Centennial was the first attempt at reviving a psychologically and economically depressed nation in the wake of the Civil War, and James Ryder, an inspired promoter, clearly understood this. In front-page newspaper ads on New Year's Day, 1876, he declared that "a good sun will rise, HIGH IN THE HEAVENS, clear away the hanging mist, and give a golden tinge of restored prosperity to all." And he closed "with an abiding faith in YANKEE DOODLE and a belief that AMERICA IS A SUCCESS."[4] With that resounding affirmation he prepared the way for Willard's *Yankee Doodle* chromo to capture the popular imagination. In 1879, while his large Centennial painting was on view in Boston, Willard renamed the image *The Spirit of '76*, the more historically resonant title by which it, the artist's many painted replicas, and the chromolithograph have since been known.

—*William Kloss*

The Look of Colonial America

COMMERCE AND CRAFTS, ARTISANS AND PATRONS

Above: Boston serpentine chest of drawers, also a superb example of the bombé form (see page 73), and parcel-gilt looking glass (see page 89), The Gallery

Opposite: New York easy chair (on right) (see page 77), John Quincy Adams State Drawing Room

By the second quarter of the eighteenth century, the art in colonial America had reached a level of maturation that is fully reflected in the magnificent objects included in this section. These objects exhibit the skills of their individual makers, of course, but they were also shaped by the international economic forces of the time; by developments in political life, especially the growing tensions with England; and, at a deeper level, by the prevailing aesthetic theories and philosophies that guided their production.

A practical test of those who settled the New World was how to cope with insufficient currency, a shortage resulting from Great Britain's policy to restrict the outflow of coin to the provinces. Spanish pieces of eight that turned up in the market were often converted into wrought silver plate by the goldsmiths. Goldsmiths (or silversmiths, as they were known synonymously) were, in effect, provincial bankers, for they were the means of providing silver plate—all of which inhibited fluid monetary exchange. In Boston, where a mint had been established by John Hull and Robert Sanderson in 1652, some locally minted coins did circulate. But by the early years of the eighteenth century, most artisans, merchants, and tradesmen acquired goods and services via commodity exchanges, bills of credit, or notes in lieu of cash. This meant that craftsmen and merchants maintained ledgers and daybooks or accounts. It is from such surviving records that information about business practices, craftsmen's customers, and some aspects of craftsmen's lives can be gleaned. For example, silversmith and patriot Paul Revere's two daybooks and family papers at the Massachusetts Historical Society are a rich source that has proved useful to identify his patrons, their political leanings, and the kind and amount of wares he produced between 1761 and 1797. Between these years his silversmithing shop made some 4,792 works.[1]

Despite such productivity in America, British mercantile theory held that the colonies would become the source of

raw material for manufacturers in the British Isles, and that provincials would then become a steady market to consume goods imported from abroad. But the prosperity that Boston craftsmen enjoyed early in the eighteenth century began to attract more craftsmen to these shores. It seems that as early as 1715 three London-trained cabinetmakers—William Howell, William Price, and Thomas Robinson—were at work in Boston, making some astonishingly beautiful and stylish pieces of furniture.[2] They were not alone— the port of Boston supported a large craft population for the size of the town until the 1740s, when a series of epidemics, a rise in the cost of fuel for heating homes (caused by a scarcity of wood), and high taxes combined to depress the economy. There is little wonder, then, that Bostonians were exceptionally vulnerable to the additional taxes later imposed by the Crown. Those craftsmen who continued with some success were well connected, with family ties to their trades and established clientele. The population of Boston changed little from about 1750 through 1790, hovering at about 18,000 inhabitants, while other port towns grew.

By the mid-eighteenth century, New Yorkers were enjoying a level of prosperity that caused New York historian and jurist William Smith, Jr., to comment: "Our affluence, during the late war [French and Indian], introduced a degree of luxury in tables, dress, and furniture with which we were before unacquainted." By the year 1775 furniture craftsmen in the city numbered some 148. In 1759 Smith also observed: "In the city of New-York, through our intercourse with the Europeans, we follow the London fashions; though by the time we adopt them, they become disused in England. . . . but still we are not so gay a people as our neighbors in Boston and several of the Southern colonies."[3]

British mercantile trade seemed to be working, but not quite in the manner expected. There was a consumer revolution going on with the value of British imports nearly doubling from 1750 to 1760—rising from £1.1 million to £2.1 million. And yet there were also large numbers of craftsmen who immigrated to the colonies to seek work from a growing class of wealthy colonists. Philadelphia's elite society—those who called themselves "gentlemen"— tripled between the years 1756 and 1772.[4]

The vitality of domestic production was destroying economic theories about how provincials were supposed to purchase goods made abroad. Benjamin Franklin noted in his *Observations concerning the Increase of Mankind, Peopling of Countries, etc.* (1755) that it was folly to draw economic conclusions about America from tables based on observations made in developed countries abroad. He believed that it would be futile to restrict American manufacturers—and unnecessary, for in the huge American market they posed no economic threat to manufacturers abroad. The population had expanded to more than 1,000,000 "English Souls in North-America," and it would double, Franklin speculated, within twenty-five years. Within a century, Franklin predicted, there would be more people in the colonies than in England. "What an Accession of Power to the British Empire by Sea as well as Land!" the diplomat concluded. "What Increase of Trade and Navigation! What Numbers of Ships and Seamen!"[5]

This argument on behalf of free trade and manufacturing for provincial Americans, while understood by some abroad,

Below: Rococo coffeepot by Bancroft
Woodcock
(see page 84)

did not appeal to officers of the Crown whose intent was to levy duties, taxes, and collect revenues for the recovery of losses of the French and Indian Wars. Colonial Americans built their civilization on what they remembered, interpreted, or imported from abroad. But now they began to assert what they felt were their basic human rights in a New World not fettered by guild restraints and free of discouraging regulations. Their advantage was being situated in an environment abundant with natural resources and with waves of new immigrants who expanded the population. American colonials competed with vigor in the world market, and in many cases home industry surpassed the workmanship of imported goods.

Evidence of this success is abundantly clear in the works of art presented here. Viewed together, they demonstrate the changes in style that take place over time and highlight regionally distinctive features of design, ornament, and construction. Furniture and silver, especially, were made in regional idioms in the population centers along the eastern seaboard, including Portsmouth, New Hampshire; Salem, Marblehead, Ipswich, and Boston, Massachusetts; Newport and Providence, Rhode Island; New York; Philadelphia, Pennsylvania; New Jersey; Delaware; Maryland; Williamsburg and Norfolk, Virginia; Charleston, South Carolina; and Savannah, Georgia. While little southern furniture is included here, works from all regions possess distinctive and recognizable features, many of which have been elucidated in recent scholarship.[6]

British subjects in America in the years 1730 to 1770 were probably unaware of two different styles of their era commonly known today as the Queen Anne and Chippendale styles. In reference to American furniture and silver, these terms are confusing and inadequate. Queen Anne is a term of fairly recent vintage used by antiquarians to define a venerable style of quiet design that emphasizes the form of objects, with ornament placed selectively on the broad surfaces so as to focus attention upon refined carving and to expose the natural beauty of wood and other mediums, dazzling the eye through light and shadow. A better term for this style, which makes its appearance as early as 1715 in Boston, would be early Georgian or late baroque. It is a suave, ele-

gant, spare, architectonic style. Its characteristics include the conjoined C-scroll ornament or the long S form in legs of chairs with compass-shaped or rounded seats and clublike feet sometimes called "horsebone" feet.

Ciphers and self-contained cartouches were engraved on silver in much the same design sensibility as cabinetmakers inlaid compass stars or carved shells to emphasize the symmetrical balance of the furniture. Also, the generous sweep of handles for tankards and other vessels displayed colonial Americans' fondness for the bold, baroque line. One of the most beautiful Collection objects to employ this line is a Pennsylvania tea table with a dished top that flows smoothly and roundly from its top edge across a broadly molded profile on its sides (cat. no. 15). The sides seem to melt organically into the shallow carved knees of the table's long, tapering legs.

In silver, the style is represented in the Collection by the Boston tankard made by Jacob Hurd (cat. no. 22). Not only does it have a dramatic sweep to its handle, it also has an S-shaped thumbpiece, a domed top, and rounded moldings that yield smooth transitions between parts.

A tall silver coffeepot (cat. no. 31) made by Bancroft Woodcock in Wilmington, Delaware, ca. 1760, displays a much different design orientation from that of the work by Hurd. The coffeepot is a symphony of movement with an S scroll that doubles over itself. This is the style of the rococo, which arrived in Philadelphia and other American port towns in the 1750s.[7] It employs lively, sweeping, sometimes asymmetrical patterns and flourishes—evident in parts of the engraved-initial cartouche on the coffeepot and in the double-bellied shape, which suggests motion rather than stability. Its S line is the slim S of Hogarth—a serpentine line of beauty rather than the fuller, baroque S line of the tankard, tea table, and other earlier works.

The swelled body of the coffeepot shares a design relationship to the tour de force bombé and serpentine shape of a chest of drawers originally owned by Ebenezer Storer, a merchant of Boston (cat. no. 21). The original fire-gilt brasses of this chest emphasize the spirited rococo nature of this style, which incorporates asymmetrical motifs that furniture historians identify with "Chippendale" design. However, as did John Singleton Copley, in portraits painted in America, furniture makers, silversmiths, and other artisans of the colonies seemed to emphasize the solid, sculptural, mass of form—well proportioned and smartly outlined but not in general given over to the asymmetry of elaborately embellished carving. For example, the Goddard and Townsend families of cabinetmakers, other craftsmen, and their patrons in Newport seemed to prefer a pattern of solid block-and-shell carving (cat. no. 18). Nevertheless, many Philadelphians on the eve of the Revolution enjoyed the opulent, naturalistic floral carving that became available through the arrival of new immigrant craftsmen from London and elsewhere in the British Isles, who were well trained in the latest fashions.

All the objects that follow make clear the fact that many American colonials and those who sailed across the Atlantic to find employment here as craftsmen were highly accomplished artisans. Although Bostonians tended to patronize their own craftsmen, imported furniture, silver, and other furnishings were a competitive reality. Paul Revere and Benjamin Frothingham (see cat. no. 10) were of the same generation. They remained loyal to English aesthetics but disloyal to the Crown after the ministers of George III mandated taxes to recoup the losses incurred in the French and Indian Wars. Being taxed without representation, colonials collectively agreed to establish nonimportation agreements that, in theory, further encouraged both craftsman and client to foster home industry. During the early years of the eighteenth century, Boston flourished. But by mid-century business was stagnant. Revere suffered crippling debts that, without help from relatives, might have put him in serious legal trouble, or worse, a debtor's prison.

During this period there were approximately 225 craftsmen working in the furniture trades in Boston. This included chairmakers, caners, turners, carvers, upholsterers, joiners, cabinetmakers, and japanners—many of whom were linked together by kinship. Boston's economy faltered in the 1740s and continued to decline even into the 1760s. In the fall of 1768 when Great Britain quartered troops in Boston, there

was some cash flow from the military, but the port blockade by the British further depressed the economy. Boston's population remained stable throughout the last quarter of the century, while Philadelphia, by contrast, grew. By 1765, the Pennsylvania city had a population of some 25,000; it continued to grow, and was the leading port town of North America throughout the colonial period. New York's population did not exceed Boston's or Philadelphia's until after the Revolution. For immigrant craftsmen, Boston became a difficult town to find employment. Design patterns innovated in Boston in the 1740s and 1750s—blockfront and bombé-case furniture—were repeated and refined by at least two generations of craftsmen there without significant innovation.

Philadelphia, by contrast, welcomed fresh waves of trained craftsmen from abroad. Morrison H. Heckscher of the Metropolitan Museum of Art made an insightful analysis of the furniture-making trade in Philadelphia and revealed two different groups of craftsmen at work: the native-born Americans and the London-trained immigrants. Those native-born, such as William Savery, Samuel Mickle, David Evans, Jonathan Gostelowe, and several others, seem to have produced furniture that was handsome and solid but without rococo ornament. Four native-born cabinetmakers—Benjamin Randolph, James Gillingham, Thomas Tufft, and Edward James—had trade cards that exhibited elaborate rococo ornament. Heckscher concludes that immigrant craftsmen seem to have been responsible for the richly carved ornament of both the furniture and the grand houses in and around Philadelphia. The best known of these foreign-trained artisans are Thomas Affleck from Aberdeen and London; Hercules Courtenay, Nicholas Bernard, Martin Jugiez, and Gabriel Valois from Paris via London; and James Connell from Ireland.[8] The taste for stylish rococo ornament that was developed in Penn's Great Town is well documented elsewhere and superbly represented by the numerous examples of Philadelphia craftsmanship considered here (see, for example, cat. nos. 32–34, 37, 40).[9] The lively carved ornament on handsomely figured wood, affirm William Hogarth's assertion that beauty consists of a flamelike motion—a slim, S-shaped line—that, like a dance, excites the eye.

Hogarth's *Analysis of Beauty* (1753) was among the publications that, in 1771, Thomas Jefferson recommended to Robert Skipwith, brother-in-law of the future Mrs. Jefferson. These essential books for a gentleman's library numbered 379 volumes, all of which have been assembled at the Brush-Everard House at Colonial Williamsburg. Only a half dozen works had to do with art criticism and theory. One was by Daniel Webb, *An Inquiry into the Beauties of Painting* (London, 1769), a copy of which had been owned by the Boston painter John Singleton Copley. Another, Edmund Burke's *A Philosophical Inquiry into the Origin of Our Ideas of the Sublime and Beautiful* (London, 1757), was an even more widely read volume owned by Americans. Its many editions and later reprintings in America suggest its great popularity.[10]

Edmund Burke, who was a Whig and a friend of those in America who resisted taxation, proposed that beauty consisted of human response to physical, sensory experiences—of pain, pleasure, and associated meanings. In his text he differentiates between things that are admired and those that are loved: "The sublime, which is the cause of the former, always dwells on great objects, and terrible, the latter on small ones and pleasing: we submit to what we admire, but we love

what submits to us; in one case we are forced, in the other we are flattered, into compliance." Contrasts between masculine and feminine attributes are used by Burke to construct his definition of the sublime and the beautiful. Beautiful works are composed of parts smooth, soft, and with gentle, swelling variations of line like those parts of a woman where "she is, perhaps, the most beautiful, about the neck and breasts; the smoothness; the softness; the easy and insensible swell; the variety of the surface." Delicacy, even fragility, and an infinite variety of muted colors were, to Burke, prerequisites of beauty. Although Burke acknowledged Hogarth's idea of the line of beauty "to be extremely just," he found Hogarth mistaken in his acceptance of the angular figure as beautiful. More important, Burke introduced the concept of associated meanings, that is to say, of memory and virtual connections between works of art and ideas associated with them.[11] This was a new approach to understanding the beautiful. It is reflective of changes in attitudes toward design and newly refined manners that began to enter into the culture of Americans between the years 1770 and 1790, as a new nation began to take shape.

—*Jonathan L. Fairbanks*

Cat. 12

Side chair

Philadelphia, Pa., ca. 1750–60

Black walnut; southern yellow pine, soft maple,
black walnut, 42 x 21 x 16 ½ in.
Funds donated by Mr. A. H. Meyer (1972.011

Chairs with "compass bottoms"—so called
because the pattern for the curvilinear seat
rails was drawn with a compass—were first
made in Philadelphia about 1730 and were
based on contemporary English forms.
Benno M. Forman advanced the theory
that this type, with its arched crest rail
and distinctive framed seat construction,
derived from Continental models and was
introduced to Philadelphia by German
immigrants.[1]

Northern European chairs are almost
certainly the ultimate origin of the type,
and the extensive use of small pins in the
construction is characteristic of German
craftsmanship. The path of transmission is
difficult to re-create, however, since many
of the design and construction features that
Forman characterized as German are also
found in contemporary Irish furniture,
which had an equally strong influence
in Philadelphia.[2]

The pierced splats on this chair (one of
a set of six in the Department of State Collection) distinguish it from most surviving
Philadelphia chairs in the Queen Anne
style.[3] Pierced splats are uncommon on
chairs without claw-and-ball feet, perhaps
because these splats came into fashion at
the same time as other features associated
with the fully developed rococo style. Surviving Queen Anne–style Philadelphia
chairs with pierced splats but without claw-
and-ball feet are all similar, with trifid feet,
volute and shell crest rails, and splats with
like silhouettes.[4] The pattern of the piercing
on the Collection's chair is the most elaborate in this group. The same pattern appears
on later chairs from Philadelphia and also
from Rhode Island and Massachusetts.[5]

According to tradition, this chair and
its mates were owned by Thomas Mifflin
(1744–1800) of Philadelphia, who was
born too late to have commissioned the set,
although he may have inherited it from his
family or that of his wife, Sarah Morris.[6]

—*David L. Barquist*

Miniature high chest of drawers

Pennsylvania, probably Philadelphia, ca. 1750–80

Cherry; yellow poplar, sweet gum, Atlantic white cedar,
southern yellow pine, 28 x 15 ¼ x 10 ¼ in.
Gift of Judge and Mrs. G. Burton Pearson, Jr. (1980.0065)

The carved feet, gracefully arched skirt, and
elegant proportions of this miniature high
chest indicate that it was the product of
a sophisticated cabinetmaker's shop, most
likely in Philadelphia. Despite the small
scale, the maker followed almost every
detail of construction and design found on
the best full-sized examples. The trifid feet
and the arrangement of the drawers, with
three in the top register, two in the second,
and single drawers below, are characteristic
of Pennsylvania high chests and chests of
drawers from the mid-eighteenth century.
Full-sized high chests of this type probably
first appeared in the late 1730s, following
the introduction of cabriole-leg chairs. This
example, however, may have been made in
the 1760s or 1770s.[1] A similar miniature
high chest appears to have been produced
about 1760, and a full-sized, flat-topped
high chest may have been made for Sarah
Pleasants Fox (1767–1825) of Philadelphia
as late as the 1780s.[2] The skirt, composed
of a series of reverse curves, is similar in
conception to the skirts on case pieces in
the fully developed rococo style, including
a high chest made by William Savery
between 1765 and 1775 and a dressing
table made by Thomas Tufft about 1775.[3]

Miniature high chests and chests of
drawers were popular in eighteenth-
century Pennsylvania. Although they were
known as "spice boxes," these chests were
used to secure small valuables such as jewelry and silver flatware rather than spices.
An inventory of "one Spice Box [and]
Sundreys therein" taken in Chester County,
Pennsylvania, in 1750, included gold and
silver sleeve buttons, silver and brass shoe
buckles, a pincushion with a silver chain,
a silver scissors and thimble, six silver
teaspoons, two silver tablespoons, a pair
of silver sugar tongs, and "Sundrey Small
things."[4] This chest has no locks and was
probably intended to safeguard less precious
possessions, such as writing implements.

—*David L. Barquist*

Cat. 14

Settee

New York, N.Y., 1740–60

Black walnut; soft maple, birch, black walnut, cherry, 38 x 65 ⅝ x 28 in.
Funds donated by the Morris and Gwendolyn Cafritz Foundation (1972.0046)

Upholstered furniture was a luxury in the eighteenth century, and for Americans, settees were rare and expensive. Perhaps as a mark of status, upholsterers and a few cabinetmakers advertised repeatedly in New York newspapers that they could readily supply this unusual form. One of the earliest references appeared in 1749, when Stephen Callow, "Upholsterer, from London," included "seattees" among his list of upholstered goods.[1] Other such advertisements were published into the 1770s, but the settee never became popular. Only four examples made in New York during the colonial period are known today.[2]

Of these four settees, the Collection's example is the earliest in style—a fully developed though somewhat austere Queen Anne idiom—and probably the earliest in date. The shape of the legs and the carving on the knees and feet match those elements in a group of Queen Anne–style chairs made in New York between 1740 and 1760.[3] Like the chairs, the settee closely resembles English furniture made in the late 1720s and 1730s.[4] In the form of its straight crest rail and C-scroll arms, it matches a settee made about 1763 for the New Yorker Samuel Verplanck (1739–1820), although the execution of the cabriole legs is quite different.[5]

The mid-eighteenth century would have been a likely period for the settee's first owner, William Beekman (1684–1770) of Brugh (Bridge) Street, to acquire new and expensive furnishings. New York City was then rapidly gaining in sophistication and wealth because of renewed attention from Crown officials and an influx of British officers. Recalling the 1750s, Anne Grant wrote that "at New York [City], there was always a governor, a few troops, and a kind of little court kept; there too was a mixed, and in some degree, polished society."[6]

Beekman was a senior member of a respected and influential family that had settled in Manhattan in 1647.[7] A successful doctor, he turned to a mercantile career in the 1740s, when King George's War opened up opportunities. Several of his sons followed his interests, and James W. (1732–1807), who inherited the settee, became one of New York's wealthiest merchants and a Revolutionary leader.

—*Gilbert T. Vincent*

Cat. 15

Attributed to Samuel Harding (d. 1758)

Tea table

Philadelphia, Pa., ca. 1750

Mahogany; Atlantic white cedar, yellow pine,
29 ½ x 24 ½ x 19 in.
Gift of Mrs. Anne C. Bienstock (1992.0028)

In this rococo masterpiece, the carver's art and the cabinetmaker's sense of proportion and sure handling of line create a graceful platform for the tea ceremony, a central part of daily life in upper-class colonial America. The table rises from the floor in a series of graceful reverse curves that lead the eye to the small tabletop, where the expensive imported tea and its attendant wares of china and silver could be displayed in an exalted fashion that heightens and emphasizes their importance. The table is supported by cabriole legs that terminate in delicate, crisply carved claw-and-ball feet. The knees are embellished with tripartite carved shells with three pendant husks below, in a hand that is seen on other Philadelphia work of this period, and the carver's skill is also evident in the pendant carved shells found in the center of the rails. The rails are skillfully shaped to curve inward, forming in essence a large coved section that lifts up and dramatizes the tabletop, creating an altarlike effect.[1] Despite a rectangular shape, such tables were often referred to as "square" tea tables in the mid eighteenth century, and they are a rare form in Philadelphia.

Like much eighteenth-century Anglo-American furniture, the ultimate source for this table's elegant form lies in Asian furniture from China and Japan.[2] Closer prototypes, as with much Philadelphia rococo-style furniture, can be found in the style and manner of Irish furniture of the period, perhaps due to the presence of Irish examples imported into the city or to the work of Irish-trained immigrant craftsmen.[3] Research by Luke Beckerdite suggests that this table is part of a group of objects that may have been carved by Samuel Harding (d. 1758) and others in his shop.[4]

—*Gerald W. R. Ward*

Dressing table

Newport, R.I., ca. 1760–85

Mahogany; eastern white pine, chestnut, 31 ⁷/₈ x 34 ¹/₄ x 21 ¹/₄ in.
Funds donated by Mrs. Richard Bethell Wilder (1967.0027)

Only approximately a dozen Newport dressing tables are known, far fewer than the number of related high chests. This table, with its open talons, is one of the most fully developed examples; its carved front legs make it singularly distinctive.

Newport dressing tables can be separated into three groups: the earliest group, with slipper feet; those with pad feet; and those with front claw-and-ball feet and rear pad feet.[1] The maker of only one table, a slipper-foot example, is documented: Job Townsend billed Samuel Ward on July 1, 1746, for "A Mahogany Dressing Table . . . 13.10.-."[2] The other two slipper-foot dressing tables are almost identical to the docu-

mented Townsend one, with the same drawer configuration, similarly carved shells within an arc, and molded overhanging tops without any applied moldings between the top and the case.[3] The second group, with pad feet, begins to incorporate the slightly later feature of an applied cove molding under the top and thus seems to date after 1750.[4] Three of the third group—the most fully developed and probably the most costly dressing tables—are closely related to the Collection's piece with their applied cove molding, similar shells all set within an inscribed arc, and open talons on the front feet.[5]

This dressing table exhibits the fine-quality, highly figured mahogany used by

the Goddard and Townsend cabinet shops. The legs are very square with crisp, hard edges, and the knee carving is robust and sculptural. On the feet, the talon and claw break the inside curve of the ankle.[6] Although there is no documentation to attribute this piece to a specific maker, some chalk script on the inside of the backboard seems to read "Jn De. . . . " The table is said to have been owned by Stephen Hopkins (1707–1785), governor of Rhode Island and a signer of the Declaration of Independence.

—*Wendy A. Cooper*

Cat. 17
Movement by William Claggett (1696–1749);
case by the Goddard-Townsend families

Tall-case clock

Newport, R.I., ca. 1745–50

Mahogany; yellow poplar, eastern white pine, black walnut,
97 ¼ x 21 ³/₁₆ x 10 ¾ in.
Gift of Mr. C. Thomas Clagett, Jr. (1989.0006)

This magnificent William Claggett clock is one of four Newport tall-case clocks that feature this unusual and commanding double cornice and extraordinary brass dial.[1] Although the related cases suggest an origin in the same cabinet shop, two of the movements are signed by Claggett and two by his apprentice and son-in-law, James Wady.[2] Born in Wales, Claggett worked in Boston between about 1708 and 1716, before moving to Newport . He is known to have made at least three types of dials, uniting them with various styles of cases, including several Boston–made japanned cases.[3] Claggett died in 1749 and was succeeded in his business by Wady; these four clocks, then, represent the height of development and refinement by a master clockmaker and cabinetmaker just prior to the mid-eighteenth century.

One of the extraordinary aspects of this clock is the elaborately engraved brass fret applied not only to the face of the arch and broken-scroll pediment but also to the facing board that surrounds the dial inside the door. Cut from cast sheet brass and probably originally gilt, this was most certainly imported by either the maker of the case or Claggett. This clock is the only one of the four that has a brass fret; the others are wood or heavy paper. Presumably, the brass fret is original, although it might have been added later in the eighteenth century.[4] It was removed during restoration (probably early in this century), and the original backing material was replaced by a thick mahogany veneer over ash or oak veneer.[5] It might be assumed that originally the fret was backed with a wool baize–type woven fabric. During restoration, however, a large fragment of hand-laid paper painted in a tortoiseshell design was found inside the face of the bonnet under an original glue block. A reproduction of this paper has been placed behind the fret to suggest what may have been the original appearance.[6]

Although both Wady cases have diminutive ogee-bracket feet, this clock and its Claggett companion have deep molded bases today and may never have had feet. The shells on the two Wady clocks compare favorably to this one, but the shell on the other Claggett clock is less flowing and not as well developed. Comparison of the mahogany panels on the front of the base of the two Claggett clocks, however, reveals that they were both cut from the same board and hence probably were made
at the same time in the same shop.

—*Wendy A. Cooper*

Attributed to the Goddard-Townsend families

Bureau table

Newport, R.I., ca. 1760–90

Mahogany; chestnut, eastern red cedar, eastern white pine,
yellow poplar, poplar (possibly aspen), 32 $^7/_8$ x 36 $^1/_4$ x 20 $^3/_4$ in.
Funds donated by The Pew Memorial Trust (1978.0067)

Bureau tables achieved a popularity in America that they never knew abroad. Neither as utilitarian as a four-drawer chest nor as practical as a cabriole-leg dressing table, the popular block and shell model must have functioned in Newport foremost as a status symbol. The survival of fifty or more Newport block-and-shell bureau tables attests to both their popularity and the prosperity of Rhode Island's merchants and entrepreneurs.[1]

The best-known labeled bureau table from Newport may be the one made by Edmund Townsend (1736/7–1811), a contemporary and cousin of John Townsend.[2] The shells on the labeled Townsend bureau are virtually identical to those on the Department of State's example, differing from the typical John Townsend shells principally in the way the inner C-scroll relates to the outer lobes at the scroll terminations. The cornice molding of the Collection bureau is like the Edmund Townsend example, having a bead below the cove different from the cavetto used by John Townsend. The ogee-bracket feet of the Collection's bureau table are similar to those on Edmund Townsend's product, with fully articulated scrolls at the base of the blocking and knee brackets that meet in the middle without a space. The original brasses with spurred bails on this example echo the scrolled rococo shaping of the backplates in a sculptural way.[3]

This bureau table is the most expensive model a client could request. It has three shells across the top drawer (the two convex shells are carved and applied, while the central shell is cut from the solid drawer front); in addition, the door of the recessed center section has concave blocking surmounted by a concave shell that echoes the larger one just above it. If a client preferred less carving or expense, he might request that the door to the compartment be made with a fielded panel having an arched top, like the one Edmund Townsend made for John Desham of New London, Connecticut.[4] For an additional fee, one could order the top drawer fabricated as a writing desk, fitted with blocked drawers and pigeonholes.[5]

—*Wendy A. Cooper*

Attributed to Robert Harrold (working 1765–1792)

China table

Portsmouth, N.H., ca. 1765–75

Mahogany, sabicu; soft maple, eastern white pine, 27 ⁷/₁₆ x 32 ¹/₂ x 22 ¹/₂ in.
Gift of Rear Admiral Edward P. Moore and Mrs. Moore (1966.0100)

This striking table documents a dramatic shift in fashion in Portsmouth, New Hampshire, during the third quarter of the eighteenth century.[1] While earlier furniture emulates late baroque design in Boston, this table falls within the mainstream of the English rococo. Its design resembles a "China Table" in Chippendale's *Director*, and its form relates to surviving English and Irish tables.[2] In all likelihood, an English immigrant, probably the noted Portsmouth artisan Robert Harrold, introduced the pattern to Portsmouth and, in the process, transformed the taste of the town's most affluent residents.

Seven china tables from Portsmouth are known.[3] All originally had a railed gallery, fretwork brackets, and serpentine stretchers rising to a central plinth and pierced finial. In addition, all but one of the tables have molded legs and plain rails. The exception,

now at the Carnegie Museum of Art, Pittsburgh, Pennsylvania, has the added embellishment of applied fretwork on the legs and rails. On six of the tables, the legs and top are solid mahogany and the rails are mahogany veneer on maple; the Collection's table varies in having its top fashioned of sabicu, a tropical wood sometimes referred to as "horseflesh." Only the tables at the Department of State and the Carnegie Museum retain their original galleries. In each case, the gallery consists of a laminate of three mahogany strips set into a groove in the top and fastened with two diagonal splines at the mitered corners. The gallery covers the nails that fasten the top.

Early histories of ownership link the tables to Portsmouth's wealthiest families. The example at the Carnegie Museum was acquired by Stephen Chase (1742–1805), a prominent local merchant, while another

bears the chalk signature of its owner, the merchant William Knight. A third table and its matching urn stand belonged to John Wentworth, Governor of New Hampshire, until 1775, and later descended in the Wendell family.[4] A fourth table, which originally had a companion stand, was owned by William Whipple (1730–1785), a leading local merchant, a signer of the Declaration of Independence, and a Revolutionary War general.[5] His estate inventory refers to the table, listing in the back parlor "1 railed Tea Table 48/ [shillings] 1 sett China 24."[6] Whipple's handsome table, adorned with an elegant tea service, served as the centerpiece of the room. The table at the Department of State undoubtedly fulfilled a similar role, although its early history remains a mystery.[7]

—*Brock Jobe*

Roundabout chair

Boston-Salem area, Mass., ca. 1760–75

Mahogany; eastern white pine, birch, 33 ¹/₂ x 29 ³/₄ x 27 in.
Funds donated by Miss Louise Ines Doyle (1972.0018)

As depicted in eighteenth-century portraits, roundabout, or corner, chairs were popular for both reading and writing. John Singleton Copley's portrait of John Bours, for example, depicts the Newport subject in a contemplative pose seated in a similar chair while reading. A contemporary portrait of George Wyllis of Hartford attributed to Joseph Steward contains even more explicit references to the sitter's writing and reading, including a roundabout chair. Eighteenth-century probate inventories confirm the frequent proximity of roundabout chairs to gentlemen's desk and bookcases and suggest that they often belonged to larger matched sets of parlor seating furniture.[1] Other English names for this form include "smoking" and "barber's" chairs, functions that were also specifically male.

In each instance, roundabout chairs permitted sitters to turn freely between a desk or table and another person in a room. The angular front corner of this Boston chair must have made swiveling less comfortable than the generously curved rails of contemporary Newport examples, which express more overtly the act of straddling.[2] The probability that the Collection's chair was once part of a larger set of matching chairs suggests that consistency of design may have required the sacrifice of comfort. Also, like many roundabout chairs, this example originally served as a commode chair, as indicated by the frame for a chamber pot fastened to the rails below the loose seat frame.

The purchaser of roundabout chairs had a range of design options. Cabriole legs with claw-and-ball feet, for example, were more expensive than straight legs or common pad feet, but less expensive than carved knees like these. The fluted arm supports on the Department of State's chair would have cost several shillings more than the plain vase-and-ring turnings found on other chairs, although simply turned supports often correspond more harmoniously

to the turned stretchers of the base. Optional crossed stretchers had little to do with the chair's stability, as opposed to the shaped crest that secured the joint between the arms and provided support for sitters inclined to slouch in the curved portion of the back between the splats. Finally, high-style chairs like this example, but without a commode seat, could be upholstered over the rails and embellished with ornamental brass-headed tacks.[3]

—*Thomas S. Michie*

Cat. 21

Attributed to John Cogswell (1738–1819)

Chest of drawers

Boston, Mass., ca. 1770–85

Mahogany; eastern white pine, 30 7/16 x 35 7/8 x 20 in.
Funds donated by the Honorable C. Douglas Dillon
and Mrs. Dillon (1969.0103)

Made of bold, stripe-figured mahogany, this chest has been acclaimed as a tour de force of the bombé form.[1] The dramatic effect of the heavy, sculptural modeling of the drawer fronts is amplified by elaborate rococo hardware imported from England, with traces of original fire gilding remaining on the reverse.[2] The placement of the hardware follows and enhances the flowing lines of the curves.

More than sixty-five pieces of the American bombé form survive, ranging from dressing glasses to chest-on-chests to chests of drawers. This chest is one of only thirteen known chests of drawers that are also serpentine and thus shaped and curved both along their sides and across their front—a form made only in Boston.[3] The earliest American bombé furniture was derived directly from English sources, but later examples, such as this one, suggest a possible Dutch or French influence.

The owners of bombé furniture constituted a virtual "who's who" of wealthy Bostonians, including John Hancock, Gardiner Greene, Joseph Barrell, Thomas Dawes, Edward Brinley, Samuel Dexter, and Ebenezer Storer, Jr. All were pewholders of the Brattle Square Church, which contained a spectacular bombé-shaped pulpit of unique design in which frame-and-panel construction is simulated with carving of single huge balks of mahogany.[4] The bombé form, as the platform for each Sunday's sermon, must have been a powerful image in Revolutionary-era Boston.[5]

Ebenezer Storer (1729–1807) was thus among distinguished peers when, as family history relates, he had this chest made. A wealthy merchant, he succeeded John Hancock as treasurer of Harvard and was a selectman of Boston. Descriptions of his mansion portray a sumptuous interior in the latest taste.[6] The house itself was valued at $15,000 at his death, an extraordinary figure for the time.[7]

The chest was made by one of Boston's leading cabinetmakers, John Cogswell, who was born in Ipswich, trained in nearby Charlestown, and was working in Boston by 1762.[8] It relates closely to five of the thirteen known chests of serpentine-bombé form: all six have identically shaped curves for their case sides, drawer fronts, case-top molding profile, and triangular base blocking. Although variations are found in other details in the six chests, clearly all the chests were made from the same patterns employed by Cogswell.

—*Robert D. Mussey, Jr.*

Cat. 22

Jacob Hurd (1702/3–1758)

Tankard

Boston, Mass., ca. 1750

Silver, 8 ½ x 7 ½ x 5 (dia.) in.; weight 28 oz. 7 dwt.
Gift of Mrs. Joel Larus in memory of her father,
Mark Bortman (1971.0124.076)

In Boston, the tankard form developed along English lines but with the adoption of certain types of ornament not commonly found on English tankards: mid-bands, finials, and figural handle terminals. The iconography of these figural terminals suggests that tankards may have been presented to young churchgoers as a token of their divine election and entrance into the communion of the church, to young men as a symbol of their entrance into adulthood, and as marriage gifts.[1] Beer and ale, the drinks most often associated with tankards, were also thought to encourage lactation, and a tankard was considered a fitting gift for a woman on the birth of her first child. The cast decoration of a warrior's head on the handle terminal of this tankard, possibly symbolizing manhood or some heroic deed, is found on many other tankards by Jacob Hurd and may have been his own design. By 1750 most tankards were made with plain handle terminals, suggesting that the form continued to be popular because it symbolized tradition, family, and position.[2]

Hurd was by far the most prolific and prominent of Boston's silversmiths in the 1740s. He received many of the most important commissions for public presentation objects and was the favorite silversmith of Boston's elite. Unlike other craftsmen of his generation, Hurd did not diversify his business, but devoted all of his energies to silversmithing. The large volume of his business and the runaway inflation in Boston in the 1740s, eventually caused his financial ruin. Forced to borrow in order to buy metal, Hurd sometimes paid interest rates of 30 percent and higher. By the time he moved to Roxbury in 1755, he was nearly bankrupt, and his financial situation had so deteriorated that he was asked to give security to the town selectmen against his becoming a public charge. When he died, in 1758—"much lamented," according to the *Boston Gazette*—his estate was insolvent.[4]

In spite of these financial difficulties, Hurd still stands as the most important Boston silversmith of his generation. His shop turned out the town's most sophisticated objects in the Queen Anne and baroque styles (see also cat. no. 23). The shop's accomplished specialists, including engravers, chasers, burnishers, and turners, also performed work for other firms, thus influencing the look of all Boston silver made during this period.[5]

—*Barbara McLean Ward
and Jennifer F. Goldsborough*

Cat. 23
Jacob Hurd (1702/3–1758)

Sauceboat

Boston, Mass., ca. 1740–50

Silver, 4¹/₁₆ x 6 ¹³/₁₆ x 4 ¹¹/₁₆ in.; weight 9 oz. 10 dwt
Gift of Jane Bortman Larus in loving memory of her parents,
Mark and Llora C. Bortman (1971.0124.074a)

This sauceboat is a fine example of a form associated with fashionable dining. When entertaining, wealthy Bostonians, like the original owner of this sauceboat, served a variety of dishes at each course. The first course generally consisted of one or two soups, fish, several roasts as well as other cuts of meat, fowl, game, vegetables, stews, and boiled puddings, while the second course included a similar list of dishes complemented by a sweet pudding or a tart. Lavish dinners required two dessert courses, one consisting of creams, cakes, and preserved fruit and jellies, and the other of fresh fruit and nuts. Sauces were an important part of the first three courses. Puddings made of eggs, sugar, milk, and meal would be served, for instance, with a sweet sauce made from melted butter, wine, and sugar that was served from a ceramic or silver sauceboat.[1] The English traveler Dr. Alexander Hamilton, in his *Itinerarium* of 1744, mentions that in Boston he was served codfish "elegantly dressed with a sauce of butter and eggs."[2]

The sauceboat form seems to have come to the colonies in delftware examples by the 1660s.[3] Ceramic sauceboats were probably always more common than costly silver examples such as this one in the Queen Anne style, which is one of a pair. Its cabriole legs, pad feet, scalloped rim, and broad lip are characteristic of Boston-made sauceboats of this period, including at least eleven surviving examples by the maker of this sauceboat, Jacob Hurd, who was the most prolific Boston silversmith of his generation.[4] Sauceboats were generally made in pairs and even sometimes in sets of four. Kathryn C. Buhler observed that they often seem to be engraved on the same side, indicating that they were meant to be displayed facing in the same direction.[5] This sauceboat and its mate, also in the Collection, are engraved with a crest of a demilion, but their original owner cannot be identified.

—*Barbara McLean Ward*

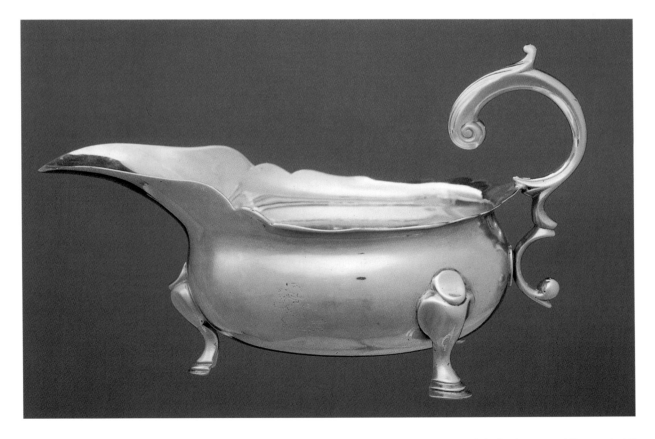

Cat. 24

Side chair

New England, probably Massachusetts, ca. 1780–1800

Mahogany; soft maple, black walnut, mahogany, 36 x 22 x 19 ⅝ in.
Gift of Mrs. Lawrence Mills (1973.0111.002)

Toward the end of the eighteenth century, a new chair-back design with hints of neo-classical ornamentation became popular in several regions of the United States. Based upon the backs of English chairs (one of which was owned in Newbury, Massachusetts, by the first decade of the nineteenth century), this back consisted of two or three horizontal, serpentine slats pierced at the center with a crowned honeysuckle, or anthemion, the most popular floral motif of the recently revived classical vocabulary.[1] Nevertheless, the chairs as a whole still remain close in spirit to Chippendale-style chairs of the mid-eighteenth century in the shape of their crest rails; straight, molded legs; and molded stiles capped by carved acanthus leaves.

The *Journeyman Cabinet and Chair-Makers Philadelphia Book of Prices* for 1795 lists a "splatt back Chair, honey suckle pattern made for stuffing over the seat rail."[2] This chair, one of a set of six in the Department of State Collection, has unusual, fully pierced honeysuckle flowers, like English examples, and yet the consistent use of soft maple for the front seat rails supports an American attribution. On other American chairs, the honeysuckle motif at the center of the slats was generally left solid; many have simplified piercings, and some are uncarved.[3]

The attribution of this set to Essex County, Massachusetts, probably follows from the Newbury chairs, long believed to have been made locally, owned by the Society for the Preservation of New England Antiquities. A second chair at Winterthur branded by William Porter may also have been made or owned in Massachusetts, where this design seems to have been particularly popular.[4]

—*Thomas S. Michie*

Cat. 25

Easy chair

New York, N.Y., ca. 1760–75

Mahogany; white oak, red oak, maple, eastern white pine,
45 x 36 ¾ x 27 ½ in.
Funds donated by Scalamandré, Inc. (1972.0108)

This chair has all the characteristics of
the standard colonial American easy chair,
a form derived from English examples of
the 1720s and 1730s, but it expresses them
in the full idiom of New York furniture.
There are the broad, generous proportions,
gently rounded crest and front rails, strongly
curved wings ending in cone-shaped arm
supports, and highly carved cabriole legs
with claw-and-ball feet of the best New
York craftsmanship. Although upholstered
chairs of this type had lost favor in England
by the 1750s, they remained popular in
America until the 1770s.

There are at least three other New York
easy chairs of this form. A nearly identical
example (Museum of the City of New
York) descended in the Van Wagenen family
of Cedar Grove, near Poughkeepsie, New
York.[1] Winterthur owns a second version,
also with acanthus leaves on the knees, but
the carving style and the squarish claw-
and-ball feet suggest the work of a different
cabinet shop. A third example appears
to have yet another style of carving.[2]

The amount of fabric required to cover
easy chairs made them expensive household
possessions in the eighteenth century.
Inventories commonly list them in bedchambers, where they might also be fitted
with a chamber pot. The chairs were often
upholstered en suite with the bed hangings
and window curtains. Although any wealthy
individual could own one, the combination
of padded upholstery and a protected niche
enclosed by the wings made these chairs
particularly suitable for sick or elderly
people.[3]

—*Gilbert T. Vincent*

Myer Myers (1723–1795)

Tankard

Probably New York, N.Y., ca. 1785

Silver, 8 ⁷/₈ x 5 ¹/₂ (dia. base) in.; weight 48 oz. 11 dwt
Gift of Dr. and Mrs. Eben Breed (1972.0038)

Myer Myers, one of America's finest silver-smiths, was born in New York City in 1723, the eldest son of Solomon and Judith Myers, who had emigrated from Holland. His master is unknown. Myers became a freeman of the city on April 29, 1746, and was a leading member of his synagogue, the congregation Shearith Israel. Through his leadership there, he became closely involved with Jewish congregations in other colonies and made silver *Rimonim* (scroll bells) for the Pentateuch for Touro Synagogue in Newport, Rhode Island, about 1765 and for the congregation Mikveh Israel in Philadelphia in 1772. He also made silver for all of the most prominent families in New York and became one of the city's leading artisans.

When the British occupied New York in 1776, Myers moved his family to Norwalk, Connecticut, where he worked until at least 1780. He removed to Philadelphia sometime before 1782, when his name begins to appear in the records of the congregation Mikveh Israel. Myers remained in Philadelphia until the end of the Revolutionary War, returning to New York in 1783. He resumed his prominent position in synagogue and city affairs and was elected chairman of the Gold and Silver Smiths' Society in 1786.[2]

Myers is famous for the sophistication of his elaborate objects in the rococo style and for the high quality of all his wares. Most of his tankards have the straight sides and flat tops typical of New York examples. This tulip-shaped tankard, however, is unusual for his work, and is a form more commonly associated with Philadelphia. It may have been inspired by objects that Myers saw during his sojourn in that city. The original engraved initials (C/RP in block letters on the bottom), and the later armorial engraving indicate that the tankard was owned by members of the Pelham family of New York. The style of the large engraved initials suggests that the tankard was made during the 1780s, probably after Myers returned to New York from Philadelphia.[3]

—*Jennifer F. Goldsborough
and Barbara McLean Ward*

Cat. 27

Card table

New York, N.Y., ca. 1760–90

Mahogany; red oak, yellow poplar, hickory, 27 ⁵/₈ x 34 x 16 ¹/₂ in.
Funds donated by the Dorothy Jordan Chadwick Fund (1975.0025)

In 1973 Morrison H. Heckscher of the Metropolitan Museum of Art published an in-depth study of the design and construction of New York rococo-style card tables, a type of furniture generally considered to be among the most successful of American designs.[1] This table is of the group identified as "Type II," a body of work distinguished by light, elegant lines, and by exuberant asymmetrical carving in the rococo style on the knees of the front legs. (The three rear legs are not carved.)

As with much eighteenth-century furniture, this table was made to be placed against the wall when not in use. The deeply incurved, serpentine sides of the table facilitate its being lifted and moved by one person. The flyleg, in the open position, reveals a "secret" drawer often found in similar tables. The top is lined with green baize and is shaped with shallow wells for counters and with square corners for candlesticks, all for the benefit of enthusiastic colonial card players enjoying a game of whist, loo, quadrille, or another popular game.

According to tradition, this example descended in the Varick family, long associated with New York. The most prominent member of the family in the eighteenth century was Richard Varick (1753–1831), mayor of New York City from 1789 to 1801. Richard played an active role in the American Revolution, first as an aide to Benedict Arnold, and then, after being exonerated of any connection with Arnold's treason, as confidential secretary to George Washington. He pursued a busy career in politics and public service after the Revolution. Although the precise line of descent of the card table is not known, Richard, who did not have children, or his brother Abraham (1750–1810), a successful merchant, are possible candidates as the original owner.[2]

—*Gerald W. R. Ward*

Cat. 28

Armchair

New York, N.Y., ca. 1755–75

Mahogany; sweet gum, eastern white pine, 39⅛ x 29 x 24 in.
Funds donated by Mr. and Mrs. Joseph H. Hennage (1968.0071.001)

Once part of a large set, this armchair is a handsome example of New York Chippendale-style design. Typical of New York furniture, it combines elements of the English George II and Chippendale styles. Cabriole legs with claw-and-ball feet, shell carving on the knees and crest rail, and eagle's-head arms are standard features of George II furniture; trapezoidal seats, pierced splats, and serpentine crest rails with ears are identified with the Chippendale style. English chairs exist with very similar patterns.[1]

The Collection's armchair so closely matches an armchair in the Los Angeles County Museum that they may be considered part of the same set, rather than from two identical sets. The original owner of the armchair at the Los Angeles County Museum (and by extension the Collection's chair) was Colonel Thomas Ellison (1701–1779) of New Windsor, New York, or his son, Thomas (1732–1796), a merchant in New York City. The Ellison family that ran an extensive and successful trading business.

At least two additional sets exist with the same splat design. An armchair and possibly a side chair, each more elaborate than the Collection's chair, came from a set that descended from Samuel Verplanck (1739–1820).[2] The Verplanck chairs are fully developed in the Chippendale style, with acanthus leaves flowing down the knees, gadrooning under the seat rail, scrolled rather than eagle's-head arms, and rocaille carving on the crest rail. Although a chair from a third set has the same splat, it is finished with carved ears and plain knees, unlike the Collection's chair.[3]

The eagle's-head arms are unusual features, found only on a few examples of New York and New England furniture. The motif appears first on George II chairs made in England; by 1750 it was used on New York furniture.[4] Another small but distinct feature is the pendant on the front rail of each chair. Most New York Chippendale chairs have

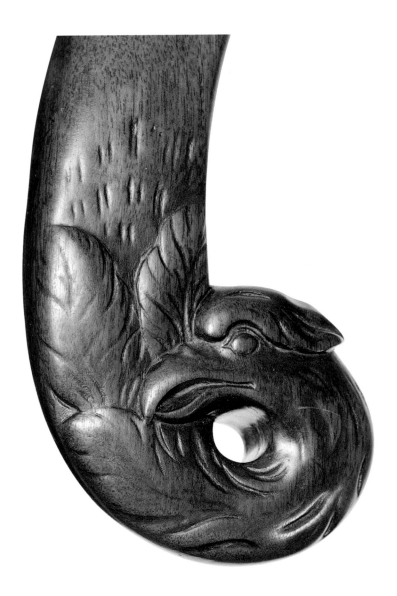

either an applied gadrooned molding or no decoration on the front rail. This unusual detail is also found on a card table that descended in the Backer family of Newburgh, New York.[5] As the table shares the same knee and foot design, it could be the product of the same maker.[6]

—*Gilbert T. Vincent*

Cat. 29

Philip Syng, Jr. (1703–1789; working 1726–1772)

Salver

Philadelphia, Pa., ca. 1760

Silver, 1 ³/₁₆ x 8 ¹⁵/₁₆ in.; weight 13 oz. 1 dwt.
Funds donated by Dr. and Mrs. Raymond Sphire (1974.0020)

The salver was introduced in the seventeenth century as a small, circular tray on a high trumpet foot, and was used for passing a beverage cup or for serving a special delicacy. The terms *salver*, *server*, and *waiter* seem to have been interchangeable during the eighteenth century; *stand* was used to refer to a small tray made to go beneath a matching vessel, such as a teapot or tureen. The word *tray* is modern.

Most American salvers in the rococo style are notable for the stiff regularity of their shell-and-scroll rims. Here, however, Philip Syng has expressed the asymmetry and fanciful spirit of the high-style Philadelphia rococo remarkably well, with a looser, more imaginative handling of the scrolls and a swirled, lively shell motif. The rim was cast in six identical sections, each centered with a shell. The joints of the sections are visible at several points around the

edge in the middle of the longest C-scroll segments. The grooved, asymmetrical feet are unusual and lack evidence of wear, suggesting that they may be replacements.

The initials "HP" are engraved on the underside of the salver, but the original owner of the object remains unidentified. Evidence of buffing on the upper surface of the salver suggests that it was originally engraved either with the crest or the coat of arms of the owner. The maker's mark, "PS" in block letters within a square reserve, is struck four times around the center of the bottom, alternating with four leaf-shaped marks.

Philip Syng, Jr., was born in Ireland and emigrated with his family in 1714. He and his brother John (1705–1738) served their apprenticeships under their father, Philip Syng, Sr. (1676–1739). Philip, Jr. rapidly became a successful businessman and

prominent civic leader. He was a founding member of the Library Company of Philadelphia and one of the original members of Franklin's Junto, a debating club that evolved into the American Philosophical Society. He was also grand warden of the Grand Lodge of Pennsylvania Masons, a vestryman of Christ Church (Episcopal), a warden and later treasurer of the city of Philadelphia, and a trustee of the College and Academy of Philadelphia. Syng's house and shop were located for many years on Front Street. He married Elizabeth Warner in 1726; the couple had twenty-one children. He and his wife retired to a farm outside Philadelphia in 1778, but returned to the city in 1785.[1]

—*Jennifer F. Goldsborough*
and Barbara McLean Ward

Philip Syng, Jr. (1703–1789; working 1726–1772)

Teapot

Philadelphia, Pa., ca. 1755

Silver, 5 ⅝ x 8 ½ x 2 ¾ in. (diam. foot); weight 15 oz. 7 dwt.
Gift of Miss Alice Harrison Warwick, Mr. John Edward Warwick,
and Mrs. Virginia Henley Ameche in loving memory of their mother,
Mrs. Alice Harrison-Smith Warwick (1966.0097.001)

This teapot, engraved with the Bayard family arms and with a history of descent in that family, is a quintessential example of the Philadelphia rococo style in silver. The relatively low stance of the pot places it early in the popularity of the inverted-pear, or double-bellied, form. The compressed domed foot is inscribed with simple concentric lines rather than the flourish of gadrooning found a decade later on such pots, and the body springs directly from the foot without the lift of an intervening pedestal. The shallow, domed cover and flush hinge, a sign of fine craftsmanship, continue the flow of gentle curves without interruption. The finial is an early example of the bell-shaped type favored by Philadelphia silversmiths of the 1760s and 1770s.

The banded effect at the joint between the body and spout is an echo of design details from the 1740s rather than the sign of a replaced spout or the mark of an incompetent craftsman. Such rococo niceties as the scrolled lower handle socket add lightness and movement.[1] Syng is known to have employed several engravers, so the lacy embellishment of this teapot may not be by his own hand.[2] Syng placed his initial mark, in block capitals within a rectangular reserve, on the bottom, on each side of a scrolled leaf mark.[3]

With such masterly works as this teapot to his credit, it is hardly surprising that Philip Syng, Jr., was one of colonial Philadelphia's most successful silversmiths, producing such commissions as the silver inkstand used in signing the Declaration of Independence.

—Jennifer F. Goldsborough
and Barbara McLean Ward

Cat. 31
Bancroft Woodcock (1732–1817; working 1754–1794)

Coffeepot

Wilmington, Del., ca. 1775

Silver, 13 1/16 x 9 7/8 x 4 5/16 (dia. foot) in.; weight 38 oz. 17 dwt.
Gift of Miss Alice Harrison Warwick, Mr. John Edward Warwick,
and Mrs. Virginia Henley Ameche in loving memory of their mother,
Mrs. Alice Harrison-Smith Warwick (1966.0097.002)

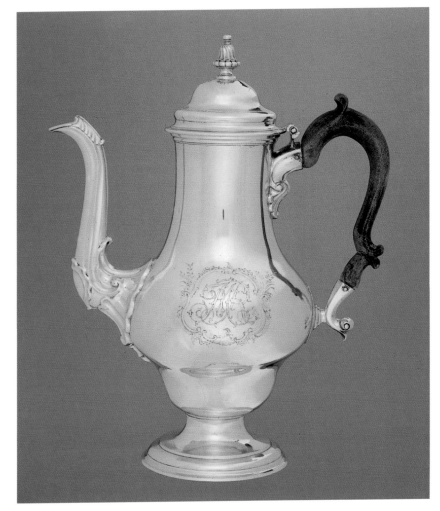

Bancroft Woodcock was born on July 18, 1732, the son of Irish Quaker immigrants Robert and Rachel (Bancroft) Woodcock, who settled in Wilmington, Delaware, shortly after 1726. His master is not known, but his style suggests that he learned his craft in Philadelphia. He opened his business in Wilmington "near the upper Market house" on July 4, 1754. In 1759 he married Ruth Andrews, and during his early career he was active in the Society of Friends. He trained at least five apprentices, four of whom were Quakers: Richard Humphreys; William Poole; his nephew, Thomas Byrnes; and his son, Isaac Woodcock. In 1790 he advertised for his runaway apprentice, Elijah Wansey, whom he described as a mulatto. Woodcock became a craftsman and landowner. For most of his life he worked alone, but in 1790 he formed a brief partnership with Thomas Byrnes, which dissolved by 1793. Woodcock maintained his prosperous shop in Wilmington until 1794, when he retired to his farm in Bedford County, Pennsylvania.[1]

Woodcock's extant work includes at least two other coffeepots of this type and numerous sugar urns, sugar bowls, and cream pots.[2] The proportions of this coffeepot are particularly fine—it is more elegant than earlier pear- and inverted-pear-shaped coffeepots, but it lacks the exaggerated attenuation of slightly later neoclassical examples. The engraved rococo cartouche and plain, rather than gadrooned, edge of the foot and cover suggest that the pot was made immediately before the Revolution rather than afterward.

Masterfully designed, Woodcock's silver embodies the high quality, simplicity, balance, and poise found in the best work of his Philadelphia peers. The delicate engraving, swirled bell-shaped finial, and the design of the cast spout on this coffeepot are almost identical to details of contemporary coffeepots by Joseph Richardson, Sr.; Joseph, Jr.; Nathaniel Richardson; and Woodcock's former apprentice, Richard Humphreys.[3]

—Jennifer F. Goldsborough
and Barbara McLean Ward

Cat. 32

Side chair

Philadelphia, Pa., ca. 1760–80

Mahogany; eastern white pine, Atlantic white cedar,
yellow poplar, 40 ½ x 23 ½ x 32 in.
Funds donated by Mrs. Elizabeth G. Schneider (1971.0080)

This chair retains the overall configuration of the tassel-back design popular in Philadelphia, but differs in minor details of its carving, which is more elaborate in some areas and less well developed in others than on related chairs.[1] The ruffled vine ornament at the center of the crest rail, for example, is more contained within the shape of the crest than are the boldly scalloped shells carved on other examples. A third variation on this design incorporates latticework in place of either a shell or vines.[2] The acanthus leaves that descend along the outer straps of the interlaced splat are richly carved here. They are less rigid than the gadrooning found on other chairs, which converges at the center of the shoe and complements the lobed shell above. The molded stiles here were less costly to execute than the cabled fluting used on more expensive chairs, and their relative plainness contrasts with the elaborately carved banister. Finally, the beaded scrolls that converge at the center of the front seat rail undercut the mass of the wood, whereas the bold shell on other variants enhances the solidity of their stout mahogany rails.

The same double scrolls appear on the front seat rails of chairs labeled by Thomas Tufft and by James Gillingham, as well as many other unattributed Philadelphia chairs, thus confirming the popularity of this design probably among several different cabinet shops.[3] The distinctive C-shaped gouge carving between the converging veins of the acanthus leaves on the knees relates closely to the carving on other Philadelphia furniture in the Collection, including a dressing table and the base of a high chest, both of which were probably carved in the same Philadelphia shop.[4] An early owner of this chair, Ella Parsons, was a descendant of William Parsons, the surveyor general of Philadelphia, who succeeded Benjamin Franklin as head of the Library Company of Philadelphia.[5]

—*Thomas S. Michie*

Armchair

Philadelphia, Pa., ca. 1765–80

Mahogany; white oak, 38 ½ x 26 ¼ x 26 ¼ in.
Funds donated by Mrs. Golsan Schneider (1976.0044)

Upholstered chairs with open arms were frequently made in large sets for aristocratic English houses, but they were uncommon in the American colonies. One reason for their rarity was their cost. On the 1772 list of prices for cabinetwork, a mahogany "[Arm]Chair Frame for stuffing over back and Seat with marlborough feet" cost £2, only ten shillings less than an easy chair frame. The carving, moldings, brackets, and "bases" (the moldings around the feet) were all listed as additional charges, which could add as much as £1 to the price.[1] With the upholstery, the cost of an armchair like this one can be roughly calculated at about £6, or almost double the cost of a carved armchair with a slip seat.

The original upholstery on this armchair and gilded tacks outlining the seat rails, arms, and back must have been intended to make a visual statement of its owner's wealth. Contemporary English armchairs of this type that retain their original upholstery have showy coverings, such as tapestry, damask, or leather. Chairs with damask or leather frequently were further embellished with tufting.[2] One unusual feature of this chair frame is the high position of the bottom member of the back frame, which suggests that the seat may have been covered with a loose cushion.[3]

Many features of this armchair indicate an origin in Philadelphia, where the most elaborate American versions of the form were made.[4] The thick rails and absence of diagonal braces in the back and seat are characteristic of American rather than English chair-making. The side rails of the seat frame are tenoned through the stiles, a construction feature found almost exclusively in Philadelphia. The foliage-carved arms and fret-carved front legs were originally fitted with casters. The arms, with their high-quality carving and the subtly twisted support moldings, are greatly superior to the carved legs, suggesting different craftsmen at work for a large shop.

—*David L. Barquist*

Cat. 34

Sofa

Probably Philadelphia, Pa., ca. 1775–1800

Mahogany; secondary woods not recorded prior to reupholstering,
40 ³/₄ x 100 ¹/₂ x 35 ¹/₂ in.
Gift of Mr. and Mrs. David H. Stockwell (1973.0099)

Sofas with the arched back, serpentine front seat rail, and outward-scrolling arms of this imposing example have survived in greater numbers from Philadelphia than from any other American city. A sofa of the same large dimensions, but with peaks in the back and a Gothic fret pattern carved on the seat rails and front legs, has been attributed to the Philadelphia cabinetmaker Thomas Affleck, for a commission of about 1766 from John and Ann Penn; the Penn sofa was made en suite with a set of armchairs, two of which are in the Department of State Collection.[1]

Furniture with straight legs and applied foot moldings, known as "Marlborough feet," became fashionable in Philadelphia about 1765.[2] The absence of peaks on the back and carving or moldings on the legs may indicate that the Department of State's sofa dates to the last quarter of the eighteenth century, when such details had become less fashionable with the advent of the neoclassical style.

This sofa was as much the creation of the upholsterer as the cabinetmaker who made the frame. The maker or original owner may have taken into consideration that the frame's massive size would be diminished visually by the addition of loose pillows and bolsters in addition to the seat cushion or "mattress."[3] The Philadelphia upholsterer further refined the sofa's appearance by outlining the frame with decorative brass tacks; originally, the arched back was also defined by a row of brass tacks along its top edge.[4] These features, together with the imported cover fabric, added greatly to the cost of the finished sofa.[5]

Equal in value to a desk and bookcase or high chest of drawers, sofas occupied a dramatic focal point in the parlor. Unlike chairs, they were not placed against the walls after company had departed but were left in position, normally next to the fireplace. A visitor to the house in Philadelphia occupied by George Washington during his presidency noted, "On the left of the fireplace was a sofa which sloped across the room."[6]

—*David L. Barquist*

Cat. 35

Tea table

Philadelphia, Pa., ca. 1760–80

Mahogany, 28 x 32 ½ (diam.) in.
Funds donated by David and Juli Grainger (1982.0071)

Tea tables with tripod bases and circular tops were first made in Philadelphia about 1740. Josiah Claypoole advertised in 1738 that he made "all Sorts of Tea Tables," which probably included the tripod-base variety.[1] In 1741 the hardware merchant Joseph Paschall sold both iron and brass "Tea Table ketches," the fittings used to lock the tilting tops in a horizontal position. In 1748 Thomas Cant recorded making a "Pillar & Claw Tea Table" that included a "Box" or "birdcage."[2] This type of table was copied from contemporary English models, although none of the design books contained illustrations of such a form.[3]

Tripod-base tea tables with birdcages were extremely popular in Philadelphia and immense numbers of them were made. They ranged from less expensive mahogany versions with "plain top & feet" that cost £2.15s. in 1771 to tables like this one with elaborately carved pedestals and "scalloped" tops (today known as "piecrust" edges) that cost more than £4.[4] The pedestal on this table, with a compressed ball at the base of the pillar, was the most popular type. Some craftsmen apparently made a specialty of supplying cabinetmakers with pedestals for tea tables; Samuel Williams advertised "mahogany and walnut tea table columns" in 1767.[5]

These pedestals were probably sold uncarved to the retailer, who contracted specialist carvers to complete the work. This table was carved by an unidentified but prolific craftsman working during the 1760s and 1770s, who also carved a high chest in the Collection.[6] He created rich effects of volume and shading through a distinctive use of detail cuts, particularly turned-over ends on the long leaves and clusters of parallel, straight cuts to shade the ends of leaves.[7] At least one other tea table has carving laid out with the same distinctive pattern, which extends onto the lower edge of the legs and the sides of the base.[8]

—*David L. Barquist*

Cat. 36

Looking glass

Probably England, ca. 1775

Mahogany veneer, soft wood, gilt gesso, glass, 58 x 27 in.
Funds donated by Bredin Foundation (1969.0105)

A pediment looking glass of this type—
strongly architectural in form, embellished
with gilt and carved floral ornament and
moldings, and capped with a gilt phoenix
finial—would have meshed well with the
woodwork and furniture of a colonial
American interior of the 1750–75 period
in all urban centers. While some examples
were undoubtedly made in this country,
the bulk of the evidence indicates that the
majority were imported from England, as
was probably the case with this example.[1]

Its size, cost, and materials made a looking glass of this type not only an imposing
work of art, but also a major signifier of its
owner's class and status, as were tall, large,
and expensive case pieces that similarly
demonstrated social position. The use of
large sheets of imported glass—technically
difficult to produce in the eighteenth century—also indicated that the owner possessed both means and taste. Reflecting
daylight and candlelight, these looking
glasses seemingly added volume and space
to interiors. Hung high on the wall, they
caused viewers to gaze upward, in a rever-
ential pose, to see their reflections amid
suitable furnishings, multiplying the effect
of the other material possessions in
the room.

—*Gerald W. R. Ward*

Cat. 37

High chest of drawers

Philadelphia, Pa., ca. 1760–80

Mahogany; southern yellow pine, eastern white pine,
yellow poplar, Atlantic white cedar, 97 ³/₄ x 45 ¹/₈ x 22 ⅝ in.
Funds donated by Mr. and Mrs. O. Ray Moore (1978.0009)

Household textiles and clothing were so valuable during the colonial period that Philadelphians generally stored them in the most elaborate and expensive piece of furniture they owned. High chests had been used for this purpose since the city was settled in 1682, but the classic, scroll-pediment high chest with applied carving was developed after 1750.[1] High chests were rarely made in England after 1740; thus, the popularity of the form among wealthy Philadelphians was a departure from their customary close adherence to current English fashion.[2] The monumental, architectural quality of the best high chests clearly was (and remains) irresistible to Americans, even when a "Chest on a frame Claw feet & Leaves on the knees & shel drawer in ye Frame . . . Scroul pedement hed" cost £21 in mahogany, a price matched only by a desk and bookcase in the price list of 1772.[3] The carving lavished on high chests like this one is ample evidence that they were intended to rival the fully draped bed as the showpiece of the bedchamber.

This high chest and at least three other high chests and a double chest were made in the same unidentified shop.[4] The chests are identical in overall design and construction, but the most striking similarity lies in their carved ornament, which was executed by the same unidentified craftsman. This carver favored long, sinuous leaves with turned-over ends and used parallel chisel cuts for shading; he also carved a tea table in the Diplomatic Reception Rooms.[5] This high chest's original flame finials and central cartouche—known as the "blazes" and "shield" in contemporary documents—are also characteristic of this craftsman. William MacPherson Hornor described one of the related high chests as the work of the cabinetmaker Joseph Delaveau, about whom nothing else has been published.[6]

—David L. Barquist

Cat. 38 and 39

Attributed to Gerrard Hopkins (1742–1800; working 1767–1800)

Two side chairs

Baltimore, Md., ca. 1770

Mahogany; southern yellow pine, spruce,
39 x 23 1/4 x 20 1/4 in.
Funds given by an anonymous donor
(1972.0062.001 and .003)

Furniture produced in Baltimore before the Revolution is relatively rare. Although the town had begun the rapid growth that would become explosive in the post-Revolutionary period, in 1770 it had only three thousand inhabitants and two principal cabinet shops. That the masters of both these shops were trained in Philadelphia has added to the difficult task of distinguishing the furniture of the bigger city from that of its neighbor to the south.

Clearly of the Philadelphia school, these two chairs (part of a set of six in the Department of State Collection) can be ascribed not only to Baltimore but also to the shop of a specific cabinetmaker. The carving of the shell in the center of the seat rail is virtually identical to the shell on the apron of a high chest bearing the label of Gerrard Hopkins.[1] This shell has certain

idiosyncrasies, such as distinctive stippling, which indicate that the pieces came from the same hand. The carving of the foliate knee brackets and cabriole legs of the chest and chairs is similarly related. Other Maryland characteristics of the chairs, not exclusively used by Hopkins, are the bold cupid's-bow crest rail, wide splat, broad proportions, and somewhat provincial design.

Gerrard Hopkins was the leader of the cabinetmaking community in Baltimore, both before and after the Revolutionary War, a man respected both for his trade and his civic leadership. Born into a large and prosperous Maryland Quaker family, Hopkins left home for Philadelphia in 1754. Three years later he apprenticed with the Quaker cabinetmaker Jonathan Shoemaker (working 1757–1793), whose attributed work is in the finest and most fashionable

Philadelphia Chippendale style.[2] Upon returning to Maryland in 1767, Hopkins set up shop on Gay Street in Baltimore, which became the principal site of his manufactory for the next thirty-three years. His first advertisement alerts Marylanders to his Philadelphia training and appeals to potential clients, Quaker and non-Quaker, by stating that he worked in "mahogany, walnut, cherry-tree, and maple . . . to be done with or without carved work."[3]

It is likely that the first owners of these chairs were John Ross Key (1734–1821) and Ann Phoebe Charlton (1756–1830) of Frederick County, Maryland, who married in 1775. They were owned later by their son, Francis Scott Key (1779–1843), the Maryland lawyer and poet best known as the author of "The Star-Spangled Banner."[4]

—*Gregory R. Weidman*

Cat. 40

Side chair

Philadelphia, Pa., ca. 1755–75

Mahogany; southern yellow pine, eastern red cedar, eastern white pine, 39 ³/₄ x 24 ¹/₂ x 22 in.
Funds donated by Mrs. Frank Hollowbush (1974.0005)

The unusual breadth of the splat, the exaggerated scale of the carved tassel and ruffle, and the pronounced contrast between carved and uncarved surfaces distinguish this Philadelphia chair (and its five mates, also in the Collection) from other American interpretations of Chippendale's engraved designs for "ribband-back" chairs.[1] Only in New York was this chair-back design as popular.[2] The overall design does not appear in any known pattern books; rather, it follows English or Irish prototypes that could have been imported here in the eighteenth century.[3]

Both carved and uncarved variants indicate the range of stylistic options from which patrons could choose according to their taste and means. Only one related set, believed to have been owned originally in the Penn family, displays the profusion of carved ornament found on this set of chairs.[4] The ruffle on the front seat rail, for example, is an unusual embellishment to which the shell is in turn applied. The carved acanthus leaves extending over the knees are another visual refinement shared by only a few other sets of Philadelphia chairs. Other details, such as the shell-carved ears, ruffled ornament at the center of the crest rail, carved shoe, and fluted stiles, added further to the considerable cost of these chairs. The commode seat frame is original.

—*Thomas S. Michie*

Armchair

Philadelphia, Pa., ca. 1755–70

Black walnut; Atlantic white cedar, eastern white pine, southern yellow pine, black walnut, 42 ⅛ x 29 ½ x 23 ½ in.
Funds donated by The National Historical Foundation (1971.4)

Made for the Loockerman family of Dover, Delaware, this armchair and six matched side chairs (also in the Department of State collection) constitute one of the largest and most elaborate sets of American Chippendale-style chairs to have survived intact. They are probably the set referred to in the 1785 inventory of Vincent Loockerman's estate as "6 leather bottomed Walnut chairs (old)" valued as 15s. apiece and "1 Ditto Arm chair" as 22s.6d. in "the blue room upstairs."[1]

The chairs were expensive because they have several costly optional elements, such as "cut-through" and "relieved" (carved) banisters, "leaves on the knees," carved crest and seat rails, and fluted stiles. These and other options correspond to those on the best work itemized in contemporary Philadelphia cabinetmakers' price books.[2] Armchairs typically cost at least one pound more than side chairs, and chairs made of walnut generally cost slightly less than those made of imported mahogany.

An odd aspect of the armchair is the absence of scroll carving on the outer sides of the hand rests. Another unusual detail on this and several stylistically related chairs is the prominent "pins" at the tops of the stiles between the fluting and the carved ears. Occurring on either side of a structural joint, they imitate pins that might secure a spline joint. These, however, are carved from the solid and are purely ornamental.

Because trades such as carving and upholstery tended to be highly specialized, large urban cabinet shops often hired independent carvers on a piecework basis. Several other chairs of this same design vary slightly in the way the carved vine passes below the shell on the crest rail and in the method of articulating the shell ears.[3] Such differences indicate different carvers, or even different workshops, responding to a common model, and they confound attribution to an individual maker based upon carving.

Related chairs have been attributed to Thomas Affleck on the strength of a chair that descended in the Hollingsworth and Morris families of Philadelphia.[4] Vincent Loockerman is known to have purchased furniture in 1774 from another leading Philadelphia cabinetmaker, Benjamin Randolph, to whom Harold Sack has attributed this set. As Morrison H. Heckscher has pointed out, however, the Department of State's chairs are stylistically datable to the mid-1760s and are unlike known labeled examples by Randolph.[5] The restrained shaping of the arms and their supports likewise suggests this earlier dating.

—*Thomas S. Michie*

Cat. 42

Basket

China, for export, ca. 1772

Porcelain with overglaze colors, 3 ⁷/₈ x 8 ¹³/₁₆ x 6 ⁷/₈ in.
Gift of Mrs. Frederick Frelinghuysen (1966.0016)

William Pitt (1708–1778), the first earl of Chatham and owner of this porcelain basket, was America's greatest ally in Parliament. The colonists "are the subjects of this kingdom," declared Pitt in his 1766 arguments against the Stamp Act, "equally entitled with yourselves to all the natural rights of mankind and the peculiar privileges of Englishmen. Equally bound by its laws, and equally participating of the constitution of this free country. The Americans are the sons, not the bastards, of England."[1] He acknowledged Britain's legal right to govern the colonies, but saw no justification for taxing them without their consent. Although Pitt was successful in having the Stamp Act repealed, he could not stop the growing hostility between American revolutionaries and the British Crown. Until his death in 1778, Pitt continued to argue against the war that developed and urged the king to

withdraw troops, warning that the armed conflict would undo the kingdom.

The basket, bearing the arms of Viscount Pitt impaling those of his wife, Hester Grenville, is from a service presented in 1772 by John Bradbury Blake, the British East India Company's agent in Canton.[2] Pitt and Hester Grenville were married about 1755. She became baroness of Chatham in her own right in 1761, and Pitt was elevated to the peerage as Viscount Pitt and earl of Chatham in 1766.[3] The arms as presented on the basket are marshaled below the coronets of an earl and baroness. The Pitt crest is shown above the arms. At the left is the earl's coronet above the letter C and, at the right, the baroness's with the letters HC.

—*Ellen Paul Denker and Bert R. Denker*

Gilbert Stuart (1755–1828)

Stephen Van Rensselaer

ca. 1794

Oil on canvas (framed as an oval),
30 1/2 x 23 1/2 in. (full-sized canvas)
Gift of Dr. Bayard Clarkson (1981.0054)

This very strong head is a virtual demonstration of Stuart's painting technique. Over a putty-colored primer, a layer of gray was applied, then a dark umber shadow tone, which underlies the splendid, high-toned face and supplies the wraparound dark shadow lending the head its strong relief. On that ground, Stuart modeled the head easily, with high flesh tones, ruddy coloring, and judiciously used highlights. Patches of umber seem to have been left uncovered in various places, such as the pupils of Van Rensselaer's eyes, his right eyebrow, and along the right side of his face, contributing to the pictorial unity of the head. Quickly and economically, Stuart made this head spring to physical and intellectual life.

At the time of the sitting, Stephen Van Rensselaer (1764–1839) was about to take the office of lieutenant-governor of New York.[1] A committed Federalist, he was the eighth patroon of this venerable family to have dominion over the vast estate near Albany. He later commanded the United States forces on the northern frontier in the War of 1812, and served in the House of Representatives from 1823 to 1829. Active in the commercial development of New York State, he promoted the construction of the Erie Canal and Champlain Canal and founded the Rensselaer Technical Institute (1826). He was "probably the foremost man in the state in point of wealth and social prominence, [and] was loved for his simple tastes, democratic behavior, and genial manners."[2]

—*William Kloss*

The Road to Independence

STATESMEN AND DIPLOMATS

Above: Window treatment featuring a gilded eagle inspired by the one in the Great Seal of the U.S., Thomas Jefferson State Reception Room

Opposite: Near-life-size statue of Thomas Jefferson in a pedimented niche, by Arthur Bruce Hoheb, after Pierre Jean David d'Angers, Thomas Jefferson State Reception Room

It is astonishing that as provincial American craftsmen were producing remarkable three-dimensional arts, as exemplified in the previous pages, and even while the Boston painter John Singleton Copley was painting some of his most beautiful portraits in this country, the ties that bound England to America were coming unraveled. The paintings and other works presented hereafter are associated with the momentous years of the Revolution. Many of them descend from or represent politicians, diplomats, and other figures who played essential roles in the formation of this country. Also included here are some significant accoutrements of statesmanship and diplomacy, such as a peace medal (cat. no. 54), a United States seal (cat. no. 55), and a skippet (a box used to protect the wax seal of major international treaties) (cat. no. 56).

The Revolution brought major changes to the artistic life of the country. Copley, for example, departed on the eve of the Revolution. After a period of study in Italy he established himself in England, where he became a major figure in British painting—never to return to Boston. Copley's magnificent portrait of Mrs. John Montresor (cat. no. 48) was painted in England during the American Revolution as a companion piece to a striking image of her husband painted by Copley in New York City, where Montresor had been stationed as a lieutenant in the British Army about 1771.

At the same time, some of the most accomplished furniture and silver was being made in the port towns of the colonies. Successful merchants had accumulated means to build great mansions and to furnish them with splendor. Much of this was possible because merchants made a practice of avoiding duties imposed by the Crown. Colonial royal governors, whose salaries were dependent upon trust and the vote of provincial assemblies, found it difficult to enforce duties on goods available only through triangular trade with the West Indies, thanks to restrictive British laws. Also, the Crown's attempts to control provincial manufacturing simply did not work.

It is estimated that by the middle of the eighteenth century the population of British North America had risen to about a million and a half individuals. As we have seen, such an increase led Benjamin Franklin to conclude that ideas about economic systems based on Old World experiences were invalid for America. The *facts* of the New World were destroying mercantile theories of the mother country. Franklin argued that in a land so vast as North America, labor would never be cheap no matter what the rate of population growth through immigration or natural increase. He further reasoned that the rapidly growing American market would create more work for manufacturers in the mother country."[1]

But such conciliatory observations were insufficient to prevent various taxes being levied on the colonists after the French and Indian Wars. First came the Sugar Act of 1764, then, a year later, the detested Stamp Act. Nonimportation agreements made by colonials then put pressure on British manufacturers and helped William Pitt obtain the repeal of the Stamp Act in 1766. This was a temporary victory, however, for in 1767 Parliament passed the Townshend Acts, which put customs duties on imports of glass, lead, paints, paper, and tea. Despite Americans' long tradition of smug-

gling, and thereby bypassing duties, the reaction was strong. In 1768, responding to threats of enforced collections and a decrease in their authority to self-govern, the members of the House of Representatives of Massachusetts Bay sent to the other colonies a circular letter that was meant to unify all colonial legislative bodies to protest authoritarian abuses and argue for self-representation. Boston's royal governor demanded that the colonial legislators retract their letter, but an overwhelming majorty of representatives voted not to rescind their letter. It then gained favorable responses from legislative bodies in all the colonies. Such civil disobedience served as an excuse for the governor to call for the arrival of British troops to occupy Boston in the fall of 1768.

This was the prelude to the events that led to the Boston Massacre, which took place in front of the Boston State House on March 5, 1770. Paul Revere depicted the clash in his most famous, and most politically inflammatory, print, donated to the Collection by a descendant of one of the victims pictured in it (cat. no. 44). Revere had associated himself with all of the groups in Boston dedicated to American liberty. By the time he made this work he was a Son of Liberty, a member of St. Andrews Lodge of Freemasons, the Loyal Nine of 1766, the North Caucus, the Long Room Club, and the Boston Committee of Correspondence. He was an admirer of John Wilkes, the radical English Whig, whose views about liberty and the natural rights of British subjects were celebrated on Revere's monumental silver Sons of Liberty Bowl, now in the Museum of Fine Arts, Boston.[2]

The events that followed are well known: the destruction of the HMS *Gaspee* in l772, the Boston Tea Party of 1773, the appointment of the committee of correspondence in Virginia in the same year. The Continental Congress adopted a declaration of rights in 1774, and a year later the Revolutionary War began with the Battles of Lexington and Concord and the Battle of Bunker Hill.[3] Also in 1775, George Washington was appointed commander in chief of the American forces, and by 1776 the British were forced to evacuate Boston. The subsequent events of the Revolution, up to and including the adoption of the Constitution in 1789, are too numerous and too well known to outline here. But it is important to observe that the diplomatic relations between American and European statesmen led to military

success. Lafayette landed at Charleston in 1777; the alliance with France took place a year later. In 1781 Lord Cornwallis surrendered at Yorktown and the Articles of Confederation were ratified. A year later Holland recognized the United States as an independent nation. Denmark, Russia, Spain, and Sweden followed.

The treaty of peace with Great Britain was signed in Paris on September 3, 1783. John Jay was one of the four American signatories to the treaty (the others were Benjamin Franklin, William Temple Franklin, and Henry Laurens). Exhausted after the treaty signing, Jay removed to London, where he was painted by Gilbert Stuart. That portrait, which hangs in the John Quincy Adams State Drawing Room, was begun in 1783 and finished a year later, when Jay, as secretary of foreign affairs, had been sent back to England by Washington as a diplomat. Jay was the first American to hold the title of foreign minister, under the Continental Congress. He continued unofficially to superintend the Department of State from the time the Constitution went into effect, on March 4, 1789, until Jefferson took office as secretary of state in September of that year.[4] While American diplomats and ministers were abroad, they experienced at first hand the courtly arts of Europe and Great Britain—a fact that undoubtedly influenced the emerging taste for neoclassicism in this country.

The Jay portrait in this exhibition is a somewhat later image painted by John Wesley Jarvis, the foremost portrait artist of New York City of the early nineteenth century (cat. no. 53). Jay is represented with dignity and restraint—a founding father who, after the 1783 peace treaty was signed in Paris, arbitrated continuing disputes between Great Britain and America with a treaty that bears his name. Concluded on November 19, 1794, the treaty marked the emergence of the new, independent nation after some twenty years of conflict and war. While he was away in London Jay was elected governor of New York, a post he held for six years. During his administration slavery was abolished in New York. Jay is reputed to have declared: "Till America comes into this measure [abolition of slavery], her prayers to Heaven for liberty will be impious."

In the imagination of Americans today, there abides a sense of these events and the noble sacrifices of many who shaped the collective ideal declared by Congress on July 4, 1776, concerning liberty and the natural rights of mankind: "We hold these truths to be self-evident, that all men are created equal, that they are endowed by their Creator with cer-

tain inalienable Rights, that among these are Life, Liberty and the pursuit of Happiness.—That to secure these rights, Governments are instituted among Men, deriving their just powers from the consent of the governed." This Declaration of Independence, drafted in Philadelphia by Thomas Jefferson and signed by representatives of the thirteen original colonies, put forth rational arguments for independence and an incendiary catalogue of abuses by King George III, including the statement: "He has plundered our seas, ravaged our Coasts, burnt our towns, and destroyed the lives of our people. . . . He is at this time transporting large Armies of foreign Mercenaries to compleat the works of death, destruction, and tyranny, already begun with circumstances of Cruelty & Perfidy scarcely paralleled in the most barbarous ages, and totally unworthy the Head of a civilized nation. . . . A Prince, whose character is thus marked by every act which may define a Tyrant, is unfit to be the ruler of a free people."

This defining document marks the moment when many citizens in this country began to understand symbolic connections between ancient governmental systems, and the new order of republican, federal, or representative government.

After the Revolution, those who served as officers under General Washington were accorded the right to wear a special medal designating them as members of the Society of the Cincinnati (cat. no. 49; see also cat. nos. 50, 51). Membership was, of course, an honor, but it carried with it no pretensions to privilege. General Washington, after victory, set an example by announcing to his officers that he was resigning as commander in chief. This occurred on December 23, 1783. No political clout, power, or privilege came to those who proudly wore the badge of the Society of the Cincinnati.

Left: Eagle inlay detail, American knife box (see page 35)

Indeed, the American general's lesson of yielding power, and his subsequent retirement as the first president of the new nation, caused King George III to observe that it "placed him [Washington] in a light the most distinguished of any man living" and made him the "greatest character of the age."[5] Many perceived Washington as the living model of the noble Roman Lucius Quinctius Cincinnatus, a celebrated Roman patriot (born about 520 B.C.), who was cultivating a small farm when chosen consul in 457 B.C., was made dictator in 456 B.C., and who gained a victory over the Aequi. Thereafter, he abdicated the dictatorship and returned to private life on his farm.

Leaders of the new government, as it emerged, adopted new artistic styles in dress, architecture, furniture, and the other arts. Foremost among the founding fathers concerned with style, invention, education, and architecture (to name but a few of his intellectual passions) was Thomas Jefferson, whose portrait, painted by Charles Willson Peale, captures in lucid detail the image of one of America's most visionary leaders (cat. no. 45). In 1789 he accepted President Washington's appointment as secretary of state, a position he held until 1793. While secretary of state, Jefferson wrote some three thousand letters and submitted a major report on American commerce.

During this period, ostentatious display of rococo ornament became equated with tyranny and the old order of an earlier generation. The new order welcomed delicate refinement or beauty as defined by neoclassical taste. It does not seem coincidental that the writing desk (made by Benjamin Randolph, and now in the Smithsonian collections) on which Jefferson drafted the Declaration was a simple mahogany writing box ornamented with a plain string inlay that signaled the introduction of the restrained style of early neoclassicism into American-made furniture.

In the center of the John Quincy Adams State Drawing Room stands another piece of furniture designed and used by Jefferson in Philadelphia in July 1776.[6] It is an English table-desk with a movable slanting top like that of a drafting table—architecturally beautiful, spare, and useful. Tradition holds that this desk was sold by Jefferson to John Dickinson, "Penman of the American Revolution," and on Dickinson's death passed to Dr. William F. Gallaher of Philadelphia. If this tradition is true, then Jefferson may have drafted portions of the Declaration on this table as well as on the small writing box. Obviously, the association of important historical events and persons with works of art help to animate otherwise mute objects. And as recent events also constitute history, it is significant to note that the Jefferson table-desk owned by the State Department was used in 1971 by the president of the United States to certify the 26th Amendment to the Constitution, establishing the right of eighteen-year-old citizens to vote.

Since traditions about ownership and events associated with objects are sometimes questioned by modern skeptics, it is refreshing when unimpeachable evidence makes connections clear. Such is the case with a small traveling writing desk owned by John Quincy Adams, eldest son of the second president of the United States (cat. no. 57). An inscription in John Quincy's hand reads: "John Adams's / bought [of] Enoch Rust Junr. / Rotterdam—April 1796." In 1794 John Quincy Adams was appointed minister to Holland. In the same month that he purchased this writing desk he proposed to his wife-to-be, Louisa Johnson. This desk was well used by Adams while he kept his diaries and wrote his voluminous correspondence to his family in America. Such a desk was not an uncommon article among travelers who maintained vigorous correspondence. A similar desk was acquired by Thomas Jefferson when he was a minister in London and Paris.

Other small objects in this section speak to the formal, official activities of the United States upon the world stage and the new government at home. Trust was the precise objective of the leaders of the new nation when peace medals were given to leaders of Native American nations. Surviving peace medals are rare today. The example presented here was made in 1793 by an eminent silversmith of Philadelphia, Joseph Richardson, Jr. (cat. no. 54). It originally was owned and worn on a thong around the neck by a Native American leader, as shown on the face of the medal. This engraved image depicts Washington on one side with a hand extended toward an Indian wearing a peace medal and smoking a peace pipe, with his tomahawk on the ground behind his foot. In the background is the image of a farmer plowing a field. It bears the engraved words: "George Wash-

ington / President 1793." The silversmith's mark is struck on the lower border. On the other side is engraved the eagle of the Great Seal of the United States. The message of this medal is clear. Washington wears his sword while the tomahawk is tossed aside. Settlement and farming takes place through *trust* and agreement or treaties with Indian nations, as confirmed by the eagle, the emblem of state.

The eagle is again represented on a silver seal of 1808, made in England by the famous silversmiths Peter and William Bateman (cat. no. 55). This seal was used for the verification of official business transactions of consular representatives in England. The eagle, depicted with a shield and holding an olive branch in one claw and arrows in the other and with its head in a cloud of stars, is based on the Great Seal of the United States, which has been in safekeeping at the Department of State since 1789.

The origin of the design of the Great Seal is a complex story, but it can be ultimately traced to ancient Rome and to the Holy Roman Empire of Charles V (1500–1558).[7] This is somewhat ironic, for there was never a more despotic person than Charles V. However, the meanings and symbolism of motifs do evolve over time and across cultures. Such adaptations and transformations of the arts of European culture are what make the shape and meaning of the American arts both complex and intriguing. The symbol of the eagle has served this nation well, both in marking official documents and in its use as a popular decorative, pictorial, or sculptural device expressive of patriotism.

While minister to France, Jefferson commissioned the painter Joseph Boze to paint a miniature of his daughter Martha at age seventeen (cat. no. 58). This beautiful image on ivory recalls the father's prudent advice to his daughter: "Some ladies think they may, under the privileges of the *déshabille*, be loose and negligent of their dress in the morning. But be you, from the moment you rise till you go to bed, as cleanly and properly dressed as at the hours of dinner or tea."[8]

Jefferson, a keen observer of political economy, had identified the problems faced by American craftsmen and manufacturers in 1774:

> By an act passed in the fifth year of the reign of his late Majesty, King George II., an American subject is forbidden to make a hat for himself, of the fur which he has taken perhaps on his own soil; an instance of despotism to which no parallel can be produced in the most arbitrary ages of British History. . . . The iron which we make, we are forbidden to manufacture; and heavy as that article is, and necessary in every branch of husbandry, besides commission and insurance, we are to pay freight for it to Great Britain, and freight for it back again, for the purpose of supporting, not men, but machines in the island of Great Britain.[9]

Despite the devastation of the Revolutionary War and its consequent dislocation of people, shops, and manufactories, America's increase in wealth and possessions after the war (examined later in these pages) caught the critical eye of Samuel Adams, who seemed not altogether happy with a society difficult to differentiate as to class: "You would be surprizds to see the Equipage, the Furniture and expensive Living of too many, the Pride and Vanity of Dress which pervades thro every Class, confounding every Distinction between the Poor and the Rich," Samuel wrote to his cousin John Adams in 1785.[10] Ostentation was his complaint. In the next generation the well-to-do learned that genteel behavior and restrained taste based on neoclassical principles could be used as a distinguishing mark of class.

—*Jonathan L. Fairbanks*

Cat. 44
Paul Revere, Jr. (1734–1818)

The Bloody Massacre

1770

Copperplate engraving on paper, hand-colored, 11 ½ x 9 ½ in.
Gift of Mr. William H. Coburn (1976.0075)

The provenance of this famous print is remarkable. It is perhaps the only impression to have descended in the family of one of the victims of the Boston Massacre of 1770. The victim's name, James Caldwell, was underlined in pencil by his granddaughter, according to family tradition. Equally notable is the fine condition of the print, since political broadsides such as this were published rapidly and passed from hand to hand as propaganda, not art objects, and they deteriorated rapidly.

The life of Paul Revere, the silversmith and patriot, is well known; little known, however, is his production of seventy-two copperplate engravings between about 1762 and 1780. Of these, at least sixteen were political prints, if the total includes portraits of political figures.[1]

The Boston Massacre was in large measure provoked by colonial radicals. The Townshend Acts of 1767 levied duties on a wide range of British imports, including paper, and were a constant annoyance to the colonists. British troops stationed in Boston felt the brunt of public opinion, from heckling to beating. On March 5, 1770, a group of men began hurling snowballs at a lone redcoat standing sentry at the customs house on King (now State) Street. He was soon reinforced by the main guard of some twenty men, who stood with fixed bayonets facing a mob of several hundred people who taunted and stoned the troops. Finally, one soldier fired without orders; the others followed suit; and what began as a "bad brawl" took a fatal turn. Moderate Bostonians did not fault the British, who, in fact, were defended in court by John Adams and acquitted of murder. But the propaganda of the Sons of Liberty, led by Samuel Adams and including Paul Revere, turned the sad event into a massacre of martyrs. Through 1776, the fifth of March was observed annually as a day of anti-British sentiment. Revere's *Bloody Massacre* was arguably the most important instrument in the creation of this pre-Revolutionary watershed.[2]

Paul Revere did not invent the image. Henry Pelham, a half brother of John Singleton Copley and a painter and engraver, designed and engraved it. Its title was *The Fruits of Arbitrary Power, or The Bloody Massacre*. Before he sent it to the printer, Edes & Gill, Pelham maintained that he had shown it to Revere. When Revere's plagiarized image was advertised (March 26, 1770) and issued before his own, Pelham wrote an angry letter (March 29):

> When I heard that you was cutting a plate of the late Murder, I thought it impossible as I knew you was not capable of doing it unless you coppied it from mine and as I thought I had entrusted it in the hands of a person who had more regard to the dictates of Honour and Justice than to take the undue advantage you have done of the confidence and Trust I reposed in you. But I find I was mistaken and after being at the great Trouble and Expence of making a design paying for paper, printing &c. find myself in the most ungenerous Manner deprived not only of any proposed Advantage but even of the expence I have been at, as truly as if you had plundered me on the highway. If you are insensible of the Dishonour you have brought on yourself by this Act, the World will not be so. However, I leave you to reflect upon and consider of one of the most dishonorable Actions you could well be guilty of.[3]

Pelham was naive to have shown Revere his design, since he was entirely correct in charging that Revere "was not capable of doing it." He must have known that virtually none of Revere's engravings was of his own invention. Revere copied whatever came to hand, most often British prints, and adapted them to his purposes by changing the captions. Since he did not pretend to be an artist, he seems to have felt no compunction about his plagiarism, especially since patriotism was his cause. His reply, if any, to Pelham is unknown. Revere's daybook for March 28, 1770, records a payment of £5 to Edes & Gill for "Printing 200 Impressions of Massacre." Pelham's "Original Print . . . taken on the Spot" was not advertised until April 2, 1770, and was also published by Edes & Gill.

The "late horrid Massacre" had taken place around ten o'clock at night (the clock hands on the First Church show 10:20 in Revere's version), a fact signified by the moon. The Old State House identifies the location. The identity of the colorist is unknown, and there are variations among the prints, though they follow a pattern. The left side of the print, with the victims, is dropped into symbolic shadow, and an ominous plume of black smoke rises from a chimney there. Above the commanding officer's head, the "Custom House" sign further locates the event while reminding the viewer of the hated taxes. Above that, Revere improved upon Pelham by introducing the large sign "Butcher's Hall." These significant indications of time, topography, and point of view are emphasized by the color.

Revere lists five men who were killed on the spot and two who later died of their wounds; of these men, a few can be identified in the image. Crispus Attucks, the black man whose head projects from the crowd near the left edge, was the most aggressive of the radicals that day and has thus received the greatest share of glory (or of ill repute, depending on the speaker's bias).

Art historian Jan Bialostocki has pointed out that the theme of the firing squad, not as an instrument of just punishment but as the perpetrator of atrocities for political tyrannies, appears in *The Bloody Massacre* for the first time. This new iconographic type in the history of art is given its most famous expression in the great painting by Francisco Goya, *The Third of May, 1808* (1814; Prado, Madrid), which indicts the cruelties of the Napoleonic troops in Spain by depicting a specific slaughter of civilians in 1808. In addition to introducing the shockingly modern theme, the Revere print "is the representation of a real happening seen from the point of view of the victims."[4]

The strength of the Pelham-Revere conception "originated in sincere outrage," an outrage also expressed in the biting verses that conclude, "Keen Execrations on this Plate inscrib'd/Shall reach a JUDGE who never can be brib'd." Henry Pelham invented, and Paul Revere broadcast, a new pictorial theme in the history of art.

—*William Kloss*

The BLOODY MASSACRE perpetrated in King—Street BOSTON on March 5th 1770 by a party of the 29th REGt

Engrav'd Printed & Sold by PAUL REVERE BOSTON

Unhappy Boston! see thy Sons deplore,
Thy hallow'd Walks besmear'd with guiltless Gore:
While faithless P—n and his savage Bands,
With murd'rous Rancour stretch their bloody Hands,
Like fierce Barbarians grinning o'er their Prey,
Approve the Carnage, and enjoy the Day.

If scalding drops from Rage from Anguish Wrung
If speechless Sorrows lab'ring for a Tongue,
Or if a weeping World can ought appease
The plaintive Ghosts of Victims such as these;
The Patriot's copious Tears for each are shed,
A glorious Tribute which embalms the Dead.

But know, Fate summons to that awful Goal,
Where Justice strips the Murd'rer of his Soul:
Should venal C—ts the scandal of the Land,
Snatch the relentless Villain from her Hand,
Keen Execrations on this Plate inscrib'd,
Shall reach a Judge who never can be brib'd.

The unhappy Sufferers were Messrs SAML GRAY, SAML MAVERICK, JAMS CALDWELL, CRISPUS ATTUCKS & PATK CARR
Killed. Six wounded; two of them (CHRISTR MONK & JOHN CLARK) Mortally

Cat. 45

Attributed to Charles Willson Peale (1741–1827)

Thomas Jefferson

1791

Oil on canvas, 25 ¹/₂ x 20 ³/₁₆ in.
Gift o0f Mrs. Henry S. McNeil in memory of
Henry S. McNeil (1988.0013)

"I have a great desire to exert my abilities in this portrait," wrote Peale while preparing to paint the secretary of state. Jefferson, only recently returned from five years in Paris as our minister to France, had settled into his new duties. The government was now established in Philadelphia, and Peale's studio at his home at Third and Lombard was frequently visited by eminent Americans— many of them friends of the artist—who sat for their portraits at his request. Peale's Museum (formally, The Philadelphia Museum) had already opened in exhibition rooms added to his studio that were lined with a growing collection of portraits (the Gallery of Great Men), as well as a rapidly expanding natural history collection— "a Repository for Natural Curiosities."

In the spring of 1791 Peale conceived the idea of his museum becoming a national museum, and at just the time that he was painting the portrait of Jefferson, he was preparing to invite many prominent citizens, including Jefferson, to become "Visitors" (trustees) of the museum. They met in February 1792 and elected Jefferson as their president. Thus Peale's portrait of the secretary of state is also that of the president of the Peale's Museum. He could not have had a better ally in his ambition for a national museum.

Two versions of this portrait exist. The first belongs to the Independence National Historical Park Collection and hangs in the gallery now established in the former 2nd Bank of the United States in Philadelphia. It was painted in the small oval format (about 24-by-20 inches) Peale established for his museum and was there until the sale of the museum in 1854. Then it was purchased by the City of Philadelphia. It has been almost continuously exhibited from the day it was completed.[1] There are few portraits of Jefferson that predate Peale's. He was in his forties and in Paris when he posed for a miniature likeness by John Trumbull (1787–88) and a marvelous bust by the great Jean-Antoine Houdon (1789). These are the best of the few surviving portraits of Jefferson from the 1780s. Peale's superb 1791 portrait in Philadelphia is imbued with a sensitive freshness, a candor, a sense almost of observing Jefferson unaware, that is mesmerizing. The intellectual and physical vigor that Houdon emphasized is there as well, but there is an almost feminine gentleness of expression that makes one feel in the easy company of a friend—as indeed Peale was.

There is no question that the Philadelphia portrait is the life portrait, for we have Peale's word that "my invariable rule is never to part with any original picture. Copies may be taken from them."[2] The striking, vivid portrait in the Collection retains the vitality of Peale's original, and the appearance of the handsome red-haired, fair-skinned man in the glow of his maturity. Something has also changed. The eyes are alight, but staring rather than contemplative. The shirt ruffle, the neckcloth, and the illusion of space between the neckcloth and the jaw are all excellently painted, yet the jaw itself seems slightly rigid when compared to the life portrait. There is a tautness in the skin of the forehead and temple that translates as tenseness and is at odds with the ease of the original. The hair is soft and supple, but there is no atmosphere around it. The rather hard contours of head and torso are perhaps the result of an overpainted background. Such divergences may of course be found in a replica by an artist. They may also be found in a copy, and the well-established practice within the Peale family of replication and copying one another's portraits might be considered.[3]

—*William Kloss*

Cat. 46

Attributed to Charles-Gabriel Sauvage, called Le Mire Père (1741–1827),
of the Niderviller factory (active 1754–1827)

Figure group of Louis XVI and Benjamin Franklin

Niderviller, France, ca. 1780–85

Bisque porcelain, 12 ⁵/₁₆ x 9 ¹/₂ x 6 in.
Gift of Mr. and Mrs. Donald F. Carpenter, in memory of
Mrs. Carpenter's parents, United States Senator from Massachusetts
and Mrs. Marcus A. Coolidge (1982.0090)

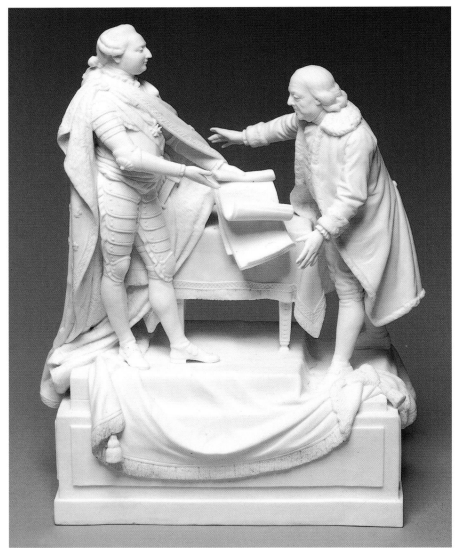

Psychologically, financially, and militarily, the French alliance was of critical importance to the success of the American Revolution. In 1776 the Continental Congress sent a delegation of three representatives to Paris to secure official French support. Although Silas Deane (1737–1789) and Arthur Lee (1740–1792) were part of the delegation, Benjamin Franklin is the best remembered of the group. He was popular with the French because of his scientific achievements, plain and rustic demeanor, and unpretentious dignity. On February 6, 1778, two treaties between His Most Christian Majesty, the king of France and the fledgling United States were signed. The treaties recognized American independence and sovereignty, pledged mutual defense if Britain tried to interrupt commerce between the two nations, and guaranteed the French possessions in the West Indies. In this bisque group, the inscription "Liberté Des Mers" (freedom of the seas) on the scroll that Louis XVI presents to Franklin refers to these provisions.

Although the treaties had been finalized in secret, their signing was known within a few weeks in French and American political circles. To recognize the new alliance formally, Louis XVI received the American commissioners at court in mid-March and there established full diplomatic relations. This figure group may represent the court reception rather than the actual signing in February, although in either case the occasion depicted was certainly auspicious. Symbolically, the power and majesty of France, embodied by the elegant figure of Louis XVI in courtly martial costume, are united with the American cause for independence, represented by Franklin, plainly clothed and gesturing humbly.

This bisque group is considered the work of Charles-Gabriel Sauvage, the foremost figure modeler employed at the Niderviller factory between 1779 and 1806.[1] The right proper rear of the base is impressed "NIDERVILLER" and incised "No 70." Although founded as a faience pottery in 1754, the factory at Niderviller began making porcelain as well in 1765.[2] With a matte surface resembling antique marble, the bisque (i.e. unglazed) porcelain used for this group and for many other figures made during the late eighteenth century in France, reflects the influence of neoclassicism.

—*Ellen Paul Denker and Bert R. Denker*

Cat. 47
John Singleton Copley (1738–1815)

Robert Chamblett "King" Hooper

ca. 1764–67

Watercolor on ivory in its original gilded copper and
vermeil brooch case (lens replaced), 1 ¼ x 1 in. (without the case)
Funds donated by Mrs. Henry A. Grunwald in honor of
former Secretary of State George P. Shultz (1979.0012)

Robert Hooper (1709–1790), the founder
of a dynasty of Massachusetts shippers,
traders, and merchants, earned the sobriquet
"King" from the wealth he accumulated
and, doubtless, from the way he displayed it.
Together with a brother-in-law, Jeremiah
Lee, the family dominated Marblehead
commerce and society in the 1760s. It has
been assumed that Copley first painted
Hooper and his wife, Hannah White, in
1767, in a pair of portraits that are now separated.[1] The miniature at the Department of
State, however, seems to show a somewhat
younger man. Hooper married Hannah,
his second wife, in 1764, which is perhaps
a more likely date for this miniature portrait
and leads to speculation that a matching
miniature of his bride was also painted.
In any case, it was King Hooper's patronage
that introduced Copley to Marblehead's
mercantile upper class, described by Jules
Prown as "low on education" and "partial
to large paintings in oil on canvas."[2]

Surprisingly, only eight to ten miniatures
that Copley painted in watercolor on ivory
are known today; all of them were executed
between about 1762 and about 1771. Since
approximately three hundred of Copley's
colonial paintings are extant, nearly all portraits, the tiny portrait of King Hooper is
a precious rarity.[3] Naturally, in such a small
work the brushstrokes are minute, and these
are often applied with a soft stippling
technique. Although the palette is generally
natural and subdued, an interesting exception is the use of red for shadows. A long
red line marks the juncture of the head and
wig, for instance, and red is also used to
model the eyelids and sockets, the pronounced crease between nose and mouth,
the nostril, the lips, and the double chin.
This artifice lends both warmth to the
complexion and vigor to the modeling.

—*William Kloss*

John Singleton Copley (1738–1815)

Mrs. John Montresor

ca. 1778[1]

Oil on canvas, original gilt frame, 30 3/8 x 25 1/8 in.
Gift of Mr. and Mrs. Richard I. Robinson (1981.0050)

Frances Tucker Montresor (1744–1826) was born in New York, the only child of Thomas Tucker of Bermuda, a lieutenant in the British Army. She married John Montresor (1736–1799), then also a lieutenant in the British Army, in New York in 1764. In 1766 Montresor was promoted to captain-lieutenant and "Engineer Extraordinary," and in 1775 he was made chief engineer in America, with the rank of captain. In the interim, he purchased Montresor's (now Randall's) Island in New York Harbor, where he and his family lived. Although he served as General William Howe's aide-de-camp at Brandywine in 1778, he was dismissed by General Henry Clinton, Howe's successor, and returned with his family to England, where he resigned his commission.[2]

The choice of John Singleton Copley to paint Frances Montresor's portrait was natural since some years earlier, in America, the artist had painted a work showing John Montresor in three-quarter profile facing left and in uniform (ca. 1771; Detroit Institute of Arts).[3] The artist, who had moved to England, was commissioned to paint a companion portrait; the two canvases have the same dimensions.

For her portrait, Mrs. Montresor affected a costume that was in the latest style, the female riding habit adapted from military uniform. "The fashion," David Mannings tells us, "must be seen against the background of war preparation in 1778, of ladies attending military reviews and wearing regimental colours."[4] The high hairdo topped off with an elegant black hat trimmed with feathers was also (rather literally) the height of fashion.

The portrait of the Captain-Lieutenant is pensive, whereas Mrs. Montresor is presented with cool neoclassical poise, in the pure profile derived from antique cameos and coins that was then much in vogue. Copley not only employs the profile pose resolutely, first drawing the contour in dark brown paint, but he also subordinates modeling to line. There is little suggestion of volume in the face, although the painting has an history of relining and abrasion, which may account for much of its flatness.[5] Denying himself the patient exploration of the sitter's features that marked his colonial portraits, Copley displays a rare single-mindedness. He succeeds through sureness of design and a bold palette. Red, white, and black, with accents of gold, focus the eye on the figure placed against the sketchy, decorative background of sky and tree. Mrs. Montresor's gray hair and white neckerchief are displays of virtuosity, as is the use of a blue ground—the blue of the sky—which is seen to admirable effect through the white shirt and collar and even through the striking revers folded across the red jacket.

Still establishing his English reputation, Copley may have employed this pose and costume in an effort to be up to date, but the painting remains unusual in combining a neoclassical design, the flowing painterliness of Thomas Gainsborough, and a flat, decorative surface. It is unlike any single-figure portrait in the artist's oeuvre.

—*William Kloss*

Cat. 49

Designed by Pierre Charles L'Enfant (1753–1825); cast by
Claude-Jean Autral Duval; embellished by Nicholas-Jean Francastel

Society of the Cincinnati badge and ribbon

Paris, France, 1784

Gold with polychrome enamels, silk ribbon (reattached),
³/₁₆ x 1 ¹/₂ x ¹⁵/₁₆ in.; 7 dwt. (1994.0013)

In 1783 Generals Henry Knox and Frederich Wilhelm von Steuben led the effort to establish the Society of the Cincinnati, a hereditary fraternal order designed to perpetuate the "friendships which have been formed under the pressure of common danger" among officers of the Continental Army and their French allies. The name was chosen because of the American officers' "high veneration for the character of that illustrious Roman Lucius Quinctius Cincinnatus," the epitome of the citizen soldier (see also cat. no. 50).[1]

The society's founding document, its Institution, describes the "order by which its members shall be known and distinguished" as a gold medal "suspended by a deep blue ribbon . . . edged with white, descriptive of the union of France and America." Cincinnatus was to be shown with "three senators presenting him with a sword and other military ensigns on a field . . . his wife standing at the door of their cottage; near it a plough and instruments of husbandry."[2] Society member Major Pierre Charles L'Enfant designed the medal in the shape of the eagle, which had been utilized in the Great Seal of the United States, with the society's medallion on its breast. Pickering's medal was one of the original forty-one badges cast in Paris by the medalist and engraver Claude-Jean Duval and decorated by the goldsmith Nicholas-Jean Francastel. It is gold with details in white, red, green, and blue enamel. The medallion on the eagle's breast is a simplified version of the one requested with fewer figures and attributes than originally stipulated.[3]

Although some officers questioned whether a hereditary society was in keeping with republican principles, it is unlikely that the owner of this medal, Timothy Pickering (1745–1829), would have shared their doubts. A native of Salem, Massachusetts, Pickering served the Continental Army as adjutant general (1777), a member of the Board of War (1777–80), and quartermaster general (1780–85), and was one of the original members of the society and signers of the Institution. Under President Washington he held several important posts, including secretary of state (1795–97; see cat. no. 5). Pickering continued as secretary of state under President John Adams but was dismissed in 1800 for openly opposing Adams's efforts to avoid war with France.[4]

—*Barbara McLean Ward*

Plate

China, for export, 1784–85

Porcelain with underglaze blue and overglaze polychrome
enamels, 1 x 9 ⅝ (dia.) in.
Funds donated by Mr. H. Richard Dietrich, Jr. (1972.0027)

The story of Lucius Quinctius Cincinnatus, the selfless Roman farmer turned soldier in defense of his beloved Rome, stirred the imagination of Henry J. Knox (1750–1806) and his colleagues and led them to organize the Society of the Cincinnati (see cat. no. 49). George Washington's "greatest pride now," wrote a visitor to Mount Vernon in 1785, "is to be thought the first farmer in America. He is quite a Cincinnatus, and often works with his men himself."[1]

The society was organized in May 1783, with Washington as president general and Knox as secretary general. During the first meeting, members chose the now-familiar design elements for the badge (cat. no. 49) and membership diploma (cat. no. 51).

Earlier, Samuel Shaw (1754–1794), an aide-de-camp of General Knox and a member of the society, had set out for China as supercargo on the *Empress of China*, the first ship to enter the American China trade. Washington's Cincinnati service, with the single Angel of Fame bearing the badge on a blue ribbon and proclaiming its importance, was the result of Shaw's first efforts to obtain china related to the society. Bordered with the butterfly version of the Fitzhugh pattern in underglaze blue, the remaining pieces of this service are perhaps the most historically important of the early Chinese porcelains made for the American trade.[2]

Although Cincinnati tea sets were later made to Shaw's order for specific persons, the service that was to become Washington's arrived in his hands under less auspicious circumstances.[3] Washington had been searching for Cincinnati china for more than two years when his friend, Colonel Henry ("Light-Horse Harry") Lee (1756–1818), reported in July 1786 on a large set available in New York City. In August, Lee purchased "1 Sett of Cincinnati China Contg, 1 Breakfast, 1 Table, 1 Tea Service of 302 ps." The china arrived at Mount Vernon in September.

—*Ellen Paul Denker and Bert R. Denker*

Cat. 51

Design by Pierre Charles L'Enfant (1753–1825);
drawn by Augustin-Louis Belle (1757–1841);
engraved by Jean Jacques Leveau (1729–1785)

Society of the Cincinnati membership diploma

1788

Line engraving on laid paper, 27 x 21 in.
Gift of Mr. and Mrs. R. Y. Mottahedah (1966.0027)

In May of 1784 the Society of the Cincinnati adopted Major Pierre Charles L'Enfant's design for its membership diploma. The copperplate was prepared in Paris by the engraver Jean Jacques Leveau after a drawing by Augustin-Louis Belle. It was then sent to America, where the wording was added by an unknown American engraver. The French members of the society, in particular, were anxious to have some written evidence of their connection with the American conflict, but it took many years before they received their diplomas. This example was signed by the president general, George Washington, and the secretary general, Henry Knox, and sent to France in 1788.[1]

The medallions at each side of the certificate display the attributes of the society's medal as described in the society's founding document, the Institution.[2] The obverse, depicted at left, shows Cincinnatus receiv-

ing the accoutrements of war from three generals while his wife huddles next to their home. An armor-clad warrior holds an American flag with the Great Seal of the United States (adopted 1782) in the center (replacing the customary stars), and his foot rests on the flags of the British Empire. At his side, an eagle discharges lightning bolts, forcing Britannia, her crown askew, and a puppylike British lion to make a hasty retreat in a fragile rowboat. On the right, the medallion's reverse shows Cincinnatus being crowned by Fame, with the sun rising over a city with open gates and vessels entering the port. The medallion hangs from a chain fastened to the sash of an angel who heralds the arrival of the French fleet and American victory. The badge worn by the society's members, in the form of an eagle (see cat. no. 49), illuminates the scene from the heavens.

Membership in the Society of the

Cincinnati was to be open to all Continental Army officers who served three years or more as well as French ministers, admirals, and commanders of the French army and navy.[3] This certificate, signed by George Washington in 1788, was issued to Claude-Gabriel, marquis de Choisy (1723–1799), who as brigadier general of infantry commanded a detachment at the Siege of Yorktown under the comte de Rochambeau. Following the surrender the marquis was promoted to the rank of *maréschal de camp*, the title on this certificate, and set sail for France from Annapolis with Rochambeau in January 1783. Louis XVI recognized the French Society of the Cincinnati in January 1784 and was patron of the order. Dissolved during the Reign of Terror in 1792, it was reorganized in the twentieth century and officially recognized by the general society in 1925.[4]

—*Barbara McLean Ward*

Cat. 52

William J. Weaver (ca. 1759–1817)

Alexander Hamilton

ca. 1794–1806

Oil on oval panel, 8 ½ x 7 in.
Gift of Mr. and Mrs. A Varick Stout (1973.0101)

This handsome, confident portrait of Alexander Hamilton (1757–1804) in a Continental Army uniform is probably a posthumous image. After his senseless death in a duel with Aaron Burr, there was a demand for portraits of Hamilton. In the shock of his abrupt demise his controversial personality was overshadowed by the memory of his public service that had culminated with six years as secretary of the treasury during which the war debt was repaid and the nation placed on a firm financial footing. Prior to that, his authorship of fifty-one of the eighty-five essays of *The Federalist* was instrumental in building support for the ratification of the Constitution. Still earlier he had served in the Continental Army, first as General Washington's aide-de-camp, and then as a distinguished field commander at Yorktown. It is the military period of Hamilton's life that the British-born artist William J. Weaver decided to commemorate in his portrait.

Weaver had probably come from London in 1794, where he had been employed by Joseph Booth at the Polygraphic Society. This establishment specialized in making inexpensive copies, called "polygrams," of painted portraits by a still-unclear method utilizing printmaking techniques and hand-finishing. What is known of this process may be discovered in two articles by Paul D. Schweizer, who has also examined the eight known versions of Weaver's portrait of Hamilton and resolved old confusion surrounding the artist's first name.[1] The State Department *Hamilton* is one of three that were painted entirely by Weaver's hand, without mechanical intervention.

Painted with a sure brush, the flesh tones of the portrait are fine, the modeling is subtle, and the powdered gray hair is soft and tactile. The white neckcloth and shirt ruffles are touched in with thin, fluid pigment. The pure profile was almost certainly derived by Weaver from a head modeled in 1792 and carved in 1794 by Giuseppe Ceracchi, an excellent and ambitious Italian sculptor, who had arrived in America in 1791. His bust of Hamilton was widely known. Weaver copied the sculpted profile and reproduced it in the small format he favored, adding the Continental Army uniform from another source.

William Dunlap, in his early history of American artists, wrote a brief entry on Weaver dated 1797 in which he said, "His portrait of Alexander Hamilton attracted attention from the strong likeness."[2] He went on to say that the portrait had been given in exchange to John Trumbull, who destroyed it. There is some reason to doubt the latter statement, and in any case we know there are several "original" images. Weaver could have made his first portrait of Hamilton—possibly this painting—anytime after the autumn of 1794, when Ceracchi brought his marble portrait bust to America. Therefore, we have not insisted on a precise date but have bracketed it 1794–1806. But the series of polygram copies should be dated 1805–1806. Weaver's "Polygraphic Art" was first announced in a *New-York Evening Post* advertisement in January 1805. And in a December 1806 advertisement in the Charleston, South Carolina, *Courier* Weaver invited patrons to his studio, where "the friends of the late General Alexander Hamilton, residing in South Carolina, will be convinced" that he could produce "as good if not better LIKE-NESSES than have ever appeared in this country."[3]

—*William Kloss*

Cat. 53

John Wesley Jarvis (1780–1840),
after Gilbert Stuart (1755–1828)

John Jay

probably ca. 1801–09

Oil on canvas, 52 x 40 ¼ in.
Lent by Mrs. Harriette B. Davis (L1979.0075)

In 1783 an exhausted John Jay had just returned to London from Paris, where he had been one of the principal American negotiators of the peace treaty that ended the American Revolution. While recuperating, Jay sat for his portrait with the expatriate artist Gilbert Stuart, whose reputation in Britain was high. The portrait remained unfinished and undelivered for eleven years, until Stuart moved to Philadelphia in 1794, where Jay, now Supreme Court chief justice, resided.

Stuart at last completed the neglected portrait, which was delivered to Mrs. Jay in New York in December 1794, and at about the same time he painted a second likeness of Jay in his judicial robes (National Gallery of Art, lent by Peter Jay). The pose of the head is repeated from the first painting, and one imagines that Stuart wanted to save time on his new commission by simply fitting the updated (older) features of Jay into the template at hand. In any case, the noble Jay portrait was a great success and, incidentally, instrumental in convincing Martha Washington to persuade the president to sit for Stuart for *his* portrait, the best known in American history.

It is not known when the English-born John Wesley Jarvis made his copy of Stuart's portrait of Jay. He was only fourteen when the original was painted, and the painting remained in the Jay family. Assuming that Jarvis copied the original and not another artist's copy, he must have seen it in New York City, where he had moved in 1801 as an apprentice to Edward Savage. The next seven or eight years were a period of development for Jarvis, and his copy of Stuart most likely dates between 1801 and 1809. His status in New York art circles increased around the latter date, when many competing artists were working in Europe. He received numerous important commissions during the next decade, culminating in a series of historical portraits of heroes of the War of 1812 painted for New York's City Hall, where they still hang.

Jarvis sometimes belittled Stuart's paintings, but like every other contemporary artist he carefully studied them. So this copy could be considered a learning exercise. But considering the great esteem in which John Jay (who lived until 1829) was held in New York, it is quite likely that this copy was commissioned. It bears many marks of the copyist. Compared with Stuart's organic, painterly improvisation, the parallel passages by Jarvis are generalized as in the ruffled shirt front, or random as in the indications of shadows and highlights on the robe. And Jarvis failed to understand the passage that made Stuart's portrait memorable—the placement and painting of the jaw. Stuart had elevated the head and jaw and modeled the jaw line with clarity and bite. Jarvis painted it more broadly, vaguely. The shadow line along the jaw has no variation in stroke or translucency—the chin seems to droop. In short, although Jarvis transmits Stuart's dignified design, he does not approach his level of inspiration.

—*William Kloss*

Cat. 54

Joseph Richardson, Jr. (1752–1831; working alone 1790–ca. 1801)

Peace medal

Philadelphia, Pa., 1793

Silver, 6 ¼ x 4 ⁵⁄₁₆ in.; weight 4 oz. 1 dwt.
Gift of Mrs. Mark Bortman in memory of her husband (1967.0037)

A number of early American silversmiths made quantities of silver tokens for distribution to various Indian tribes.[1] Most were simple ornaments designed for trade, as emblems of friendship, or even as enticements to promote conversion to Christianity. The grandest were pledges of peace or tangible evidence of treaties between the American government and Indian tribes or nations. Few examples have survived, as most were either buried with their Native American owners or melted down when their original significance was lost.

This presentation medal, roughly the size of a man's hand, is believed to have marked a treaty between the fledgling United States and an Indian nation. The symbolic depiction of an Indian chief and George Washington exchanging a peace pipe in the foreground, with a man and an ox plowing a field in the background, appears on other extant medals. Contemporaries asked why Washington retains his sword while the chief has discarded his tomahawk.[2] The reverse is engraved with the arms of the United States as they appeared on official seals for treaties. The plaque is encircled with a simple molded band, each end of which protrudes at the top and is pierced to form a suspension loop. An imprint of fabric, probably made during the casting process, appears on one side of the medal. Charles Bird King's *Portrait of Sagoyewatha* (known as Red Jacket, Albright-Knox Art Gallery, Buffalo, New York) shows the Seneca chief dressed in European-style clothes with a remarkably similar medal tied high at his throat.[3]

Joseph Richardson, Jr., employed James Smither, Jr., as an engraver from at least 1795 until as late as 1802. It is possible, therefore, that Smither is responsible for the stiff but competent work on this medal.[4]

Although Joseph Richardson, Jr., and his brother Nathaniel are listed in the Philadelphia County militia records at the time of the Revolutionary War, they were staunch Quakers. Perhaps the first peace medals presented on behalf of an American organization were the medals, struck in 1757, commissioned by the Friendly Association of Regaining and Preserving Peace with

the Indians by Pacific Measures. Joseph Richardson, Sr., was the maker of a large number of them and a member of the association, a group primarily of Philadelphia Quakers. A note, apparently written two years after this medal was made, was found tucked into Joseph, Jr.'s surviving letter book. It refers to an order for 50 pairs of armbands, 42 pairs of wristbands, and "12 Medals 2 Size Engraved as heretofore/ 9 do [ditto] 3 do the Year 1795."[5]

—*Jennifer F. Goldsborough*
and Barbara McLean Ward

Cat. 55

Peter Bateman (1740–1825) and William Bateman (1774–1850);
working together 1805–1815

Consular seal

London, England, 1808–09

Silver; ivory handle
4 7/8 x 1 5/16 (dia. seal) in.; weight 7 oz. 17 dwt.
Funds donated by Mr. and Mrs. Philip Park Robertson (1983.0017)

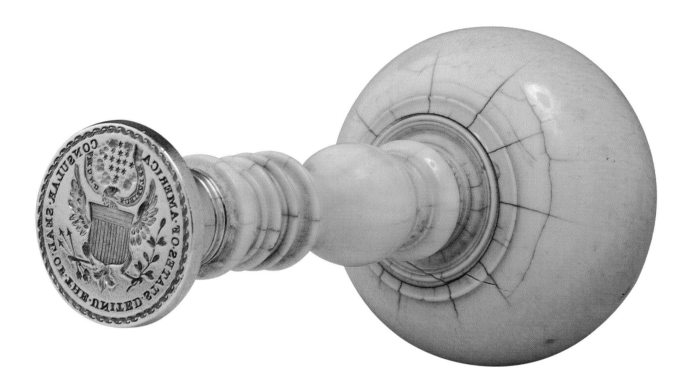

The substantial, turned-ivory handle of this piece ends in a silver ferrule and disk, cut with a representation of the arms of the United States including the motto E PLURIBUS UNUM in deep intaglio carving, all in mirror image. The seal may have been used to verify official business transacted by our early consular representatives in England. It bears the mark of Peter and William Bateman, one of the best-known silver-making firms of the period in England .[1]

Seven members of the Bateman family, starting with John, worked in silver and gold. John's widow, Hester, the most famous of the Bateman family because of her success as a woman in a male-dominated field,

first entered her mark as a "smallworker"— a jeweler and crafter of small silver items— in 1761, and continued to work as a spoon maker and silversmith until her retirement in 1790, when her sons, Peter and Jonathan, registered their mark.

When Jonathan died in 1791 his widow, Ann, worked with her brother-in-law, Peter, until 1800, when her son, William, entered the partnership. Ann retired in 1805. William and his uncle, Peter, worked together until Peter retired in 1815, and William carried on alone until he sold the business in 1840.

—*Jennifer F. Goldsborough*

Cat. 56

Attributed to Seraphim Masi
(working 1822–ca. 1855)

Skippet

Probably Washington, D.C., ca. 1840

Silver, 5 ³/₁₆ (dia.) in.; weight 19 oz. 12 dwt.
Funds donated by The Honorable Ronald S. Lauder
and Mrs. Lauder (1980.0013)

Skippets are boxes, usually of silver or gold, used to protect the official wax seals on important official documents. They were used by the United States in the nineteenth century, and only for major international treaties. Most skippets by American silversmiths survive in foreign archives. The design of the seal itself is usually reproduced on the top of the skippet, and the base and cover are generally pierced to accommodate the cords that attach the wax seal to documents.

The majority of American skippets are unmarked, but several District of Columbia silversmiths are known to have made them as special commissions for the government. For example, Charles A. Burnett (1760–1849) made the silver skippet for the Treaty of Ghent in 1815. Jacob Leonard (who worked about 1810 to 1825) was paid for four silver-gilt skippets in 1819. Seraphim Masi made four skippets in 1824, one in 1825, and several others over the course of his career, including several gold skippets for Commodore Perry's expedition to China in 1852. Samuel Lewis (working from about 1850 to about 1870) made skippets until 1870, after which the practice of using these protective but expensive boxes was discontinued.[1]

This unmarked skippet is a fine example of a rarely seen form that is unique to the purpose and mission of the Department of State. Inscribed with the words E PLURIBUS UNUM in block letters in a banner, the skippet is nearly identical to the silver-gilt, unmarked skippet attached to the Convention of Adjustment of Claims with Mexico, which was ratified February 8, 1829, and to a silver skippet attached to the Convention of Transit Way across the Isthmus of Tehuantepec with Mexico, signed in 1851.[2] The seal design was cast as a rather heavy plaque and is backed by a thin disk of plain silver to form the top of the cover of the shallow, drum-shaped box. The background of the plaque has been scraped and the raised design very carefully refined with chasing. The box itself is simply made of sheet silver. This skippet appears to date from the period when Seraphim Masi is known to have been supplying such items to the federal government.

—*Jennifer F. Goldsborough*

Cat. 57

Writing box

England or Rotterdam, Holland, ca. 1796

Mahogany; beech, 6 ¹/₄ x 20 x 10 ¹/₈ in.
Funds donated by The Grainger Foundation, Inc. (2001.0001)

Of standard form and style for the early neoclassical period, this portable writing desk is distinguished by its documented ownership by John Quincy Adams (1767–1848). Reflecting the family's penchant for documentation, the desk is inscribed in ink on the back of the upper folding writing section: "John Adams's / bought [of] / Enoch Rust Junr. / Rotterdam —April 1796."[1] The inscription is attributed to John Quincy, rather than his father John, on the grounds that its graceful, fluid style strongly resembles the handwriting of the young diplomat and varies considerably from the more controlled and rigid penmanship of the elder statesman.

In 1796 John Quincy Adams was in the middle of a three-year appointment as the United States minister to Holland. The inscription indicates he purchased the desk from Enoch Rust, Jr., possibly as a used article of furniture, in April of that year. At that time, however, Adams was in London, squiring his future wife among other things, and he did not return to Holland until early June.[2] Thus he may have added the inscription at a later time, misremembering the date of purchase slightly when doing so, or he may have ordered the desk from Rust (probably a former owner or a merchant rather than a cabinetmaker) in April and acquired it later.

A prolific correspondent and nearly compulsive writer, like the rest of his family, Adams made good use of this desk, as attested by the presence of columns of figures, shadowy inscriptions, ink stains, and other graffiti on its wooden surfaces.

The Collection includes several important desks associated with great American statesmen, including a similar example owned by Thomas Jefferson.[3]

—*Gerald W. R. Ward*

Cat. 58
Joseph Boze (ca. 1744–1826)

Martha Jefferson

1789

Watercolor on ivory, 3 ½ x 2 ½ in.
Courtesy of the American Embassy, Paris (1966.0099)

When Thomas Jefferson was appointed United States minister to France in 1784, he took with him his eldest daughter Martha (called Patsy). Jefferson's pleasure in his assignment to France was clouded by the recent death of his wife, Martha Wayles Skelton (September 6, 1782). To his official duties was now added the responsibility of raising three daughters. He took twelve-year-old Martha with him to Paris, leaving the two younger girls in the care of relatives.

They reached Paris on August 6, 1784, and Jefferson searched for permanent lodgings and for a suitable boarding school for Martha.[1] Only five months after their arrival came the sorrowful news that Jefferson's two-year-old daughter, Lucy, had died. Martha's surviving sister, Mary, was brought to Paris in 1787 and also was enrolled in boarding school. The *demoiselles de* Jefferson remained there until the spring of 1789, when their father was preparing to accompany them back to America and then return to France.

Joseph Boze probably painted this miniature portrait of Martha, now seventeen, at just that time, while Jefferson was waiting for a leave of absence to be granted. An inscription on paper mounted under glass on the reverse reads: "Mlle Martha Jefferson fille de Monsieur Thomas Jefferson Ministre Americain à Paris MDCCLXXXIX." The watercolor and the inscription are mounted in a gilded copper case tooled with a floral motif. Martha is shown half-length, wearing a simple, high-waisted pale yellow dress trimmed with a small white ruffle collar and a blue waistband. Her eyes are large in relation to her mouth, but this may just be the artist's convention. Her most striking feature is her light red hair, dressed in helmet-style, with side curls and ringlets falling over her forehead. Behind her, delicately painted, is a distant grove of trees and the sky, bluer toward the top to set off her hair and accentuate her blue eyes.

Joseph Boze had come from Martigues, near Marseilles, to Paris, where he studied with the great pastel portraitist Maurice Quentin de La Tour. Boze also painted portraits in this popular medium, and in watercolor for his highly regarded miniatures. He won the royal patronage of Louis XVI and Marie-Antoinette, yet also painted Robespierre in 1791. He moved to England for a time, but returned to France to testify in favor of the queen at her trial, a bold action which earned him eleven months in prison. Since he survived until the Bourbon Restoration, he ended his career once more in royal favor.

Although Jefferson was granted his leave of absence in mid-June 1789, he only received the letter at the end of August. He and his daughters left Paris on September 25. Back home at Monticello, Martha was soon engaged; she was married on February 23, 1790, to Thomas Mann Randolph, Jr. Her father's expectation of returning to his post in Paris was disappointed when President Washington appointed him secretary of state. Jefferson was never to return to Europe.

—*William Kloss*

Cat. 59

Raphaelle Peale (1774–1825)

General Josiah Harmar

ca. 1799–1803

Watercolor on ivory, 3 x 2 ½ in.
Gift of Ambassador and Mrs. Robert Newbegin (1969.0028)

General Josiah Harmar (1753–1813) owes his place in diplomatic history to his role in the exchange of ratifications of the Treaty of Paris. Ratification was required from the legislatures of nine states represented by the Continental Congress. The long process was not completed until mid-January 1784; the deadline for receipt of the ratification in Paris was March 3. Harmar, recently made colonel, was appointed a bearer of dispatch to deliver the ratification. Winter storms delayed the Atlantic crossing, and Harmar placed the document in the hands of Benjamin Franklin on March 29, nearly four weeks late, but the British raised no objections.[1]

On August 12 of the same year, Harmar was appointed commander of "the first national peacetime military force in American history."[2] His small regiment was dispatched to Ohio in a largely unsuccessful attempt to protect the settlements there while driving squatters out of the Northwest Territory. Harmar was brevetted brigadier general in 1787, and he holds (with Governor Arthur St. Clair) the dubious distinction of waging the first official federal campaign against the Indians (October 1790), in which he was forced to retreat. Although he was officially absolved of wrongdoing, his reputation was severely damaged and he resigned at the end of 1791.[3]

In the absence of documentation, the dates of execution suggested for his portrait, ca. 1799–1803, are based on circumstance and style. Harmar appears to be about fifty years old in the watercolor. In 1799 he had completed six years of service as adjutant general (the officer in charge of a state militia) of Pennsylvania, the last major post of his career. The portrait, therefore, may be a modest valedictory. Raphaelle Peale, eldest child of Charles Willson Peale, though better known today for his still lifes, had painted miniatures at least as early as 1795. He made some of his finest dated miniatures between 1799 and 1801, when he was establishing an independent career in Philadelphia.[4]

Not blind to the advantage of his father's reputation, Raphaelle boldly advertised in *The Philadelphia Gazette* on September 11, 1800, and must have attracted some clients: "A NAME!/ RAPHAELLE PEALE/ To make himself eminent, will paint MINIATURES, for a short time, at Ten Dollars each—he engages to finish his pictures equally as well for this, as his former prices, and invariably produces/ASTONISHING LIKENESSES."[5]

There is no way to judge the accuracy of his likeness of General Harmar, because no other portrait seems to exist. The direct realism of the miniature is convincing, however, and the work compares well with others of this period.

Characteristic of the artist are the long, free strokes used in the hair and in the face of the Harmar portrait, the emphatic eye sockets, the sloping shoulders, and the pronounced blue tones in the background and the face. Spontaneous, even wayward in his approach, Raphaelle Peale brought an unaccustomed brio and freshness of characterization to the habitually sedate American miniature portrait.

—William Kloss

Cat. 60

Adolphe Phalipon (active ca. 1825–1880),
after Ary Scheffer (1795–1858)

Marquis de Lafayette

1825

Oil on canvas, 26 x 22 in.
Funds donated by the John Jay Hopkins Foundation (1993.0001)

On October 17, 1824, the Dutch-born Parisian artist Ary Scheffer wrote a letter to the speaker of the House of Representatives informing him that he had "sent by the ship *Cadmus* . . . a full-length portrait of General Lafayette painted by me, which I pray you to do me the honor to accept for the Hall of the House of Representatives over which you preside. As the friend and admirer of General Lafayette and of American liberty, I feel happy to have it in my power to express in this way my grateful feelings for the national honors which the free people of the United States are at this moment bestowing on . . . the man who has been so gloriously received by you as the 'Nation's guest.'"[1] Although the portrait only reached Washington a month after Lafayette had addressed Congress in the House chamber, it has hung there continuously since January 20, 1825, in fitting tribute to a great hero of our Revolution. The "national honors" then being extended to Lafayette, and to which Scheffer alluded, accompanied the thirteen-month tour of America that the general undertook, in which he traveled to every state in the nation. Not only did the citizens, whose admiration and love for him were unbounded, have the opportunity to express their gratitude, but Congress voted him a gift of $200,000 and a township and returned him to France on a United States warship, thus simultaneously restoring his personal fortune and his political influence.

It is against this background that the bust-length portrait in the Diplomatic Reception Rooms must be viewed, for it was painted to meet the demand for portraits of Lafayette that ensued after his return to Paris. It was painted by a virtually forgotten pupil of Scheffer named Adolphe Phalipon, who copied Scheffer's portrait in 1825.[2] It is not known which of his teacher's portraits of Lafayette he was copying. Scheffer's life portrait of his friend was painted in 1818–19, when Lafayette was sixty-one and had just been elected to the Chamber of Deputies. It was shown at the 1819 Paris Salon. The civilian, *republican* costume of the general reflected his political principles, and its unpretentious simplicity was admired. In 1822–23 Scheffer made two replicas, one of which was given to the marquis, while the other went to America. Scheffer apparently retained the 1819 original, and of course there may have been a painting of the head that preceded that. But Phalipon's reliance on Scheffer's portrait is exact and unmistakeable.

It is a superb copy, subtly and precisely painted, delicately modeled with shifting light and shadow. The sober, thoughtful expression that Scheffer memorably captured is faithfully preserved.

—*William Kloss*

Cat. 61

Snuff box

Probably Bilston, England, ca. 1790–1800

Enamel on copper, ⁷/₈ x 1 ¹³/₁₆ x 1 ⁵/₈ in.
Gift of Dr. and Mrs. Roger G. Gerry (1991.0026)

This small box was probably made during the last quarter of the eighteenth century or in the early nineteenth century in Bilston, England, one of several south Staffordshire towns noted for its production of small enamel-on-copper wares.[1] Most motto boxes of this type were made as souvenirs, but a few, including this one, have political or patriotic associations. The simple inscription—"American INDEPENDENCE For ever," painted in brown on a white background—indicates that this box was produced for an American consumer. While seemingly straightforward, this motto was politically charged in the volatile political climate of the 1790s and early 1800s, when the Fourth of July and other commemorative celebrations took on partisan meanings. This box, which celebrates independence rather than echoing popular Federalist toasts such as "the Constitution" or "The Constituted Authorities," may have been meant as an expression of support for Thomas Jefferson, leader of the Democratic Republicans and author of the Declaration of Independence.[2] It is also possible that it was meant as a statement of a more neutral character. When asked to provide a toast for the local Fourth of July celebration in 1826, John Adams, who, like his old political rival, Jefferson, was on his deathbed, replied "I will give you 'Independence forever!'"[3]

—*Barbara McLean Ward*

A Nation United

NEOCLASSICISM IN THE FEDERAL ERA

*N*eoclassicism swept away the taste for the old, heavily ornate, rococo designs of an earlier generation. This new style, popular in the first few decades after the Revolution, represented more than mere ornament: it was a new way of thought, attitude, manners, and of understanding the symbolic connections between the ancient and modern worlds.[1] It was an especially potent and appropriate style for the art and architecture of the new republic, and the Department of State Collection, as this section reveals, is rich in material from this period.

At the elite level of society, George Washington set the example for his countrymen's taste in the best and earliest examples of neoclassicism within Mount Vernon's Banquet Hall (which he finished by 1785). Its lacy stucco ceiling ornament with swags, garlands, and oval paterae recalls the designs of English architect Robert Adam. Washington wrote that it was his intention to do the room in a plain, neat style. He was fully aware that he set an example of taste for republican virtue.

Those who aspired to be refined and genteel found their models not only in British and Continental fashion but also in books about manners and furniture. Among the most significant such works for furniture were George Hepplewhite's *Cabinet-Maker and Upholsterer's Guide* (London, 1788), Thomas Sheraton's *Cabinet-Maker and Upholsterer's Drawing Book* (London, 1791–93), George Smith's *Cabinet-Maker's and Upholsterer's Guide, Drawing Book*, and *Repository of New and Original Designs* (London, 1826), and the popular London periodical Ackermann's *Repository of Arts, Literature, Fashions, etc.* Individuals who desired to express genteel culture through the possession of stylish and beautiful objects found that Edmund Burke's *Philosophical Inquiry into the Origins of Our Ideas of the Sublime and the Beautiful* advised that smoothness was a quality "essential to beauty." In fact, Burke stated, he could not "recollect any thing beautiful that is not

Previous pages: Duncan Phyfe sofa (see page 163), armchairs (see page 162), and card table (see page 161), Dolley Madison Powder Room

Below: Urn inlay detail

smooth." Refinement of parts, gradual variation, and delicacy of color were other essential aspects of beauty to be seen not only in the design of buildings, in furniture, silver, and other decorative arts but also in the clothing, posture, and movement of the person.[2]

Between Hepplewhite's publication and Smith's, at least three phases of neoclassicism may be detected—each step in design evolution moved from light and delicate form and ornament toward more robust, heavier, and classically academic forms. Such stylistic shifts are of less importance than the fact that artistic control of the mind and body, and of man-made surroundings—artifacts, houses, and public buildings—embodied stylistic and symbolic connections with the ancient classical past. Gentility favored leisure and consumption; it also helped to confer social power and status to those who owned property and were polished in their manners.

The genteel style of neoclassicism, quickly adopted by the middle class, swept nineteenth-century America. By the 1830s Greek-style temples, built of marble or of wood and painted white, became the fashionable democratic building mode in the United States. Middle-class, genteel society required abundant consumer goods, a desire that led to speculative manufacturing for the masses. This period from 1790 to about 1830 (often termed Federal or republican in its earlier phases, and Empire in its heavier, later manifestation) witnessed the production of venture cargo furniture for export and sale at dockside throughout the world, as well as a heady market for imported goods and substantial industrial growth involving warehousing and the mass retailing of goods for rapidly expanding markets.

New styles of advanced taste are often introduced into the decorative arts first in silver. In 1774 the Philadelphia silversmith Richard Humphreys (1750–1832), for example, was commissioned by the First Continental Congress to fashion a two-handled presentation urn for Charles Thomson (1723/4–1824), an Irish immigrant to Philadelphia who became secretary of the congress from 1774 to 1789. Thomson was a highly respected and learned friend of Benjamin Franklin.[3] This silver urn (now owned by the Philadelphia Museum of Art) is the earliest landmark—a threshold example—of the introduction of neoclassical design in the colonies.[4] (Its counterpart in the mid-eigh-

teenth century was the baroque-style, two-handled loving cup made in Boston by Jacob Hurd.) Although neoclassical motifs can be found in American objects that are earlier than the Humphreys urn, this is a monumental and clear example of a form derived from classical antiquity. It seems likely that Humphreys had been given an example of fashionable English silver to copy for Thomson's presentation piece. Ironically, the cartouche on the urn's side was engraved by Philadelphia seal cutter James Smither (active 1768–1778) in an elaborate asymmetrical or rococo style. In 1778 Smither was accused of treason, so he departed with British troops bound for New York, but he returned to Philadelphia in 1786 after the war.

The neoclassical urn shape continued to be a favorite form in silver and in furniture throughout this period, and was also used as a decorative element for inlays, tombstones, and architectural ornament. Philadelphia silver urns are often embellished with minute beading that circumscribes the vessel's base and rim. This is a device that is useful to distinguish Federal-period Philadelphia-area silver from that made in other cities. Such beading is to be found in this exhibition on a covered sugar urn (cat. no. 89). A pineapple finial and pierced gallery surmount this elegant object made by Joseph and Nathaniel Richardson for James Smith and Jemima Russell, who were married in 1787. Their initials are intertwined in the engraving on the side of the urn, which descended directly in the Smith family to the donors. As was customary in the eighteenth and early nineteenth centuries, the title to silver and other domestic movables passed down from mother to daughter through the female line of the family.[5]

In contrast to domestic silver, some was ceremonial. At the expiration of his presidency, George Washington gave an English Sheffield-plate (or fused-plate) wine cooler to his secretary of state, Timothy Pickering (cat. no. 5). This handsome and spare object with its bulbous body and lion's-head handles bears an engraved inscription that records the gift. There could hardly be a more appropriate object for the Department of State to own, as it not only represents the office of the secretary of state but also records the respect by Washington accorded a former comrade in arms. In addition, the gift reflects the civility that Washington maintained throughout his life.

Right: Cupboard with Chinese export porcelain decorated with the American eagle of the Great Seal, James Monroe Reception Room

The American eagle of the Great Seal of the United States became, in the early Federal period, an important symbol for the new nation. This motif fairly drenched furniture, silver, and other objects as the most preferred ornamental detail. A card table made in Providence, for example, features a shield-bearing eagle under stars inlaid in a panel on the center of its skirt (cat. no. 101).

The bald eagle was also an emblem incorporated into the design for the badge for the Society of the Cincinnati (see cat. no. 49) by Major Pierre Charles L'Enfant (1754–1825) in 1783. It was Major L'Enfant who laid out the plan of the nation's capital city, Washington, D.C. The eagle of the Great Seal and that of the badge found an enthusiastic audience not just among American craftsmen but also among the manufacturers of wares exported from England and China to the expanding American market. Some of the State Department's notable examples of Chinese export china decorated with the badge of the Society of the Cincinnati includes six plates and a dish from the Washington dinner service (cat. no. 50) and a partial tea set brought back by Samuel Shaw on the *Empress of China*, which became, in 1784, the first American vessel to enter the China Trade.

Sometime after Shaw's first voyage (when he did not have the medal in hand for the Chinese artisans to copy) the supercargo brought back the pieces that he presented in 1790 to William Eustis of Boston. Shaw made several trips to Canton, where he was appointed first counsel by Congress. He died in 1794 on his fourth voyage. It seems reasonable to suppose that the partial set of Shaw's porcelain owned by the Department of State was made within a few years of the time when the ship *Columbia-Rediviva*, in company with a sloop named the *Lady Washington*, departed Boston in 1787 en route to the mouth of the Columbia River in the Pacific Northwest. Here, Bostonians initiated a fur trade with Native Americans, transporting the fur to Chinese merchants in Canton in exchange for spices, tea, and silk. *The Columbia* returned home in 1790, after circumnavigating the globe.[6]

Such achievements by Americans, coming in almost all enterprises within the decade following peace, are astonishing. It must have been exhilarating for Americans to sense themselves part of an era of extraordinary exploration, technological advancements, and important historical events. The federal processions held in many towns throughout the country included hundreds of craftsmen and tradesmen carrying banners celebrating "Free Trade." In the 1788 procession of New York City, the parade was led by Thomas and William Ash, Windsor and rush-seat chairmakers whose banners announced: "The federal states in union bound, O'er all the world our chairs are found." Whether this was a boast based on fact or merely hopeful expectation is immaterial. What American craftsmen did believe was that with free trade they could rise from being mere provincials to become masters of their own fate as large-scale exporters of works made by their own hands.

While free trade around the world enlarged horizons for Americans, important advances in style and technology also encouraged craftsmen to celebrate the achievements of home industry and the refinement of taste. Reflections of such refined taste can be illustrated by the earliest piece of American silver made for presidential use. It is a coffeepot owned originally by John and Abigail Adams (cat. no. 82). Its urn-shaped form supports a high-domed lid crowned by a finial that echoes the urn body in miniature. The coffeepot seems to have been made sometime shortly before the year 1800. It was fabricated either by Nathaniel Austin in Boston, whose mark it bears, or it is the work of Revere, and was merely retailed by

Below: Urn inlay detail, Baltimore sideboard (see page 154)

Right: Portraits of Mr. and Mrs. John Quincy Adams by Charles Robert Leslie (see pages 164–67), upholstered arm chair (see page 86), and Portsmouth china table with a pierced gallery (see page 71), John Quincy Adams State Drawing Room

Austin. Regardless, it is a handsome and spare work that mixes stylish neoclassical practicality with beauty.

The stance of this coffeepot expresses the dignity of manner that was becoming a model of gentility throughout America. Its presence seems to epitomize the seriousness and purposefulness recommended in Lord Chesterfield's *Principles of Politeness and of Knowing the World,* a manual that shaped many people's behavior.[7] Polite behavior or gentility, together with a developed taste for refined goods, spread throughout democratic, middle-class America. Such taste helped to form a vast marketplace that nurtured a need for skilled craftsmanship and abundant manufacturing in this country.

Refinement and gentility, it has been observed, "bestowed concrete social power on its practitioners." Most importantly, refinement and gentility inspired trust.[8]

A silver tea set with fluted sides (cat. no. 88) in the new style of neoclassicism was made by Paul Revere after the Revolution. His earlier teapots were spherical in form or baroque with curvilinear rococo ornamentation. Most of Revere's tea equipage made before the Revolution was made for Tories. Registering their protest through nonimportation agreements, Whigs and patriots in Boston refused to drink tea throughout the 1760s and 1770s. Instead, they drank rum that could be smuggled past the revenue collectors. Indeed, among the generation of Bostonians most recently passed away, it was customary to call rum "Boston tea." After the Revolution, Revere produced an abundance of teapots and tea equipment—usually, but not always, in the newest, neoclassical style. This called for urns and oval-shaped forms decorated with neat but fashionable bright-cut engraving like that on the fluted teapot and stand that Revere made about 1796 for the merchant Moses Michael Hays.

Hays's name appears twenty-five times in Revere's daybooks. He was grand master of the Grand Lodge of Massachusetts in which Revere was an officer, and successfully conducted business in Boston, Newport, and New York. In the last city Hays was also a patron of the prominent silversmith Myer Myers.

Silversmithing was only one aspect of Revere's remarkably active life. He was fully aware of the important roles he

Below: Eagle detail, Fitzhugh Chinese export porcelain (see page 151)

played in the unfolding events of American history. Revere made sure that as the nation grew and prospered, so did his own career. He practiced many trades—ranging from dentist to cannon- and bell-founder. As the nation took shape, Revere evolved from small-scale craftsman to large-scale industrialist. That he sat for self-portraits made by superb artists at three different phases in his life attests to his awareness of his place in the scheme of things. The first was by Copley in 1768, the second was a profile drawing by St. Memin about 1800, and the third was by Stuart in 1813.

In the latter part of Revere's life he undertook his most ambitious enterprise by developing copper-rolling mills in Canton, Massachusetts. This he commenced with a loan from the fledgling United States government (which he promptly repaid). His mill produced sheet copper to protect the hulls of ships—both commercial and in the nation's new navy. His copper was also used for roofing, including the dome that architect Charles Bulfinch designed for the new Massachusetts State Capitol. Revere was a man of enterprise who recognized opportunities. He grew with

them, and retired as a gentleman—to become the legendary self-made, patriot American.

While Revere adapted quickly to changing fashions, not all craftsmen of the Federal period were stylistically progressive. Cabinetmaker John Shaw of Annapolis was able to produce furniture in the latest style, but the card table that bears his label dated 1790 (cat. no. 100) continues a form that he made in the 1770s. Obviously, there was a market for spare, somewhat old-fashioned furniture, or Shaw would not have placed his label on the work.

By comparing that simple table to a sideboard made in Baltimore about 1785 (cat. no. 97) one can readily appreciate the high levels of style achieved in Maryland as the town of Baltimore became a major center of trade. This sideboard's pattern of inlay is what makes it readily identifiable with Baltimore craftsmanship, even though it comes very close to looking like the work of a London-trained artisan. Indeed, members of the firm that made this piece had trained in London, but despite that fact they adopted the design patterns favored by Baltimoreans.

With open trade across the Atlantic, the American consumer could choose from an abundance of furniture, clocks (cat. nos. 75–81), and porcelain (cat. no. 84) imported from France. Yet most citizens seemed to exhibit a strong affinity for works by craftsmen who followed the lead of England. This is a curious matter, for the Revolution had only recently taken place, and the British again attacked the United States in the War of 1812, burning the White House. But artistic style and politics do not necessarily neatly intertwine. Citizens in this country still spoke English, and throughout the Federal period, despite political differences, were less inclined than ever before to claim stylistic independence.

The style of furniture that made its appearance about 1810 from the workshop of Duncan Phyfe and others takes its cues from the English Regency. Reeded parts of furniture of this period recall the bundle of rods or fasces surrounding axe heads of Roman antiquity. On the back crest rail of a New York sofa (cat. no. 107) the theme of the Roman fasces is explicitly carved—these motifs, together with two horns of plenty, must have surely represented to Americans of the period not simply antiquarian motifs but emblems of unity, power, and abundance.

Major style shifts occurred between the Hepplewhite-inspired shield-back chair of the 1790s to the square-backed chairs made by Phyfe and his contemporaries (cat. nos. 105, 106). The latter recalled in somewhat archaeologically correct terms classical Roman furniture. Phyfe's shop at times employed as many as one hundred workmen. This was an era of manufacturing prosperity. While tools and techniques for craftsmen remained largely the same, production methods changed, becoming more efficient. Surplus products led to stockpiling, warehousing, and export of furniture, ceramics, and glass to distant ports. Venture cargo from Salem, Massachusetts, involved the shipment of furniture made in that town for sale in ports as distant as Capetown, South Africa. Under the spread wings of the American eagle, trade with China continued to bring tea, silk, porcelain, and other luxury goods to meet the demands of America's rapidly expanding and consuming middle class. American-built clip-

per ships were beginning to prove their superior speed.

Jesse Baldwin, a New York City merchant and importer, obtained from China a pair of porcelain cider jugs, which he probably intended to sell. But sell he did not, for the jugs descended directly to his great-great-granddaughter, Sarah Carson Robb, from whom, in the twentieth century, they were purchased by Elinor Gordon, a distinguished dealer in Chinese export porcelain. On their sides are painted images of the American eagle. These eagles displayed a new iconographic twist. Instead of the eagle of the Great Seal that holds olive branches and arrows, this eagle holds a trumpet and shield on which is depicted a fouled anchor. In the eagle's beak is a banner that proclaims IN GOD WE HOPE. One of these jugs is included here (cat. nos. 73, 74).

American ceramic manufacturers competed with imported porcelain and pottery from China, England, and the Continent. In the 1820s and 1830s William Ellis Tucker of Philadelphia was the first in America to successfully produce and market porcelain. While there had been an attempt in the early 1770s to establish a porcelain factory in Philadelphia, that effort failed after only two years.[9] Tucker's success was such that he and his business partners employed some 40 workers and produced more than 140 forms. Most of the works from the Tucker factory took stylistic cues from popular French porcelain, although the coloring of the floral garlands and bouquets on the Tucker water pitcher in this section (cat. no. 96) is similar to that on the earlier Chinese-export cider jugs. Indeed, the rose-colored floral bouquet was also popular throughout ceramic wares in England and the Continent. What the Tucker pitcher represents is an extraordinary era of manufacturing enterprise and confidence. American resourcefulness in the pursuit of refinement, beauty, and commerce in the early years of the nineteenth century was aimed to serve a democratic market—the ever-expanding middle class.

The same could be said for the lighthouse clock made at about the same time by Simon Willard of Roxbury, Massachusetts (cat. no. 90). Willard, who lived a very long life, patented many designs for his technological inventions. His clocks are celebrated as some of the nation's best works of the Federal period. On the one hand, the Willard clock can be seen as patterned on the form of the Eddystone lighthouse in the English Channel off Plymouth, England. On the other hand, its form is also like that of a classical column. The clock presented here exhibits a stylistic nod to French design in the classical taste—a taste that was favored by many furniture craftsmen and patrons in Boston throughout the first thirty years of the nineteenth century.

Upon his death Willard was the first to be buried at Forest Hills, the newly established, romantic garden cemetery in Jamaica Plain, near Boston. To mark Willard's grave, a magnificent eight-foot-high Gothic revival tombstone was carved in sandstone by sculptor and stonemason Alpheus Cary.[10]

It was Cary who, in 1818, introduced the young aspiring sculptor Horatio Greenough (1805–1852) to stone carving. Greenough, in turn, traveled to Italy to learn the art of sculpture, in order to make the colossal Greek revival marble monument of George Washington that was intended to be placed as a memorial under the dome of the then new United States Capitol Building. Greenough's marble Washington, created 1832–40, is posed as a Zeus-like figure, naked to the waist. Ordinary American citizens objected to seeing Washington unclothed, so the monument was moved out of doors. It is now displayed in the National Museum of American History.[11]

All of this is cited in order to offer some perspective on the direction in which classicism was headed in America. The trend was from the lacy forms of early neoclassical style of the late eighteenth and early nineteenth centuries toward the more ponderous sculptural mass of archaeologically correct classical revivalism that began to be popular about 1820. These expressions of the art and architecture of antiquity were but the first of many successive, yet overlapping, revival styles that would come to characterize the arts of the westward-expanding nation in the mid- and late nineteenth century.

—*Jonathan L. Fairbanks*

Mantel

New York, N.Y., ca. 1810–20

White pine, 66 x 88 x 10 ¾ in.
Gift of Dr. John W. Wholihan (1978.0064)

This elaborate mantel comes with a distinguished historical association: a bronze plaque, once attached to it, read: "This Mantle Taken from House No. 1 Broadway, New York The residence of John Kennedy 9th Earl of Cassels Built in 1760 Taken down in 1881 / Lord Howe's Headquarters Last building in New York over which the British Flag was displayed." Although that rich colonial history has traditionally been linked with the mantel, it appears instead to date from the beginning of the nineteenth century.

The Kennedy house was built on the site of the first Dutch fort on Manhattan Island. The original house on the site was built in 1664, but the Georgian-style house known as the Kennedy mansion was built for Archibald Kennedy (1685–1763), a British colonial official who came to New York as a young man. Kennedy served in several local governmental capacities and was one of the most prominent men of his day. Like other colonial officials, he purchased land in and around Manhattan Island, including the land where 1 and 3 Broadway were erected in 1760. At Kennedy's death, his son and namesake, Captain Archibald Kennedy, RN, succeeded him as owner of the property.

During the Revolutionary War, the area immediately surrounding the younger Kennedy's house was in the center of political action. During the early days of the Revolution, George Washington lived at 1 Broadway, considered at the time to be one of the finest houses in the city and "the favorite resort of the officers of the army."[1] Later, during the long British occupation of the city (1776–83), the Kennedy mansion was the home of Sir Henry Clinton, Sir Guy Carleton, and Sir William Howe.

Upon the death of Captain Kennedy, his heirs, sons John and Robert Kennedy, of Teignmouth, England, sold 1 Broadway to Nathaniel Prime on December 13, 1810, for $35,000. Prime, a wealthy stock and commission broker with offices on Wall Street, may have installed this mantel in his new house as part of a remodeling project. According to Walter Barrett, writing in 1862, "Old Nat Prime was an extraordinary man—stout, thick, short, and heavy in person, yet he was a wonderfully shrewd calculator. . . . Mr. Prime bought the house on the corner of Broadway and Battery Place. . . . He lived here many years, and saw his sons and his daughters intermarrying with the first families in New York. Thirty years ago, Mr. Prime was deemed the third richest man in New York. . . ."[2] So notable was Prime that Gustave de Beaumont, traveling companion of Alexis de Tocqueville, wrote in 1831, "Mr. Prime, our banker, who is the wealthiest man in this country, also puts himself out to be nice to us."[3]

Furniture known to have been in the house during Prime's tenancy suggests that he sought to create a fashionable interior in the latest neoclassical style. A parlor suite owned by Prime (now at Boscobel) was at the height of fashion in 1810.[4] The Kennedy house mantel appears to date from the Prime period of ownership. Similar mantels, with gouged flut-ings, carved fans, and sunbursts with protruding buttons, are known in houses north of New York City and have been described as "Hudson Valley" type.[5]

Helen Wilkinson Reynolds pictured several examples of mantels in this style in her book on Dutchess County, New York, architecture. Mantels in the homes of Bartow White, James Given, Colonel John Storm, and Obediah Brown, all built about 1810, are remarkably similar to the Kennedy house mantel, suggesting that Prime may have commissioned a carpenter from that area to carve his mantel. These mantels are said to have been made by "a traveling carpenter, who lived a year with the family and was paid a dollar and his board. . . . [He] did not use books of design to guide him, but evolved his style himself."[6]

—Page Talbott

Cat. 63 and 64
Attributed to Richard Whittingham, Sr. (active 1795–1818)
or Richard Whittingham, Jr. (active ca. 1810)

Pair of andirons
New York, N.Y., 1795–1810

Brass, iron, 27 x 12 (at feet) in.
Funds donated by Miss Henrietta E. Bachman (1974.0090.001 & .002)

This pair of andirons is distinguished by its fine proportions and distinctive decorative details.[1] At the knees on the cabriole legs are unusually prominent spurs, sharp ended but with a distinctive curl at their tips. The legs terminate in finely reticulated claw-and-ball feet. The urn finials are engraved with swags of foliage and roses tied up with ribbons; the pedestals are engraved on the front with a motif of two crossed flags and a centered pole or staff with a liberty cap at the top. Where the poles cross is a cloverleaf. One flag has concentric circles of eight dots and eleven stars, a symbol of the new United States; the other has three stripes suggesting the French national colors. On the ground are a broken spear and a toppled crown lying on a naturalistic rendition of turf, probably representing the toppling of the English monarchy. On the sides is an octagonal medallion within a circle, a neoclassical motif used frequently by craftsmen after 1780. Edging the pedestals is a deeply chased design of triangles with dots and a line of dashes. The bases of the columns do not overhang their square plinths, and there is a distinctive pattern of curves and notches on the lower edges of the plinths.

The tall, attenuated columns topped with smooth, engraved urns represent a new style, as do the patriotic designs engraved on the pedestals. New York became the capital of the United States briefly in 1789, after which the government moved to Philadelphia. Symbols celebrating the new status of the American colonies appeared in all media. These andirons recognize the contribution of the French to independence. Another pair attributed to the Whittinghams is engraved with an urn and weeping willow that illustrate the nation's response to the death of George Washington in 1799.[2] The Collection's pair, another pair marked "Whittingham N. York," and the attributed "weeping willow" pair have the same zigzag-and-dot pattern on the pedestals, similar medallion motifs, and the same cuts on the lower front edge of the plinths. The urns in all three pairs seem to have been made from the same casting.[3]

Whittingham varied the legs and feet on his andirons. This pair has full claw-and-ball feet very much in a Philadelphia style. The wood pattern for their casting may well have been carved by a Philadelphia craftsman.

The Whittinghams were born in England, where Richard, Sr., was trained as a brass founder in Birmingham. The family came to the United States in 1791 and landed first in Philadelphia. Richard, Sr., worked in New Jersey until 1795, when the family moved to New York.[4]

—*Beatrice B. Garvan*

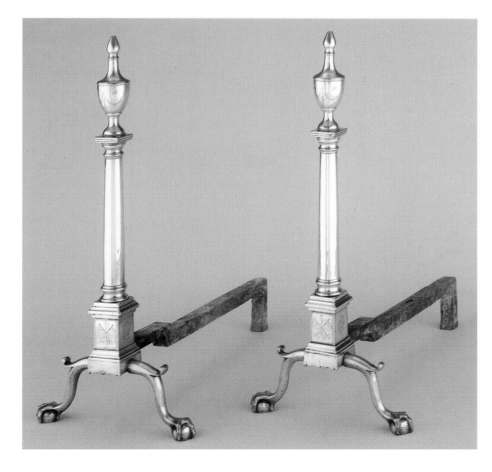

Garniture

China, for export, ca. 1780

Porcelain with underglaze blue and overglaze colored
enamels and gilt, 13 ½ (largest vase) in.; 3 ½ (dia.) in.
(1991.0027.001–005)

Vases in groups of five or more were
among the most popular decorative
items ordered from China by Europeans,
particularly the Dutch, during the
eighteenth and early nineteenth centuries.
The standard set of these so-called
garnitures, usually three covered round
vases of baluster form alternating with
two flaring beakers, was used to decorate
rooms and chimney pieces in the homes
of the wealthy.

This set is especially ornamental.
Underglaze blue borders of scrolls,
garlands, and diaper patterns frame scenes
with Chinese figures in architectural or
landscape settings rendered in the "man-
darin palette" dominated by purple, gold,
iron-red, green, and sepia overglazes.
Although generally associated with the
Dutch market during much of the eighteenth century, garnitures such as these
with elaborate decoration became desir-
able in the emerging American market
by the later years of the century.

—*Ellen Paul Denker and Bert R. Denker*

Cat. 70
David Wood (1766–ca. 1850)

Shelf clock

Newburyport, Mass., ca. 1815–20

Mahogany; mahogany, eastern white pine, yellow poplar,
basswood, satinwood veneer, 32 ⁷/₈ x 11 ³/₄ x 5 ³/₄ in.
Bequest of Caroline Ryan Foulke (1988.0037)

Few details are known of David Wood's
life between the opening of his shop in
Newburyport in 1792 and his last advertisement in 1824, in which he announced
"new and second hand clocks for sale
at the shop to which he has recently
moved." Like many New England clockmakers, Wood also served as a sales agent
for Simon Willard, his chief competitor in
Boston, who in the 1780s had developed
the first inexpensive, preindustrial shelf
clocks, which inspired this and so many
other New England examples.

Shelf timepieces like this one were less
costly alternatives to eight-day tall-case
clocks. Compact and made without striking mechanisms, they required smaller
amounts of brass and far less labor to produce. However, the elaborately inlaid cases
on many of Wood's timepieces belie their
modest cost and stand among the most
stylish case furniture produced during the
Federal period. Patriotic incidents drawn
from the recent history of the new republic are appropriately commemorated on
the painted iron dial, possibly by Lemuel
Curtis of Boston.[1] The addition of quar-
ter-columns in the front corners, brass
handles on either side of the upper case,
a veneered door, and French bracket feet
enhance the resemblance between this and
much larger, more substantial case furniture.

No document has yet come to light
that links any of Wood's clock cases to a
specific cabinetmaker. Three contemporary Newburyport clockmakers—
Samuel Mulliken, Daniel Balch, and Paine
Wingate—are all known to have ordered
clock cases from the Newburyport cabinetmaker Jonathan Kettell (1759–1848),
yet Wood's is one of the few names of
local clockmakers that does not appear
among Kettell's accounts.[2]

At the Metropolitan Museum of Art a
shelf clock in an architectural case with a
pagoda top may be one of Wood's earliest
clocks. A second group has pierced and
gilt pewter fretwork, and a third group, to
which this clock belongs, has solid crests
with inlay ranging from circles and stars
to the more unusual radiating pattern of

mahogany and satinwood veneers, such
as that seen on this example.[3]

Inexpensive shelf clocks were one of
this country's major contributions to the
history of clockmaking. Although this
clock was the product of a traditional
system of master craftsmen and apprentices, it marks the end of an era, for mass-
production methods first developed in the
New England clock industry soon would
pervade every branch of American manufacture.

—*Thomas S. Michie*

Pair of vases

France, possibly Paris, ca. 1810–30

Porcelain with overglaze enamels and gilt
13 ½ x 6 ⅞ x 5 ⅞ in. (1980.0066.001); 13 ½ x 6 ¾ x 5 ⅛ in. (1980.0066.002)
Gift of Israel Sack, Inc.

Jesse Benton Frémont remembered a dinner party in the White House during Andrew Jackson's administration when "... we were taken to the state dining room where was the gorgeous supper table shaped like a horseshoe, and covered with every good and glittering thing French skill could devise."[1] Indeed, the preponderance of French objects in the While House by the beginning of John Quincy Adams's administration was so overwhelming that Congress felt moved to stipulate in the 1826 Appropriation Act for White House furnishings that purchases were to be of American-made objects "as far as practicable."[2] This caveat, however, had no effect on china purchases. All presidents, beginning with George Washington and continuing throughout the nineteenth century, chose French porcelain for their tables. Furthermore, early nineteenth-century American porcelain tended to follow French styles in design. Little wonder, then, that fine mantel vases such as this pair were fashionable items in the American carriage trade.

Although these vases are not marked, their exquisite portraits of Washington and Benjamin Franklin may have been executed in Paris on porcelain that may have been made there as well.[3] During the early nineteenth century, foreign buyers favored Paris porcelains, which were considered "more elegant and cheaper" than the wares from the national factory in Sèvres.[4] This preference had arisen, in part, because Parisian manufacturers catered aggressively to the desires of foreigners in providing both forms and decorations to suit American and English as well as Continental tastes. The firms continued to do business from Paris even after their factories, and sometimes also their decorating studios, were moved closer to clay sources in Limoges.

—*Ellen Paul Denker and Bert R. Denker*

Cat. 73 and 74

Covered jugs

China, for export, ca. 1802–10

Porcelain with overglaze enamels, 9 ³/₄ x 7 ⁷/₈ in.
Funds donated by the Monica and Hermen Greenberg Foundation
(1985.0008.002)

During the early years of the new republic, the Great Seal of the United States, or one of its variations, was used frequently to decorate Chinese export porcelains for the American market. Patriotism was easily displayed to guests by using china embellished with the eagle and shield. Chinese decorators were happy to satisfy this demand and used as pictorial sources the numerous coins, government documents, shipping papers, newspapers, billheads, and letterheads bearing the seal, or eagles derived from it, that were carried to the Far East by captains and supercargoes. Although the version displayed on this covered jug is different from the official seal, the elements of eagle, shield, and stars suggest the ultimate design source.[1]

The specific design source has been identified as the masthead of the *Rhode-Island Republican*, a newspaper published in Newport by Oliver Farnsworth between 1802 and 1805.[2] The device consists of a spread-winged eagle that holds in its beak a banner with the motto IN GOD WE HOPE while grasping in one talon a shield with a fouled anchor and in the other talon the trumpet of Fame; a halo of sixteen stars (for the number of states) is above its head. Iconographically complex, the device combines the familiar elements of the eagle and halo of stars from the Great Seal with the shield and fouled anchor that have long been associated with Rhode Island. An official arms for the state was not adopted until 1882; however, the elements of the shield and anchor in conjunction with the word "Hope" or the motto IN GOD WE HOPE had been used in various media to signify the state from the late eighteenth century.

The covered jugs (and a related punch bowl) in the Collection have been identified as coming from a group of two bowls and four jugs that were once owned by Jesse Baldwin, a New York City merchant and importer.[3] These pieces may originally have been made on speculation for the Rhode Island market, but, failing to sell in that state, were offered in New York. The Collection's jugs descended with the second punch bowl in the Baldwin family, while the Collection's bowl and the other pair of jugs took different paths.[4] Indeed, the Collection's bowl has been associated with John Jay (1745–1829), the prominent lawyer and statesman from New York, but this relationship is now considered tenuous.

—*Ellen Paul Denker and Bert R. Denker*

John LeTellier (working ca. 1770–1800)

Seven-piece coffee and tea service

Probably Philadelphia, Pa, ca. 1794

Silver, 15 x 11 ⁵/₈ x 5 ¹/₈ (dia. base) in. (coffeepot); weight 50 oz. 5 dwt. (coffeepot)
Funds donated by Mrs. Wiley T. Buchanan, Jr.,
in memory of the Honorable Wiley T. Buchanan, Jr. (1982.0038.001–.007)

This is among the earliest of the large matched coffee and tea sets made in the United States. The locked tea caddy, in particular, is a most unusual addition to the set. Before the Revolution, American coffee and tea services were usually assembled over a period of several years and could consist of stylistically diverse pieces, possibly even produced by different smiths in different cities. For another twenty years after this set was made, few Americans possessed the affluence or advanced taste to purchase a silver coffee and tea service all at one time. This splendid set glorifies the neoclassical style of the 1790s. The urn-shaped coffeepot, ornamented with restrained, bright-cut borders, is particularly characteristic of the Philadelphia taste for elegant, attenuated forms. Fluted bodies or walls are not as frequently seen in Philadelphia silver as in silver made in Boston and New York, but they add structural strength to the relatively thin walls of rolled sheet silver made possible by machining (available in

Philadelphia as early as the 1760s), as well as providing a decorative play of light and shadow. The fluted, pedestal plinth and fluted, or faceted, urn finial of this piece are exceptional refinements. Typical of neoclassical coffeepots, the most conservative form in the set, this piece retains rococo elements in its cast shell handle sockets and curved, shell-ornamented spout.

None of the pieces of the set has the narrow bands of minute beading so common on Philadelphia neoclassical tea and coffee pieces of the 1780s and early 1790s. Instead, repetitive bright-cut engraved borders incorporating a half-daisy motif define the top and bottom of each body, presaging the milled borders used after 1800. The fluted, pedestal-based slop bowl is typical of the neoclassical style in its relatively large size and wide, spreading form. Instead of large, ornamental script initials, the conjoined "CC" on each piece is simple and contained within a rather small, squarish shield reserve. The

initials are those of the fashionable Cornelius and Catherine Comegys of Philadelphia and Chestertown, Maryland, who married in 1794 and may have received the set as a wedding gift. It is thought to be similar to one made by LeTellier for President James Madison but lost when the British burned the White House in 1814.

LeTellier is listed in numerous books as also working outside of Philadelphia. He may simply have solicited work in Chester County, Pennsylvania, and Wilmington, Delaware, during the 1790s rather than actually operating a shop in those locations. It is likely that he maintained his business in Philadelphia, where his obvious talents could reach a large and fashionable clientele. LeTellier had a son, also named John, who may have used the same marks.[1]

—Jennifer F. Goldsborough

Cat. 82
Probably by Paul Revere, Jr. (1734–1818);
retailed by Nathaniel Austin (1734–1818)

Coffeepot

Boston, Mass., ca. 1800

Silver, 14 1/8 x 12 3/8 x 5 (dia. base) in.; weight 37 oz. 4 dwt.
Gift of Mrs. Joel Larus in memory of her father, Mark Bortman
(1971.0124.002)

This is the earliest known piece of American silver made for presidential use. It is inscribed with the initials of John and Abigail (Smith) Adams. John Adams (1735–1826), second president of the United States, was born in Massachusetts and educated at Harvard College. A leader in the Revolutionary cause, he served in both Continental Congresses and helped to draft the Declaration of Independence. He was later one of the representatives who negotiated the Treaty of Paris ending the Revolutionary War in 1783, and acted as the first United States minister to Great Britain, between 1785 and 1788. Adams was elected vice president under George Washington and became president of the United States in 1797.[1]

This coffeepot, which dates stylistically to Adams's term as president, is the only major piece of silver known that bears Nathaniel Austin's mark, "NA" in block letters within a square reserve, here placed on the shoulder near the rim to the left of the handle. Nathaniel Austin was born in Charlestown, Massachusetts, within months of the birth of John Adams. He and his younger brother, James (b. 1750), probably received their training in the shop of their uncle, Josiah Austin (1720–1780). Nathaniel began his silversmithing business in Charlestown, but his shop was wrecked in the bombardment of 1776, and he and his wife, Anna (Kent) Austin, moved across the river to Boston.[2] Nathaniel Austin purchased twelve scalloped teaspoons from Paul Revere, Jr., in 1787, six of which survive and bear Austin's mark. A teapot and stand with the same cipher bear Revere's mark overstruck with the mark of Josiah Austin, a mark also used by Nathaniel throughout the 1780s.[3] It therefore seems likely that this coffeepot, so different from anything else made by Austin, was made in Paul Revere's shop. Although the coffeepot cannot be attributed to Revere's shop definitely, it shows the refinement associated with Revere's work, and the engraved acorn border is similar to the borders on marked Revere silver, if a little sketchier and less finished.[4]

The combination of an urn-shaped pot with a domed cover is unusual. The rather narrow, ribbonlike border of repetitive engraving and the fine reeding (instead of beading) on the base, shoulder, and rim help to date this coffeepot to about 1800. The engraved reserve in the form of a belt or garter is an unusual touch.[5] A Sheffield-plate coffee urn owned by the Adamses and engraved with the same cipher is in the White House collection.[6]

—*Barbara McLean Ward*
and Jennifer F. Goldsborough

Cat. 83

Louis Mallet (active ca. 1790–1824)

Mantel clock

Paris, ca. 1795–1820

Bronze; dial gilt bronze, 25 ½ x 7 ¾ x 7 ¾ in.
Gift of Mrs. Patrick D'Orsi (1970.0027)

Writing from Paris in 1779 to his daughter Sally, Benjamin Franklin observed, "Pictures, busts, and prints (of which copies are spread everywhere) have made your father's face as well known as that of the moon."[1] Few Americans of any era have been the subject of more portraits than Benjamin Franklin. From Feke to Greuze, Houdon to Wedgwood, his likeness exists in bronze, terra-cotta, marble, earthenware, and porcelain as well as on canvas. From the earliest portrait, in the 1740s, until his death in 1790, images of Franklin appealed to audiences in France and Britain as well as the United States.

In 1777 and 1778, while Franklin was serving as one of the United States commissioners to negotiate a treaty of alliance with France, three sculptors—Jean-Jacques Caffieri, Jean-Antoine Houdon, and Jean-Baptiste Nini—undertook portrait busts and medallions of Franklin.[2] The full-length, bronze figure of Franklin on this clock by Louis Mallett is a reduction of a terra-cotta statuette by François-Marie Suzanne, a contemporary of Houdon and friend of Jacques-Louis David. Said to be an excellent likeness of Franklin, whom he may have known, Suzanne's statuette was in fact a posthumous portrait submitted to the annual Paris Salon of 1793.[3]

Louis Mallett is notable for having been appointed clockmaker to the duc d'Orleans, later crowned King Louis Philippe of France. Other clocks by him incorporate busts and figures of George Washington, suggesting that he may have specialized in clocks for export to America.[4] With its bronze dial conforming to the pedestal, the design here emphasizes the figure of Franklin more than many other contemporary clock designs, in which the figures typically form part of larger compositions integrated with the clock case.

Franklin himself purchased a French bronze clock about 1780 as a present for his daughter Sally.[5] It was around this time that "French clocks" were becoming popular ornaments on mantelpieces of wealthy Americans, particularly those who had taken the Grand Tour or who sought works of art with patriotic rather than sentimental subjects.[6]

—*Thomas S. Michie*

Cat. 84

Jean Nepomucène Hermann Nast

Plate

Paris, France, 1806

Porcelain with overglaze enamels and gilt, 9 ¹/₈ (dia.) in.
Funds donated by The Folger Fund (1999.0002)

James Madison (1751–1836) and his vivacious wife Dolley were long at the center of Washington's dynamic social scene even before he became the fourth president of the United States. This plate from a French dinner and dessert service that belonged to the Madisons remains as a symbol of that city's vibrant social life, the admiration of Americans for things French during the early years of the republic, and the continuing close diplomatic relationship between France and the United States.

The Madisons acquired the service in 1806 through the efforts of their personal friend, Virginian Fulwar Skipwith. Madison was secretary of state at the time and had recently finished negotiating the Louisiana Purchase. Skipwith was apparently a clever broker as well. He reported in a letter to Madison that he had purchased the set not from the Sèvres manufactory as he had originally intended, but for 40 percent less from Jean Nepomucène Hermann Nast, a Paris porcelain manufacturer.[1] When the Madisons moved into the White House in 1809, the set probably went into storage. Official china purchases made during his presidency were of the plain sort to fill in losses from the sets in use during Thomas Jefferson's administration. But after British soldiers burned the White House in August 1814, a deed meant to punish the young nation for its continued diplomatic ties to France, the Madisons were forced to set up housekeeping with some of their own furnishings in Octagon House. This service undoubtedly played a role in helping Washington social life resume and normalcy return to the battered city.[2] Although the Madisons were not able to reoccupy the White House again during his administration, the table service is considered White House china nonetheless.

—*Ellen Paul Denker and Bert R. Denker*

Bowl

Boston, Mass., ca. 1795

Silver, 3 x 6 ¼ (dia. rim) in.; weight 11 oz. 13 dwt.
Gift of Mrs. deRosset Myers (1973.0064)

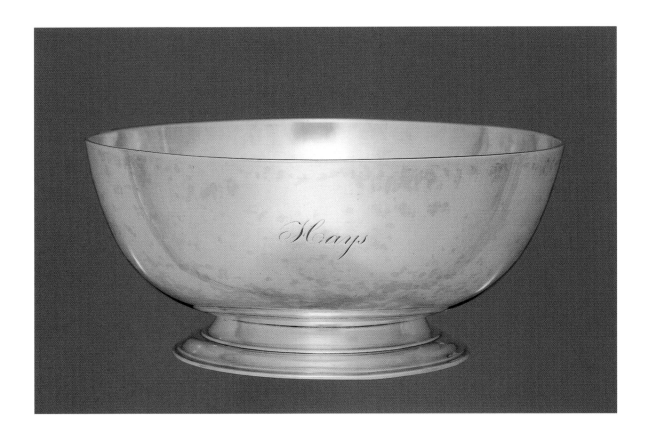

This bowl was made for the prominent Boston merchant Moses Michael Hays (1738–1808). Hays was born in New York, the son of Judah and Rebecca Hays. He began his mercantile career in New York, but by 1769 he had removed to Newport, where he had already established a considerable business. A leader among New York's Freemasons, he served as grand master of King David's Lodge and took its charter with him when he moved to Newport, reestablishing the lodge there in 1769. As deputy inspector general of the Rite of Perfection for the West Indies and North America for the Ancient and Modern Order of Masons, he traveled to Philadelphia and Jamaica during the early 1770s. By 1776 he had established business connections in Boston and apparently had moved his family to the city, although he maintained extensive ties to Newport until 1782. In that year, he became a member of the Boston Lodge and, in 1788, was elected grand master of the Grand Lodge of Massachusetts, an office he held until 1792.[1] Paul Revere, the maker of the bowl, put his support behind the Grand Lodge in 1782 and served as deputy grand master, first under Joseph Warren (1784–85) and then under Moses Michael Hays (1790–92). During this time, Hays and Revere also became business associates (along with others) in the formation of the Massachusetts Mutual Fire Insurance Company.[2]

This bowl may have been made as a presentation to Hays, perhaps in appreciation for his service to the Masonic order. Revere's daybooks, which survive for the period 1761–97, include few orders for bowls of this type. Its form resembles the famous Sons of Liberty punch bowl made by Revere in 1768, but it is closer in size to a standard slop bowl.[3] Solder lines on the underside of the bowl suggest that the base rim has been reattached.

—*Barbara McLean Ward*

Cat. 86
Paul Revere, Jr. (1734–1818)

Sugar basket

Boston, Mass., 1787

Silver, 4 ¹¹/₁₆ x 6 ¹/₈ x 4 ⁹/₁₆; weight 9 oz.
Funds donated by Miss Louise I. Doyle (1991.0036)

This sugar basket was originally owned by the prominent Jewish merchant Moses Michael Hays of Boston and is one of more than twenty-five pieces of silver that Hays ordered from fellow Mason Paul Revere.[1] The order for this basket is listed in Revere's daybook under the date December 6, 1787. Hays received a credit for 47 ounces of silver, and Revere recorded the purchase as a Silver Sugar basket weighing 9 ounces. He charged Hays £3.3s. for the silver and £3 for fashioning.[2]

The basket displays many elements typical of the neoclassical style, with its boat shape, beaded rim and base, and floral bright-cut engraving. The form of this basket is simpler and more restrained than the basket with rayed flutes originally owned by Edward Tuckerman and his wife Elizabeth (Harris) Tuckerman that Revere made about 1798 (Museum of Fine Arts, Boston). Other sugar baskets by Revere include a fluted and engraved basket made for Jonathan Hunnewell (Metropolitan Museum of Art) and a plain example (Cleveland Museum of Art).[3] Judging from surviving pieces, Revere more often fashioned sugar bowls in an urn form with high concave covers.

Its plain surface suggests that the State Department basket may have been made to be used with the drum-shaped teapot, also engraved "MRH," which Revere made for Hays and his wife, Rachel Myers Hays, about 1783.[4] The basket also bears the full-name "Hays" engraved in script, and it descended in the family.[5]

—*Barbara McLean Ward*

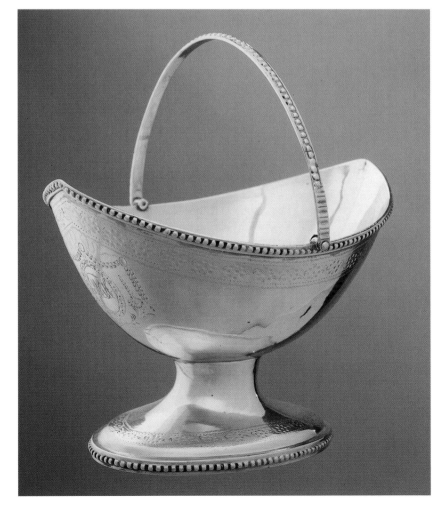

Plate

China, for export, ca. 1805–10

Porcelain with overglaze enamels and gilding, 1 1/8 x 9 7/8 (dia.) in.
Funds donated by Mrs. Alexander O. Vietor (1968.0011.042)

Trained as a military engineer, Sylvanus Thayer (1785–1872) studied in military schools in Europe for the United States government prior to his 1817 appointment as superintendent of the United States Military Academy at West Point. By 1833, when he requested to be relieved of his command, he had transformed the academy into a disciplined and efficient institution.[1] Thayer's pride in his own military accomplishments and those of his young nation was displayed at table in the fine set of China-trade porcelain plates that are now traditionally associated with him. The example illustrated here shows a triumphant eagle, borrowed from the Great Seal, perched atop a cannon surrounded by tokens of war and American flags. In contrast, the elegant borders of a leaf chain and flowered double festoons are quietly neoclassical.

Few American China-trade services from this period are as decorative or as patriotic as this one, but Thayer was not the only customer to order the design. A second set of plates survives from the Nichols family of Salem, Massachusetts.[2] Punch bowls, a mug, a cider jug, and a pair of cylinder vases with the same eagle-and-trophies motif, but with different borders, are also extant.[3]

The circumstances surrounding the occasion for the purchase of this particular service are unknown, but the various borders that were used with the central motif suggest that the different pieces could have been ordered from about 1805 to as late as about 1817.[4]

—*Ellen Paul Denker and Bert R. Denker*

Cat. 88

Paul Revere, Jr. (1734–1818)

Teapot and stand

Boston, Mass., ca. 1796

Silver, teapot: 6 7/16 x 11 1/8 x 3 3/4 in. (1991.0035.001);
stand: 7/8 x 7 3/8 x 5 1/4 in. (1991. 0035. 002)
Weight 40 oz. total

This teapot and stand set is one of approximately fourteen sets to survive from Paul Revere's shop.[1] In a letter to his agent in England, Frederick William Geyer, Revere mentions that: "They enclosed me in the case of plated ware a book with drawings which is a very good direction for one to write by."[2] Kathryn C. Buhler lists four teapots with shaped panels bordered by fluted sections made by Revere between 1786 and 1789 that closely resemble a teapot illustrated in the trade catalogue from about 1785 of Love, Silverside, Darby & Co., of Sheffield, England.[3] Although the fluted form of this pot is a design attributed to Revere, it was also produced by other Boston silversmiths such as Benjamin Burt, and undoubtedly was inspired by imported Sheffield-plate wares and pattern book illustrations.

Revere's daybooks reveal that the silversmith made only nine teapots before the Revolution, and more than fifty teapots during the last two decades of the eighteenth century. As Deborah A. Federhen has observed, this increase in production, while attributable to a renewed affluence among his patrons, also suggests that the flatting mill that Revere acquired in 1785 enabled him engage in more efficient production practices. Unlike his earlier pear-shaped teapots that were raised from flat ingots, teapots of this fluted design were made from sheet silver formed around wood patterns and then seamed.[4]

The initials "JH" within the cartouche on both the teapot and the stand are for Judith, the eldest daughter of Moses Michael Hays and his wife, Rachel Myers Hays. Judith married Samuel Myers, her first cousin and son of the New York silversmith Myer Myers, in 1796. Judith and Samuel Myers settled in Richmond, Virginia, where Samuel Myers established a successful mercantile firm in partnership with his half-brothers Moses Mears Myers and Samson Mears Myers.[5] The teapot and stand descended in the family until acquired by the Collection.[6]

—*Barbara McLean Ward*

Cat. 89
Joseph Richardson, Jr. (1752–1831) and
Nathaniel Richardson (1754–1827); working together 1777–1790

Covered sugar basin

Philadelphia, Pa., ca. 1785

Silver, 8 ⅞ x 4 ⅜ (dia. rim) in.; weight 13 oz. 5 dwt.
Gift of Mrs. Morris Hill Merritt, Mrs. Duffield Ashmead III,
and Mrs. Robert D. Langmann (1981.0039)

Joseph Richardson, Jr., and Nathaniel Richardson carried on the family silversmithing business established by their grandfather Francis Richardson (1681–1729) in Philadelphia before 1701. Their father, Joseph Richardson (1711–1784), continued the business until his retirement in 1777, when he passed it on to his sons. Nathaniel never married and continued to live most of his life with his brother Joseph. In 1790 Nathaniel changed occupations and worked as an ironmonger and hardware merchant until his death. Joseph Richardson, Jr., married Ruth Hoskins in 1780 and continued as a silversmith until 1801, when he decided to devote himself entirely to his duties as the second assayer of the United States Mint in Philadelphia. Although they were talented and successful silversmiths in one of the oldest firms in Philadelphia, Joseph, Jr., and Nathaniel found it advantageous to import English silver, jewelry, and plated silver to supplement their stock.[1] They also jobbed out work to other Philadelphia silversmiths and employed the services of several engravers. The engraver James Trenchard did work for the Richardson brothers during the 1780s and is probably responsible for the large "JJS" initials on this sugar dish, whose beautiful embellishments indicate the hand of an engraving specialist.[2]

The urn-shaped covered sugar basin was one of the most popular forms to emerge in the neoclassical style. Characterized by a mirror-smooth, "tight skin" surface, purity of line, and perfect proportions, this form was given its ultimate refinement by Philadelphia silversmiths between 1785 and 1800. The elegant verticality of Philadelphia sugar basins belies their substantial size and weight. Ornamentation was especially minimized in Philadelphia Federal silver, possibly in reaction to the florid decoration often encountered on pre-Revolutionary rococo silver of that city.[3]

In this particularly fine covered sugar basin, the Richardsons have emphasized the restraint and delicacy of neoclassicism. Through imported goods—the makers specifically asked for pierced salt dishes and pierced-rim waiters in ordering silver from England during the early and mid-1780s—they may have been inspired to add a similarly pierced border to their tea equipment. They were among the first Philadelphia silversmiths to do so.[4] The pierced gallery is a regional feature exclusive to silver made in Philadelphia and its sphere of influence.

—*Jennifer F. Goldsborough*

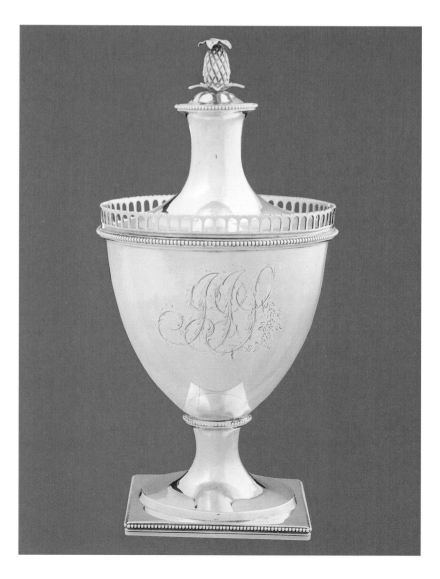

Cat. 90

Works by Simon Willard (1753–1848)

Lighthouse clock

Roxbury, Mass., ca. 1822–30

Mahogany, mahogany veneer; American chestnut,
eastern white pine, 29 ³/₄ x 10 ³/₁₆ (dia.) in.
Gift of Mrs. Clifford Allen Bellows,
in memory of her husband (1985.0018)

Simon Willard was an inventive clockmaker, well known for his patented
designs featuring a variety of technological innovations. Perhaps the best known of
these is his banjo clock, patented in 1802.[1]
Considerably less popular was his lighthouse clock, patented in 1819 as an alarm
clock. The first examples of these were
equipped with an alarm mechanism, but
the later ones were made without alarms.[2]

"Eddystone Lighthouse" clocks,
intended to resemble the famous Eddystone light in the English Channel off
Plymouth, England, are all of essentially
the same shape, although many variations
exist. The clock in the Department of
State, inscribed on the dial "SIMON
WILLARD," is cylindrical with an octagonal
base, while others were made with a rectangular body on a cubic base, either plain
or paneled, a cylinder on a square, or
a cylinder on a cylinder.[3] It descended
in the Bellows family.[4]

Another variable element of these
clocks is the feet, which were made in ball
form (gilt or plain) and paw-foot form.
The Collection's clock has gilt ball feet,
as well as a swirl-and-dot chased ormolu
surround at the base of the cylinder where
the two parts of the case meet. This is a
particularly dressy feature: other clocks
have a plain wood collar or a less elaborate ormolu one. Made in the style of
classical revival furniture in Boston, the
case (by an unknown maker) of the
Collection's clock features broad expanses
of handsomely figured mahogany,
enhanced by contrasting ormolu and
brass ornaments.

Under the clear glass dome—a modern
replacement—is a white porcelain dial
with Roman numerals and the maker's
name.[5] The dial has an ormolu surround,
and on the octagonal base is an ormolu
mount with an urn and foliate design.

—*Page Talbott*

Partial dinner service

China for export, ca. 1800–20

Porcelain with overglaze enamels, 1 ½ x 9 ¾ (dia. plate) in.
Funds donated by Mrs. Henry S. McNeil (1990.0016.002, .005, .007 & .008)

The dinner service is decorated in a pattern called "Fitzhugh," which refers to a group of Chinese export porcelain having certain identifying characteristics made between about 1780 and 1840. The decorative elements of this group include a central device—a medallion, eagle, monogram, or coat of arms—surrounded by four clusters of flowers and emblems associated with the four accomplishments of the Chinese scholar: music, painting, analytical skill, and calligraphy. The whole is enclosed by an elaborate border, either a trellis–diaper and spearhead border often called "Nanking," or a complex design made up of butterfly, cell diaper, and floral motifs. Some examples that fall into this group, such as George Washington's Cincinnati china (see cat. no. 50), lack the four floral and emblematic clusters. The clusters and borders may be painted in blue, brown, orange, green, yellow, rose-pink, lavender, gilt, black, or gray.

The name and definition of the Fitzhugh group developed over a long period of time.[1] In 1966 J.B.S. Holmes discovered that members of the English Fitzhugh family had played important roles in the British East India Company over three generations. In England, true Fitzhugh porcelains are those that mimic pieces associated with William FitzHugh, a supercargo (agent) at Canton who shipped china to England in the late 1700s. His pattern displays the characteristic center medallion, four floral groups, and the trellis–diaper and spearhead border.[2]

Fitzhugh patterns seem to have been more popular with Americans than with the English, reflecting the rise to prominence of the American traders at the time. Consequently, there is more variation in American-market Fitzhugh porcelains. The present set centered with an eagle, bearing a ribbon with the motto E PLURIBUS UNUM and a shield with floral cluster, is a characteristically patriotic American adaptation of the Fitzhugh pattern.

—*Ellen Paul Denker and Bert R. Denker*

Covered tureen and stand

China, for export, ca. 1760–70

Porcelain with underglaze blue and overglaze polychrome enamels,
7 1/2 x 14 x 10 5/8 in. (tureen and cover, 1986.0043)
2 1/2 x 14 3/4 x 11 1/2 in. (stand, 1986.0046)
Funds donated by Mr. and Mrs. Henry N. Flynt, Jr.,
in memory of Mr. Flynt's mother, Helen Gier Flynt (tureen);
Funds donated by Janet A. Hooker Charitable Trust (stand)

Colorful and exotic "tobacco-leaf" china was made between 1750 and 1800 for table services, garnitures, and tea services. Its patterns have been classified broadly by the palette employed: one type pairs the rose palette of colors with a blue underglaze; the other unites the same palette with green, brown, and iron-red enamels.[1] The emphasis in both types is on the lavish use of colors derived from the mixture of opaque white enamel, beginning during the reign of Yung Cheng (Yong Zheng, 1723–35), with the palette of translucent colors from the earlier porcelains of K'ang-hsi (Kangxi, 1662–1722). Elaborate floral patterns using the rose palette predominated in China-trade porcelain during the second half of the eighteenth century. The dense patterns of the tobacco-leaf group made them the most costly. Both broad and feathery leaves or plumes are included in the tobacco-leaf group, suggesting that no single plant was used as the dominant design source. There is some belief, however, that

the broad leaves resemble the annona, or custard apple.[2] Furthermore, the flowers seem to have been taken from hibiscus or passion blossoms, and motifs reminiscent of pomegranates may also be seen. Lotus pods were frequently used as the handles on tureens. Phoenixes (*feng huang*), squirrels ("pine rats" in Chinese), and Oriental figures were sometimes included as well.[3] East Indian textiles have been suggested as a possible design source, but the European or Chinese designers who invented these patterns for copying by the Chinese decorators probably relied on a general impression rather than a particular fabric.[4]

—*Ellen Paul Denker and Bert R. Denker*

Cat. 96

William Ellis Tucker, with partners
and successors (active 1826–1838)

Pitcher

Philadelphia, Pa., ca. 1830–38

Porcelain with overglaze enamels, 9 ¼ x 8 x 5 ¾ in.
Gift of Mr. and Mrs. Joseph D. Shein (1973.0082)

In 1852 Thomas Tucker reflected upon the
evolution of his brother's facility for making
porcelain: "My father had a china store on
Market Street [Philadelphia], and in the year
1816, he built William a kiln in the yard
back of the store, when William commenced painting upon the white ware in
the store, and burning it in the kiln."[1]
William's experiments in firing clay pieces
were successful in 1826, first in
"queensware" (probably a white earthenware) and later in porcelain. "After many
experiments and much labor," continued
Thomas, "he was successful in making a
very beautiful porcelain in a small way."

These early accomplishments continued.
Beginning in 1831, William Tucker
expanded the business by acquiring land
and mineral rights for raw materials from
New Jersey, Delaware, and Pennsylvania.
He moved and enlarged his operation,
which eventually included some forty
American and foreign workers. The necessary capital came largely from partnerships
bought by three wealthy Philadelphia
Quakers for their sons, John N. Bird
(1826–27), John Hulme (1828), and
Alexander Wills Hemphill (beginning in
1831). Hemphill's father, Judge Joseph
Hemphill, continued as the principal owner
after William Tucker died suddenly of a
fever in 1832.

Tucker's factory is often noted as the
first truly successful venture in making
porcelain in the United States with American materials. Despite the longevity of
Tucker's manufacturing concern and the
quantities of wares produced there, his
distribution was limited primarily to the
mid-Atlantic region, from New Jersey to
Maryland.

In 1832, when Thomas Tucker recorded
the shapes and decoration then in production, more than 140 different forms were
being made, including table pieces and vases.[2]
The most characteristic of these was the
"Vase pitcher," number seven in the shape
book, represented in the Collection by this
pitcher with polychrome enamel decorations
and by another example in monochrome
enamels, each typical of the factory.[3]

— *Ellen Paul Denker and Bert R. Denker*

Cat. 97

Attributed to John Bankson (1754–1814) and Richard
Lawson (1749–1803), active 1785–1792

Sideboard

Baltimore, Md., ca. 1785

Mahogany; mahogany veneers, satinwood, yellow-poplar, white oak,
40 ¹/₂ x 72 ³/₈ x 27 ⁷/₈ in.
Gift of Mr. and Mrs. Mitchell Taradash (1967.0007)

This magnificent sideboard precisely mirrors the qualities of its place and time of origin.[1] The wealth and sophistication of Federal-period Baltimore are reflected in its stylish design and highly ornamented facade while the cabinet represents Baltimore craftsmanship in its most English expression. A key example of why that city's Federal furniture has been called the most English of all American regional schools, this sideboard has even greater importance as one example of the largest and most significant group of Baltimore's early Federal furniture.[2] It is one of about thirty closely related case pieces that exhibit the distinctive design, ornamentation, and construction derived from early neoclassical London furniture. The form—a shallow bow-front case, with a single center drawer over a shaped skirt which is flanked by two deep drawers—is identical to four other examples from the group. The form is derived from English prototypes of the 1770s and indicates that the Baltimore examples predate such publications as George Hepplewhite's *Cabinet-Maker and Upholsterer's Guide* (1788).

Further demonstrating the closeness to English furniture are the inlays—the glory of the early Baltimore group. Among the characteristic designs are the ruffled fan in the center of the apron, the quarter-blossoms in the spandrels, and the chain of large ruffled bellflowers with a central spine. The most extraordinary inlay is the floral spray set in a fluted urn, typical of the elaborate and original pictorial inlays that embellish the group, ranging from naturalistic foliage and animals to hunting scenes, classical figures, and allegorical monsters.[3] The overall use of satinwood cross-banding with light and dark stringing to highlight the edges of drawers, doors, and oval panels in mitred frames is characteristic of the broad range of English-inspired Baltimore Federal furniture as well as the early group of related case pieces.

This highly English-style sideboard and its related group are the work of the large cabinetmaking firm headed by John Bankson and Richard Lawson. The key individual in bringing this sophisticated English style to Baltimore was Lawson, a

Yorkshire native who worked for thirteen years at Seddon and Sons, the largest furniture-making firm in London in the last quarter of the eighteenth century. Arriving in Baltimore not long after the close of the Revolution, by July 1785 Lawson joined in partnership with Bankson, formerly of Philadelphia and a retired major in the Continental Army who brought to the firm connections with leading Revolutionary War figures. Bankson's contacts combined with Lawson's knowledge of the new neoclassical style as practiced in London was a recipe for success, and the firm quickly became the acknowledged leader of the Baltimore cabinetmaking community.[4] Their work probably influenced other local craftsmen and led to the creation of the most stylish Federal furniture made in America.

—*Gregory R. Weidman*

Commode

New York, N. Y., ca. 1800

Mahogany, mahogany veneer, light- and dark-wood inlay;
yellow poplar, pine, 38 ³/₄ x 53 ¹/₄ x 24 in.
Bequest from the estate of Mrs. Richard C. Rockwell (1995.0017)

Although Americans achieved political independence from England in the Revolution, the patriots' victory was not accompanied by a similar strong desire for stylistic or artistic independence. This beautifully inlaid commode, fashioned in New York City by a skilled cabinetmaking shop, is testimony to this retention of a penchant for things English. Its demilune form is directly taken from the design for a commode published as plate 78 in Hepplewhite's *Cabinet-Maker and Upholsterer's Guide*. This influential English pattern book, first published in London in 1788 and into its third edition by 1794, was included in the libraries of a good many American furniture makers and housewrights.

The Collection's commode differs slightly from the Hepplewhite plan in having a central section of four drawers, flanked by cupboards, although as Hepplewhite notes these commodes are made of "various shapes." Because they are "used in principal rooms, [they] require considerable elegance," and "the top and also the border around the front, should be inlaid." The maker of the Collection's commode followed this advice, as its top is decorated with a spectacular inlaid sunburst and stringing forming a radiating, semicircular pattern, echoing the Hepplewhite plate.

Commodes of this general style were made in Boston, Salem, Maine, and elsewhere, as well as in New York, demonstrating the homogenization of design that is characteristic of much high-style Federal-period furniture and that was caused by the proliferation of pattern books and price guides.[1] Some examples are fitted with drawers and compartments that allow them to function as sideboards or so-called butler's desks.[2] Most commodes, however, like the Collection's example, were primarily chests of drawers that evidence suggests were used principally in bedchambers to store linens.[3]

—*Gerald W. R. Ward*

Cat. 99

Jug

England, 1795

Earthenware with blue and black underglaze slip
and black and gilt overglaze, 9 ¼ x 8 ⅞ x 6 in.
Gift of Mrs. Jerauld Wright (1981.0031)

Following the Revolution, the United
States began to develop as a wholly separate market. Beginning in 1784, the Chinese produced trade porcelains with
decorations meant for American buyers.
Similarly, English pottery manufacturers
soon realized that wares decorated to
commemorate American events or to
appeal to American sentiments would
have a ready market.

Large, cream-colored earthenware
jugs (also called pitchers in America and
today called Liverpool or Liverpool-type
jugs) with black, transfer-printed decoration, such as ships, Revolutionary heroes,
or the Great Seal, were among the earliest wares made in England specifically
for the American market.[1] Appearing in
the United States by 1790, they were
popular through the first two decades
of the nineteenth century, first in a tall
baluster form with a sharp, beaklike
spout and strap handle, and later as a
globular collared jug identified with the
Empire style.

Although creamware was considered
rather elegant when decorated in black,
the combination of a cobalt-blue glaze on
a yellowish body could not satisfy consumers' desires for the blue-and-white
"Nanking" patterns available on porcelain
from China. In 1779, Josiah Wedgwood
(1730–1795) introduced "pearl white"
wares (today called pearlware) to answer
this need.[2] With a body made white by
the addition of kaolin from Cornwall,
pearlware was given a bright glaze with a
bluish tinge that coordinated well with
decorations painted or printed in blue.
The fashions for such wares in America
closely followed the date of their English
introduction.

This pearlware jug is hand-painted
with a ship that flies an American flag and
is inscribed "WT / 1795" within a wreath
below the spout. On the reverse, a female
figure (perhaps Hope) with a large anchor
commemorates the American shipping
industry and the role of "WT" in it. The
jug also reflects the coexistence of
creamware and pearlware objects in the
American market. Its shape typifies early

creamware Liverpool jugs; it was rendered
in pearlware to accommodate the blue-
dipped background of the decorations.[3]
Compared to the common, shell-edge
pearlware used in American homes, this
handsomely decorated jug would have
been perceived as rare in its day.[4]

—*Ellen Paul Denker and Bert R. Denker*

Cat. 100

John Shaw (1745–1828; working ca. 1768–1816)

Card table

Annapolis, Md., 1790

Mahogany; walnut, white oak, yellow poplar,
southern yellow pine, 29 7/8 x 35 7/8 x 17 5/8 in.
Gift of Mrs. Augustine J. Todd (1980.0030)

John Shaw is the most famous name in
Maryland cabinetmaking of the eighteenth century. His renown has two principal causes. First, contrary to the practice
of the vast majority of American cabinetmakers, he chose to label much (if not all)
of the furniture produced in his Annapolis
shop; thus, Shaw's work can be readily
identified. Second, his fame was assured by
his obtaining a large number of contracts
from the State of Maryland to furnish
major public buildings. Due to their
important histories, many of these unusual
documented pieces have survived.

Shaw came to Annapolis from Glas-
gow, Scotland, in 1763, when the town
was in its heyday as the cultural and political center of the colony. Working as a
journeyman by 1768 and independently
by 1770, he was in partnership with
Archibald Chisholm from 1772 to 1776.
Shaw's commissions for the Maryland
State House began in 1775, and he was
the armorer for the State of Maryland
during the Revolution. He was most successful, however, when he was in business
on his own in the 1790s, the period of the
greatest number of his labeled pieces and
his extensive commissions for the Maryland State House, including the furnishings for the Senate Chamber and the
Governor's Council Chamber.

This handsome but simple early
Federal-period card table bears one of
Shaw's standard labels, engraved by the
Annapolis silversmith Thomas Sparrow
(born 1746; working 1764–1788) and
dated 1790 in ink.[2] The table is identical
to another labeled example in its three
distinctive sections of figured mahogany
veneers across the apron and the characteristic rounded molding of the edges of
the top and the bottom of the apron.[3] In
partnership with Chisholm, Shaw made
tables of this sort as early as the mid-
1770s; this table is typical of Shaw in
its conservatism.

This table descended in the Washington family. It was owned by the donor's
grandmother, Lucy Washington (Mrs.
William Bainbridge Packette), at Harewood, Jefferson County, West Virginia; she
inherited it from her parents, George
Steptoe Washington (about 1770–1809)
and Lucy Payne, a sister of Dolley Payne
Todd (Mrs. James Madison). The Washing-
tons had married about 1790, so perhaps
the table was a wedding present. George
Steptoe Washington inherited Harewood,
built in 1771, from his father, Samuel
Washington (1734–1781), a brother of the
first president.

—*Gregory R. Weidman*

Card table

Providence, R.I., 1790–1820

Mahogany; mahogany veneer, light- and dark-wood inlay, satinwood;
eastern white pine, cherry, hickory, 28 ¹⁵/₁₆ x 35 ¹³/₁₆ x 17 ³/₈ in.
Intended bequest of Mr. James R. McElwain (L1969.0083)

This fine Federal-period card table has been attributed to Massachusetts, but many characteristics of its construction and ornament point strongly toward Providence as the place of its manufacture. It is fashioned in an unusual shape—square with round corners—that is found on a substantial number of Providence tables but rarely seen elsewhere. The use of overlapping, flyleg construction and the secondary woods also suggest a Providence origin.[1]

Although the inlaid urns on the leg pilasters also appear on Boston tables, and the "checkerboard pattern" inlay is found on Boston and New Hampshire tables, the eagle on the center of this facade is not common on other card tables. Several features distinguish this inlay from other closely related examples, including the use of eighteen stars, the eagle facing to its left, a lesser degree of articulation in the bird's wing feathers, and the visibility of one leg.[2]

The satinwood veneer adds considerably to the visual appeal of this table and was an expensive option when it was built. Cabinetmakers prized satinwood for its fine "straw colour cast" and its "cool, light, and pleasing effect in furniture."[3] "Close in the grain, of a pale yellow colour, and elegantly veined, it presented an agreeable variety to the more sombre coloured woods" such as mahogany.[4]

—*Gerald W. R. Ward*

Cat. 102

Side chair

Salem, Mass., ca. 1800–1815

Mahogany; birch, soft maple, eastern white pine,
35 ¼ x 17 ⅞ x 17 ⅝ in.
Funds donated by Mrs. Golsan Schneider
(1971.0069.007)

In 1971 the Fine Arts Committee acquired an extraordinary group of nineteen square-back side chairs ornamented with carved eagles in the crests. According to tradition, all had belonged to Benjamin Williams Crowninshield (1772–1848), the eminent Salem merchant, United States congressman, and secretary of the navy under Presidents Madison and Monroe.[1]

The chairs display minor differences and probably represent an assemblage of surviving examples from five sets owned by members of the Crowninshield family. In one variation, the eagle in the crest looks to the left, has three layers of feathers on the wings, and is set against a star-punched background as seen here. On the other variety, the eagle looks to the right, has two layers of feathers, and fits within a plain tablet. In addition, the banisters are narrower, and the veining of the three palmlike petals at the neck of the banisters is more vertical. The chairs also differ in the design of their rear legs and the treatment of their upholstery. In the first type, the legs taper inward at a slight angle; on the other, they have a more graceful curve similar to that on other Salem seating furniture.[3]

Production of both versions was apparently limited to Salem.[4] No exact English precedent is known and similar patterns from other American communities have yet to surface. The only related design is a popular Salem square-back chair with overlapping Gothic arches and a carved tablet based on plate 9 in the third edition of Hepplewhite's *Cabinet-Maker and Upholsterer's Guide*.[5] A skilled local artisan probably developed this eagle-crested design as an alternative to the Hepplewhite plan, but it never became as prevalent as its Gothic-arched counterpart.

The carving on the Crowninshield chairs may be the work of a specialist. The noted carver Samuel McIntire (1757–1811) charged one Salem cabinetmaking firm for "cutting" and carving chair backs in 1795.[6] During the same period, Daniel Clarke and Joseph True performed similar work in Salem, and, as a result, attribution of an object to a particular artisan is difficult without conclusive documentary evidence.[7]

—*Brock Jobe*

Convex mirror

Probably England, ca. 1800–20

Eastern white pine, sylvestris pine, spruce, basswood
or lime, gilt, 51 ⅝ x 36 ¾ in.
Funds donated by Mrs. Mary N. Mathews (1984.0077)

This mirror displays lavishly carved oak leaves, graceful gilt candle arms ornamented with leaves and drapery tassels, and a spread-winged eagle. The abundance of vigorous, naturalistic foliage sets the mirror off from others of the same type, such as one considered to be of New York manufacture (New York State Museum, Albany) and another in a private collection labeled by Thomas Fentham of London.

According to Robert C. Smith, this mirror typifies an English neoclassical mirror imported to this country between 1800 and 1820, a time when Fentham was one of the principal manufacturers.[1] The variety of woods used suggests English manufacture, as does the high quality of the oak-leaf carving, made of basswood or lime rather than of cast composition, as is more typical of American-made mirrors. The bobeches are restorations.

The eagle does not by itself point to an American origin or intended American market for the mirror. Charles F. Montgomery noted that "the eagle has been a popular decorative device for centuries, [appearing] as a crest on such frames made in England."[2] Helen Comstock remarks that the eagle on the Collection's mirror is no different from those on English or French convex mirrors, many of which were exported to America.[3] Nevertheless, this classical symbol made such mirrors favorites among American patriots.

Smith has suggested that the eagle, "a regal and animated motif, was probably a survival of a feature of English Palladian mirrors, where in its theatrical pose . . . it represented a baroque intrusion into an otherwise conventional classical setting." He illustrates a design for a mirror from William Jones's, *Gentlemens or Builders Companion* (London, 1739), which was based on an English neo-Palladian door-case. Smith traces the use of the eagle on mirrors from Jones to Chippendale to Hepplewhite, suggesting the continuity of this design as well as underscoring its non-American origins.[4]

—*Page Talbott*

Cat. 104

Card table

Probably New York, N.Y., ca. 1805–20

Mahogany, mahogany veneer, satinwood veneer; yellow-poplar,
birch, eastern white pine, 29 ¹/₁₆ x 36 x 17 ³/₄ in.
Funds donated by The Diplomatic Rooms Endowment Fund
(1980.0071)

This table has been attributed to Duncan Phyfe based on similarities between it and other examples, most notably a four-post pedestal side table of nearly identical design in *Furniture Masterpieces of Duncan Phyfe* (1922), Charles Cornelius's authoritative book.[1] The finish is probably original.

Perhaps the most ubiquitous decorative element in Phyfe's work is the acanthus leaf seen here on the upper side of the curved legs and the vase-shaped portion of the four legs. Typically, the acanthus is combined with such details as the delicate reeding that starts at the base of the acanthus leaf and continues down the leg to the foot. Cornelius notes that Phyfe's wood-carving technique simplifies the acanthus of classical decoration into a series of rounded grooves and ridges.[2]

Common decorative features on Phyfe-attributed tables are straight fluting, seen here on the edge of the platform, and whorled fluting, used on the bulbous section of the columns below the vase. These whorls animate the table, moving the eye from the base up toward the double elliptical top, which is devoid of carving but elegant in shape and in surface color.

Since Cornelius published his work on Phyfe in 1922, many documented examples of New York–made furniture in Phyfe's style but not made by him have been identified. Moses and Stephen Young, for example, made a labeled table now in the Department of State that is very similar to one pictured in Cornelius.[3] Furthermore, several examples of furniture labeled by Michael Allison cast doubt on past Phyfe attributions. Research has revealed that certain carvers and specialized journeymen provided piecework for several New York shops, and that cabinetmakers in the major East Coast cities had access to price books such as *The New-York Revised Prices for Manufacturing Cabinet and Chair Work* (1810), among other titles.[4] Lacking a labeled card table matching this one, it should be attributed more conservatively to that group of New York City cabinetmakers with the same decorative vocabulary as Phyfe's.

—*Page Talbott*

Cat. 105 and 106
Attributed to the shop of Duncan Phyfe (1768–1854)

Two armchairs

New York, N.Y., ca. 1800–10

Mahogany; cherry, hard maple, 33 x 20 ⅛ x 21 ¼ in. (1980.0080.001);
Mahogany; cherry, eastern white pine 33 x 20 ¼ x 22 in. (1980.0080.002)
Funds donated by The Kathleen Price and Joseph M. Bryan Family Foundation

These armchairs, attributed to the workshop of the master cabinetmaker Duncan Phyfe, illustrate the variety of decorative and design elements available to New York patrons in the early nineteenth century. Many of these elements reflect the popularity of symbols from ancient Greece and Rome, and directly derive from patterns described in *The London Chair-Makers' and Carvers' Book of Prices for Workmanship*, first published in 1802, reissued in 1807, and later emulated in the United States in *The New York Book of Prices for Manufacturing Cabinet and Chair Work*, published in 1817 and printed by J. Seymour.

So ubiquitous were these types of chairs that each element was listed and priced according to complexity of workmanship and amount of labor required. Hundreds of chairs made in New York City from 1800 to 1825 are known, and although Duncan Phyfe's establishment was prolific, it is unlikely that it produced all of these chairs. Such chairs are better seen as illustrations of a style favored in one city, with attributions to Phyfe given guardedly.

An analysis of these chairs in the Collection suggests, nonetheless, that they were indeed made in Phyfe's workshop. One (above right) contains many of the most popular features of chairs attributed to Phyfe: the crest with a carved panel featuring the ribbon, bowknot, and reed design; double crossbar splats with rosette-carved centers; bowed serpentine arms with a reeded facade; acanthus-carved, urn-shaped, turned-arm supports; a bell-shaped seat with a reeded facade; reeded front legs with bulbous, tapered feet; and raked, square rear legs.[1]

The second armchair (above left) is the more modern and elaborate version of this high-style New York form. Two embellishments make this a more expensive example: the front legs turn outward and end in brass paw feet, and there are urns at the termination of the rear stiles and on part of the arm support. With the exception of the paw feet, this chair is very similar to a set that William Bayard purchased from Duncan Phyfe in 1807.[2]

—*Page Talbott*

Cat. 107

Attributed to the shop of Duncan Phyfe (1768–1854)

Sofa

New York, N.Y., ca. 1810–20

Mahogany, mahogany veneer; cherry, soft maple, 35 1/4 x 73 1/4 x 23 in.
Lent by Mrs. James Balling (1980.0079)

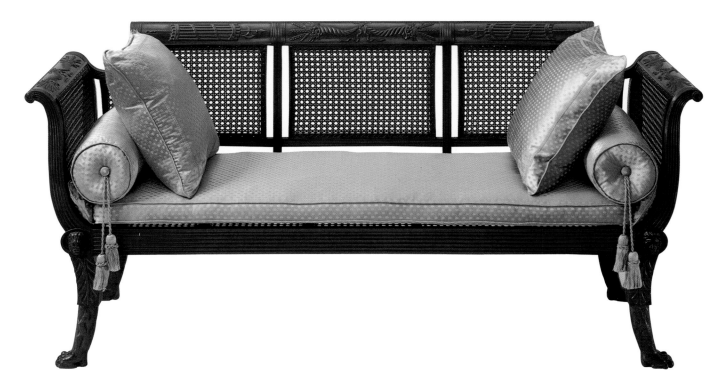

A large number of Sheraton- and Empire-style sofas have been attributed to the workshop of Duncan Phyfe because of trademark carving on the top rail, seat rail, and legs, but such a plethora of sofas decorated with cornucopia, thunderbolts, bowknots, and acanthus leaves could not all have originated in Phyfe's shop. This caned settee, however, may be sufficiently linked to documented Phyfe examples that it can be safely attributed to that master cabinetmaker.

The hairy legs and paws of the sofa, for example, are relatively rare in New York furniture of the early nineteenth century, although a documented set of chairs made by Phyfe for the Livingston family uses these same motifs, a feature that was available, according to the New York price books, at extra charge.[1] The well-known sketches by Phyfe among the Bancker papers at Winterthur—probably executed in 1815 or 1816—include a drawing of a lyre-back side chair with hairy legs and paw feet.[2]

Several settees of this general form are now in public collections. One sofa,

nearly identical in the shape and carving of the back rail and side wings, rests on a base consisting of two curule stools ornamented with gilded lion heads and paw feet.[3] Like the sofa in the Department of State, this settee is caned (a relatively rare feature), but, in all likelihood, it was intended to be fitted with cushions.[4]

Although the use of applied lion heads is rare on American furniture, this motif was popular in England and appears on furniture illustrated by Thomas Sheraton, Thomas Hope, and George Smith, among others, in their widely circulated design books. Animal monopodia (a miniature head and body on a single, life-sized foot) and lion's-paw feet and lion masks are among the most distinctive decorative features of the Regency style.[5]

—*Page Talbott*

Louisa Catherine Johnson Adams

John Quincy Adams

Cat. 108
Charles Robert Leslie (1794–1859)

Louisa Catherine Johnson Adams

1816

Oil on canvas, 36 ½ x 29 in.
Gift of Robert Homans, Jr., Lucy Aldrich Homans, and
Abigail Homans, in memory of their father, Robert Homans (1975.0039)

On June 25, 1816, T. B. Johnson, Louisa Adams's brother, wrote from New Orleans requesting portraits of his sister and brother-in-law for himself. John Quincy Adams had assumed his post as minister to the Court of St. James a year earlier, soon after the conclusion of the Treaty of Ghent (1814). As it happened, Adams had just made the acquaintance of Charles Robert Leslie, "a young American Painter, who lives with Mr. Alston. . . . [He] has a picture of some reputation, at the present exhibition, at Somerset House; and is patronized by the President of the Academy, Mr. West."[1] The combined support of these highly regarded artists, Washington Allston and Benjamin West, was invaluable to Leslie early in his career. Allston's painting *The Dead Man Restored to Life by Touching the Bones of the Prophet Elisha* had created a sensation in London in 1814. Benjamin West, formerly historical painter to George III, had by then been president of the Royal Academy of Arts for nearly a quarter of a century. West had been born in Pennsylvania and was always a staunch supporter of American artists; like Allston, Leslie was American, although he would remain in England. These facts, together with the intense nationalism prevailing in the United States after the War of 1812, make Adams's choice of Leslie to paint these portraits seem inevitable.

Louisa's sittings commenced on September 5, 1816. When John Quincy saw the portrait in progress on September 14, he thought the likeness "not so good as mine." Each subject sat some fourteen times until the end of October.[2] When both pictures were finished, Louisa wrote to Abigail Adams (November 11, 1816): "Our Portraits are most striking likenesses and should they reach America are to be exhibited at Philadelphia."[3]

The thoroughly Regency style of the painting is striking. The elegant yet casual pose, the poetic aura, the sumptuous textures and colors all bespeak Thomas Lawrence, not Benjamin West. It is impressive that Leslie, who turned twenty-two on October 19, should command this style with such conviction, but he had already given evidence of a precocious talent in his *Self-Portrait* (1814; National Portrait Gallery, London).[4]

Mrs. Adams, born in London in 1775, seems at home in this very English style. Her mother was an Englishwoman and her father, Joshua Johnson, was an American merchant who was forced to leave England during the American Revolution. Consequently, Louisa Adams spent much of her childhood in Nantes, France. In 1790 Johnson was appointed American consul in London, and it was at the consulate in 1794 that John Quincy Adams, just appointed minister to The Hague, first met Louisa. "Louisa was charming, like a Romney portrait, but among her many charms that of being a New England woman was not one," her grandson, Henry Adams, was to write. "Try as she might, the Madam could never be Bostonian."[5]

Leslie has made much of the contrasts between this couple, even though they are united by their frank, undissembling faces. Mrs. Adams's sloping pose, the consonant flow of her gown and robe, her relaxed wrist and dangling glove are all placed in expressive contrast to the weighty, forthright presentation of her husband. For Louisa, Leslie reserved the parklike landscape with an elegiac evening sky; for John Quincy, the firmly held book.

—*William Kloss*

Cat. 109

Charles Robert Leslie (1794–1859)

John Quincy Adams

1816

Oil on canvas, 37 x 29 in.
Gift of Robert Homans, Jr., Lucy Aldrich Homans, and
Abigail Homans, in memory of their father, Robert Homans
(1975.0038)

Among the multitude of characterizations of Adams, this portrait is striking for the serenity the artist captured in America's then-Minister to Great Britain (1815–17). On September 11, 1816, only four days after Leslie began work on the painting, Mrs. Adams wrote to her mother-in-law, Abigail, "Mr. A. tells me his picture is likely to prove an excellent likeness at which I am much delighted as I think he never looked so well or so handsome as he does now." He was generous in granting Leslie some fourteen sittings through October 31, and the young artist made the most of the opportunities.[1]

A sense of physical and mental well-being pervades the figure. Nearly frontal, the substantial block of his body and head is drawn and modeled to convey strength of purpose and intellect. In its air of good humor and candor untinged with irony or asperity, it is rare among portraits of Adams. Mrs. Adams was moved to write a poem in praise of the artist's success, in which she singles out precisely these qualities:

> On the Portrait of my Husband
> The Painter's art would vainly seize
> That harmony of nature,
> Where Sense and sweetness joined with ease
> Shine forth in evr'y feature.
> That open front where wisdom sits
> That Eye which speaks the soul
> That brow which study gently knits
> That soft attemper'd whole—
> That vast variety of Mind
> Capacious, clear, and strong
> Where brilliancy of wit refin'd
> Enchants the list'ning throng
> That sense of right by God impres't
> That virtuous holy love
> Of excellence whats'ere is best
> Imparted from above
> These Painter if thou canst impart
> Shall fame immortal raise
> And e'en the greatest in thy Art
> Shall carol forth thy praise.[2]

Adams holds a book, his forefinger marking his place, while his other fingers draw our attention to the design embossed on the binding—Adams's seal, just received from a London engraver. Leslie at first "did not incline to" Adams's request to include the seal, and it is somewhat oddly placed on the back cover of the quarto volume. The seal had deep significance for Adams. This is its first appearance.[3] It combines an eagle and a lyre, and it bears a Latin motto, NUNC SIDERA DUCIT, which may be rendered "it now leads the stars," an extremely erudite reference. Adams elucidated the motto in his diary entry for September 7, 1816, the very day of his first sitting to Leslie. It reads, in part:

> . . . Orpheus is said to have charmed Lions and Tygers, . . . by the harmony of his Lyre. . . . The meaning of this Allegory is explained by Horace. . . . Orpheus was a Legislator whose eloquence charmed the rude and savage men of his age to associate together in the State of civil Society. . . . It was the Lyre of Orpheus that civilized Savage Man. It was only in Harmony that the first human political institutions could be founded. After the Death of Orpheus, his Lyre was placed among the Constellations, and there, according to the Astronomics of Manilius, still possesses its original charm. . . . It is the Application of this Fable, and of this passage of Manilius, to the United States, the American political Constellation, that forms the device of the Seal. The modern Astronomers have connected a Vulture with the Constellation of the Lyre. . . . Instead of that bird, . . . I have assumed the American Eagle as the bearer of the Lyre. The thirteen original Stars form a border round the Seal. . . . The motto from Manilius is upon the Lyre itself. The moral application of the emblem is, that the same power of harmony which originally produced the institutions of civil government . . . now presides in the federal association of the American States. That Harmony is the Soul of their combination. That their force consists in their Union; and that while thus United, it will be their destiny to revolve in harmony with the whole world by the attractive influence of their Union. *It is*

the Lyre of Orpheus that now leads the Stars [emphasis added]. . . . The Lesson of the emblem is Union.[4]

This extraordinary exegesis, together with his demeanor in the portrait, suggests Adams's pride in representing America in London at this moment of resurgent nationalism following the successful conclusion of the War of 1812. In 1829 he wrote that "the Seal which you will find upon this Letter is a pythagorean Emblem of my whole political System."[5]

The portraits of Adams and his wife (cat. no. 108) were sent to America in late February 1817.[6] The subjects soon followed them, for in the summer John Quincy Adams returned to become secretary of state (1817–25) in the administration of President James Monroe.

—*William Kloss*

The Nation Expands Westward
DISCOVERY, BOUNTY, AND BEAUTY

Thomas Jefferson's vision of a nation with abundant land for the thousandth generation of citizens to come resulted in an exponential increase of territory with the Louisiana Purchase. The Far West and the Northwest Territory were already being explored and partially settled at the time of this acquisition, in 1803. However, most of the western part of the continent—beyond the great rivers of the Mississippi, Missouri, and the Platte—was largely unknown and unsettled territory. For many, it seemed to be in the "natural" order of things that the entire continent, east to west, become connected to the new nation. The works of art in this last section illuminate and affirm this discovery of the continent and the growing democratization of these United States.

The Far West was as much an attitude or state of mind as it was a measured space. Those who chose or were forced to live beyond the borders of established villages or cities cared little about national boundaries. Mapmakers could outline the shape of the continent from waterways, but the great space beyond the Missouri River was largely uncharted. This changed as the transcontinental expedition of Lewis and Clark made its way across the continent, gathering remarkable specimens and valuable information about the land and its peoples to the mouth of the Columbia River and the Pacific Ocean.

The nineteenth century was an era of extraordinary change. The pace of events quickened—as new forms of transportation accelerated movement of goods and people from sail to steam, from horse and carriage to train, and as canals and locks connected coastal harbors to inland lakes and rivers, enabling barges to transport heavy cargo to the interior. Social experiment and religious ferment encouraged freethinking settlers to move away from what they considered corrupting influences of cities. For example, in 1846 the Mormons (Latter-day Saints) pushed westward from Nauvoo, Illinois, en route to the valley of the Great Salt Lake. This

was the year of the beginning of the Mexican War, when much of the West became United States territory. Just three years later, the gold rush launched thousands of prospectors to California. Parlor-car travel from coast to coast was assured by 1869, when the Atlantic and Pacific were connected by rail. As the continent became the new nation, the abundance of this empire, its sublime landscape, and its varied people were celebrated with images made by artists of the "American canvas."[1] These are the images, expressive of diverse talents and viewpoints, presented in the following pages.

From the nineteenth century to today, our national identity has been inextricably linked to the great American landscape. This is made clear not only in the paintings made by American artists who traveled to witness at first hand the Far West but also through the numerous traveler's guidebooks, novels, and other western literature that captured the imagination of readers both here and abroad. Poets paid tribute to the western lands. William Cullen Bryant's little book *Selections from the American Poets* (New York: Harper & Brothers, 1840) included a work of his own titled "The Prairies." It begins:

> These are the gardens of
> the desert, these
> The unshorn fields,
> boundless and beautiful,
> For which the speech of
> England has no name—
> The Prairies. I behold them for
> the first,
> And my heart swells,—

Thomas Jefferson's curiosity about all aspects of the American continent was insatiable. Foremost was his interest in New World maps and discoveries in natural history. While he was in Paris in 1786 he met the naturalist Compte de Buffon who had claimed that American animals were degenerates of European species. Jefferson provided him with specimens of American moose, elk, and deer that proved

otherwise. As a searcher for the truth, Jefferson was not impressed with conventional wisdom but was nourished by observable facts. He held American Indians in high esteem, even establishing a room at Monticello devoted to Native American artifacts. He was deeply moved by the prehistoric fossils that he collected for more than twenty years and displayed in his entrance hall. He wrote about fossils for Philadelphia's American Philosophical Society, of which he was president.

In that same town, his colleague at the society, the artist Charles Willson Peale, established in 1784 an art and natural science museum, which once occupied the State House (now Independence Hall). Peale's Museum displayed American species both extinct and extant. Also, Peale's own portraits of American leaders were included in the museum together with bones of a mammoth that he had exhumed.[2]

The intellectual ferment after the Revolution fostered a "diffusion of knowledge" for the betterment of humanity. The new nation entered the "official" world of natural history studies, liberated from preconceptions but lacking the institutional patronage of great European intellectual societies. Americans had to prove their "academic patriotism" by making New World discoveries known through their writings. A diverse "brotherhood" of gentlemen, some of whom were formally trained and others self-taught, established the Academy of Natural Sciences in Philadelphia in 1812 above a cake shop. But their real work as intellectuals took place at Peale's Museum, the University of Pennsylvania, and at the American Philosophical Society where they gathered to deliver papers; announce new findings; and record, collect, and classify the natural world.[3]

It was in such a heady atmosphere of national pride and awareness of new opportunities for discovery that, in 1802,

Jefferson sent his envoy-extraordinary, James Monroe, to Paris to negotiate the purchase of the whole Mississippi valley from Napoleon Bonaparte for $15 million. Monroe was partnered in the effort by Robert Livingston, the American minister in Paris. The purchase, completed in 1803, radically expanded the nation westward. It made good sense to Jefferson, for he reasoned that it would provide land for settlement for centuries to come. The real extent and natural wonders of the West were unknown, and that inspired him to send out the exploratory party headed by Meriwether Lewis and William Clark on their perilous journey to the Pacific Northwest.[4]

Parts of the West Coast and the Northwest Territory were already settled, but what lay in between was a vast space generally known as the "Great American Desert." Being a seeker of truth, Jefferson desired facts and specimens from this uncharted territory. Like space explorers of modern times, Lewis and Clark ventured across the vast continent and brought back abundant specimens and detailed reports. One of the most impressive artifacts sent to Jefferson is an American bison robe (about 1797), with painted images recording battles between the Mandan, Sioux, and the Ricaras. It once hung in Monticello's entrance hall and now is preserved at the Peabody Museum, Harvard University.

Expeditions of exploration to the West continued in the next generation, yielding information gleaned beyond the farthest rivers. An engineer, Major Stephen H. Long (1784–1864), took a specially constructed steamship on an expedition (1819–20) up the Missouri carrying artists Samuel Seymour and Titian Ramsay Peale. Seymour and Peale were the first artists of consequence to pictorially document and publish accounts of the Rocky Mountains and its wildlife. Exploration of the Far West continued with Prince Maximilian zu Wied, who in the early 1830s gathered specimens and with artist Karl Bodmer created pictorial records. These he published in his handsomely illustrated report: *Reise in das Innere Nord-Amerikca in den Jahren 1832 bis 1834* (1830–41).

The Far West was becoming known, with images of the land seeping into the awareness of Americans at about the same time that those who had fought in the War for Independence were becoming senior citizens and were being

honored by a new generation of their countrymen. The marquis de Lafayette (1757–1834), an officer who had served Washington throughout the war in ways too numerous to recite, returned to the United States after years of political fame and trials in France. Back in America, during fourteen months in 1824–25, he made a triumphal tour of the twenty-four states that then constituted the Union.

As a citizen of the world and a republican, Lafayette was accorded a national celebration on this return visit. He is known to have regarded the Constitution of the United States as the most perfect document of its sort in existence. Congress voted him $200,000 as recompense for his services. The superb likeness reproduced earlier in this book (cat. no. 60) was painted in 1825 by Adolpe Phalipon. The portrait represents a reflective face—a handsome image that was repainted on a pair of French porcelain vases that are also owned by the Department of State.[5]

The two presidents who followed Jefferson—James Madison and James Monroe—were fellow Virginians. The Collection portrait of Madison, the fourth president, was painted in 1826 by Charles Bird King (cat. no. 120). It captures the face of one who participated in the shaping of the Constitution and who was a joint participant with Hamilton and Jay in writing *The Federalist*. For eight years Madison served as Jefferson's secretary of state. That reason alone would make this portrait a State Department treasure. He was president when war was declared against Great Britain on June 18, 1812; survived the burning of the Capitol by British forces in August 1814; and concluded the peace with the Treaty of Ghent on December 24, 1814. His wife, Dolley, is known for having furnished the White House with some of the most advanced classical-style furniture of the day in America—works made in Baltimore after designs by architect Benjamin Henry Latrobe, many of whose drawings are in the collection of the Library of Congress. An example of Madison's china, made in France while he was secretary of state, displays an elegant classical border in the latest taste (see cat. no. 84).

The fifth president, inaugurated in 1817, was James Monroe. He had studied law under Jefferson before being elected to the Assembly of Virginia in 1782. As a delegate to the General Congress in 1783 he was witness to and played an important part in the completion of Independence. He served Madison as secretary of state between 1811 and 1817, and also was secretary of war, from 1814 to 1815. During his administration, Spain ceded Florida to the United States. His celebrated policy, the Monroe Doctrine, declared that any attempt on the part of European powers to extend their system of government to any portion of the Western Hemisphere is "dangerous to our peace and safety." He shared with Madison and Jefferson a sense of the continent being part of a natural whole. Americans are fortunate to have had three brilliant Virginians to serve as presidents successively as the nation quite literally took shape.

The portrait of James Monroe, painted by fashionable portraitist Thomas Sully of Philadelphia in 1829, shows the president in his declining years (cat. no. 121). He was seventy-one years old when the painting was made. Yet the portrait is sufficiently idealized in its soft handling of paint to evoke a cheerful countenance—one seeming to look forward to the future, rather than toward the past. The French porcelain dessert service made for President Monroe in 1817 has a border illustrating trophies that represent Strength, the Arts, Commerce, the Sciences, and Agriculture.[6]

In March 1825 Henry Clay (1777–1852) was appointed secretary of state by President John Quincy Adams. Clay had long been speaker of the house, and was an eloquent supporter of the Missouri Compromise, which brought Missouri into the Union. From Lexington, Kentucky, Clay was admired in the western country as an incomparable "stump" orator. His portrait, painted by Edward Dalton Marchant, represents the vitality and ardor of the sitter, who had cham-

pioned the War of 1812 and who served as a commissioner for the treaty of peace with Great Britain, signed in 1814 in Ghent (cat. no. 110). He ran against James Knox Polk (1795–1849) in the presidential election of 1844. Clay objected to the annexation of Texas that Polk supported. Polk was elected, becoming the eleventh president, and his annexation of Texas led to the Mexican War and the Spanish cession of Upper California and Mexico. Settlement of disputes with the British government over the Oregon Territory led to the 49th parallel agreements.

Images of leaders who shaped the course of the nation offer one way to suggest both change and continuity. Another way to understand America is through images of land and sea, still lifes, and genre scenes. The Collection of the Diplomatic Reception Rooms is richly endowed with such images. Indeed, at the State Department the western experience is best conveyed through pictorial imagery of places rather than through portraits, and through paintings rather than through the decorative arts.

The story begins chronologically with a work by Joshua Shaw, *View on the Kiskeminitas* (cat. no. 116), painted in 1838. This landscape shows a peaceful scene conventionally divided into three sections. The near view, or foreground, is a pictorial translation of Edmund Burke's concept of beauty—things are small, smooth, and delicate. The middle distance, where cows rest and a stream meanders, represents the "picturesque" part of the painting. In the distance is an energetic, sublime view of an industrial city, with its factories' engines billowing smoke.

It is the sublime, distant view that dominates the imagination of landscape painters throughout most of the nineteenth century. The painting *A Glimpse of the Capitol at Washington* follows the same arrangement of parts (cat. no.

123). At the horizon stands the monumental Capitol—certainly the most majestic or sublime structure of its time in America. The foreground and middle ground show efforts to domesticate the land, which nevertheless remains picturesque and without much ordered success.

The *View of Boston Harbor* by Fitz Hugh Lane certainly captures the excitement of trade and commerce as represented by the grand vessels under sail (cat. no. 111). Yet centered on the horizon in the distance is the gold-domed State House, designed by Charles Bulfinch—nerve center of all that takes place in this wonderful world of action.

A pair of eighteen-karat-gold goblets that depict a steam-engine-driven train were made in New York (cat. nos. 118, 119). They highlight the fact that rail power at midcentury inspired awe and touched the sublime. No other subject could be more masculine than a steam engine depicted on a gold goblet. Could these vessels have been made of gold discovered in California—the precious metal that inspired the forty-niners to trudge across the continent or take to the sea in clipper ships in their rush to the goldfields?

The still life painted by Severin Roesen in mid-nineteenth-century Pennsylvania may be viewed in two contexts—as an ambitious and effusive revival of seventeenth-century Dutch super-realism, or as a symbol of the glorious natural abundance experienced in this country (cat. no. 125). By midcentury it was the fashion for Americans to display images reflecting abundant fruit and flowers above their sideboards which themselves were carved with game and other objects of nature's bounty. Resting on the counter and shelves of sideboards, at the time were silver bowls, urns, and water pitchers like one made by Samuel Kirk of Baltimore (cat. no. 124). Kirk was well known for his eclectic use of motifs, introduced in the 1840s, that revived high baroque forms of the seventeenth century. His signature pieces display richly wrought repoussé workmanship—hammered floral ornament raised from within his vessels. In this case, the outside surfaces display beautifully chased floral detail surrounding a pagoda. Americans' taste for natural

abundance as captured by Roesen's painting is thus also reflected by the ornament of Kirk's silver. Nature representing God's handiwork was a pervasive theme in all the arts (see cat. no. 8, for another example).

Democratic, or popular, arts—that is to say, arts for the people—were mass-produced by a printing process called lithography introduced into America in 1818. The process was quickly perfected, making possible the distribution of good-quality images at low cost for an eager-to-buy middle-class market. William Sidney Mount's image *The Power of Music* was made to depict American rural life; not as it was, but as what it was supposed to be—that is to say, idealized (cat. no. 128). No doubt Mount was witness to many of the elements in this scene as he made preparatory sketches for oils that he painted in his studio on Long Island. But the painting from which this print was drawn on lithographic stone was an artistic composition like those made later by Norman Rockwell. Like Rockwell's prints, these sold well for their publisher.

Goupil, Vibert & Co. used a different process to produce the prints *The County Election* and *Stump Speaking* (cat. nos. 126, 127), after paintings by George Caleb Bingham. These complex compositions best lent themselves to copperplate engraving by Philadelphian John Sartain. Sartain employed many different methods, including mezzotint engraving, in order to achieve the rich, velvety blacks that distinguish these prints. After printing, they were hand-colored with watercolors in order to capture the essence of the original oils. These prints document the broad range of citizens attending the election and voting process—democracy in action on the edge of the frontier at Arrowrock on the Missouri River.

Western America—the frontier—was as much an attitude or state of mind as it was a time and place. The American West of the mountain man and fur trader, of the explorer and overland pioneer settler, the cowboy and rancher, the gold-seeker and outlaw—has been the subject of many displays. It is a subject too vast to encapsulate here, no matter

Right: John Mix Stanley, Barter for a Bride *(see pages 204–05) above Philadelphia Queen Anne side chairs (see page 64), The Gallery*

how important the expansion into the West was in the development of the American character and spirit.

But it could be observed that at the very moment in our country's development when the eastern seaboard was undergoing cultural refinement and achieving remarkable levels of physical comfort and social tranquility in an ordered society, people moving westward into the frontier forsook such comforts in order to participate in new forms of social experiments, technologies, and transportation. Stagecoaches, canals, steamships, and trains penetrated the landscape. In the imagination, the great American West represents the sublime rather than the beautiful aesthetic of Burke's analysis. As the sublime western landscape became domesticated through settlement, it became picturesque.

The era of overland migration was also a period of religious ferment and diversity. In 1844 Israel Daniel Rupp of Lancaster, Pennsylvania, published *An Original History of the Religious Denominations at Present Existing in the United States* (Philadelphia: J. Y. Humphreys), which inventoried forty-one different faiths and supplied descriptions of each written by leading clergy. Left out of Rupp's *History*, of course, were the beliefs of Native Americans, and of immigrants from Asia who helped to build the railroads. Nonetheless, the book chronicles a vast diversity of flourishing denominations: Presbyterians, Baptists, Catholics, Congregationalists, Quakers, Moravians, Methodists, Mennonites, Millenialists, Shakers, Schwenkfelders, Universalists, Restorationists, Amish, Episcopalians, and Mormons, to name more than a few. It is clear from Rupp's book that each denomination was undergoing transformation. Changes within faiths and society at large were made manifest in exoduses across America's landscape. Most visible, as mentioned, was the large overland pioneer migration of Mormon pioneers from Illinois to Utah.

At the time of this massive movement of settlers, writer-historian Francis Parkman (1823–1893) of Boston was mounted on horseback, heading toward the Rocky Mountains, experiencing the rigors of the frontier life, recounted later in his exciting narrative *The California and Oregon Trail* (1849). This book, reprinted many times, helped to establish his literary career.

Books were no more popular than lithographed images of the West, many of which were published by Currier & Ives. Two of the most popular were colored images—*The Rocky Mountains. Emigrants Crossing the Plains* of 1866 (cat. no. 130) and a lithograph of a train crossing the continent made in 1860 (cat. no. 131). The latter print was anticipatory

Below: Detail, Cyrus Dallin, Appeal to the
Great Spirit *(see pages 212–13)*

*Bottom: Detail of Theodore Roosevelt in
Frederic Remington's* Our Elk Outfit
at the Ford *(see pages 208–09)*

of the transcontinental connection
made between eastern and western
rails that resulted in the driving of
the golden spike in Utah in 1869.
All Currier & Ives prints present
the world the way it was supposed
to be, with stirring images that
reflect the spirit of an ideal, democratic America, rather than particular details of the actual.

Much more descriptive of an
actual event directly observed is an
oil painting made by John Mix Stanley, who in the fall of
1853 was an illustrator with the Pacific Railroad Survey in the
Washington Territory (cat. no. 129). This painting, one of the
finest of Stanley's to survive, depicts courtship among the
Blackfoot. It is a studio production, of course, but nonetheless
it is based on direct observations with probable use of sketches
and daguerreotypes to accurately record an actual event.

While the landscape of the American West was being
explored, described, and settled, a retrospective survey of
America's past was being written by the distinguished historian George Bancroft (1800–1891) of Massachusetts. His
monumental ten-volume work, *History of the United States
from the Discovery of the American Continent*, was based on
research in primary documents. The first volume appeared in
1834. During President Polk's administration, Bancroft was
appointed secretary of the navy. He established the naval
academy at Annapolis and made
important improvements to the Naval
Observatory in Washington, D.C.,
before resigning to become minister
plenipotentiary to England. That post
provided him opportunity to research
archives in London, Paris, and elsewhere. In 1849 he moved to New
York City to complete his historical
undertaking. His last volume, which
concluded with the completion of the
American Revolution in 1782, was
published in 1874. While Bancroft was
writing about the past, the great conflict of the Civil War raged between
Union and Confederate forces.
Although Bancroft's history was about

the past, it was an affirmation of
unity. His final volume ended with
the statement that, in 1782, former
colonies pledged mutual citizen-
ship and perpetual union—making
them one people. In February
1866, after President Lincoln's
assassination, Bancroft delivered
before Congress a moving oration
honoring Lincoln, certainly the
nation's most heroic figure in this
era of manifest destiny.

One of the most famous painters whose works celebrated the grandeur of the American West was Thomas
Moran. His painting *The Cliffs of Green River, Wyoming*,
although dated 1900, is based on observations made in
1871, when he traveled on the Union Pacific Railroad into
Utah territory (cat. no. 133). The cliffs on the Green River
did present a colorful and inspiring sight for the visitor
from the East, who passed many miles of flat, desolate land
before coming upon the site in southeastern Wyoming.
Moran's painting shows the cliffs more majestic than they
are. His coloring is factually correct, but it is highly
unlikely that he actually saw the mass of Indians on horseback that he used to enhance the foreground. On close
inspection, these figures seem more like images of Arabian
horsemen popularized by French painters of the last quarter of the nineteenth century. Nonetheless, Moran's
imagery profoundly influenced
Americans who were in search of
nature's marvels. Indeed, Moran provided illustrations for wood engravings reproduced in popular books
promoting sightseeing by rail in
Pullman cars that crossed the continent in merely four days. That was
the claim made by William M.
Thayer, who used some of Moran's
images in *Marvels of the New West: A
Vivid Portrayal of the Unparalleled
Marvels in the Vast Wonderland West of
the Missouri River* (1892). It was
Moran's sweeping vista of the Grand
Canyon of the Yellowstone that
helped to persuade Congress in

1872 to establish Yellowstone National Park.

A tougher West was pictured by New York artist Frederic Remington. His small black and white illustration *Our Elk Outfit at the Ford* (E86) deals with people and a real situation as experienced close up by Theodore Roosevelt (1858–1919). The illustration highlights the following incident, recalled in an article written by Roosevelt for *Century Magazine* in 1888: "But as the river was high and the horses were weak, we came within an ace of being swamped at one crossing." Roosevelt is the horseman second from the left. Roosevelt's love of the great outdoors, of nature, and the grandeur of the American West led his administration (1901–9) to establish five national parks and four federal game preserves, as well as eighteen national monuments protected by the Antiquities Act. He also added 125 million acres to the national forest reserves and developed the structure for today's National Wildlife Refuge System.

It is not surprising that the one of the most handsome American coins—the buffalo nickel—came about through Roosevelt's friendship with American sculptor James Earle Fraser (1876–1953), who became president of the National Sculpture Society and who created a magnificent monument honoring Roosevelt at the entrance to the American Museum of Natural History, New York. On the base of that monument, the American bison is beautifully carved in low relief.

The rapid population decline of the American bison seemed also to represent the end of an era. Frontier days were by no means over, but, for many at the turn of the century, the character of the continent seemed changed. The sculptor Cyrus E. Dallin, born in Springville, Utah, had great concern for his friends, the Native Americans. In 1888 he traveled to Paris and there studied sculpture at the Académie Julian. A visit

of Buffalo Bill Cody's Wild West Show in Paris inspired Dallin to draw upon his youthful experiences in the West. This led to his making a series of works that honored Native Americans. He believed that his generation would witness the demise of the descendants of those who were here before settlers arrived from Europe.

His first work in the Indian series was *Signal of Peace*; it stands in Philadelphia's Fairmount Park together with his second work of the series, *Medicine Man*. For the St. Louis World's Fair, he created in 1903 a heroic Indian warrior with a raised clenched fist called *The Protest*. This Indian, like the others, was mounted on a horse. Dallin's fourth monument, and his most famous, represents a mounted Plains warrior with his arms lifted in supplication. *Appeal to the Great Spirit* was completed in 1908; a small version of that sculpture is included here (cat. no. 134). In 1912 a heroic version of this sculpture was placed in front of the Museum of Fine Arts, Boston, where it continues to attract photographers and admirers from all countries of the globe. Certainly honoring the Native Americans was the right thing to do. But growing numbers of Native Americans today refute the myth of their imminent passing.

Although mistakes have been made in the past, it is clear that the United States is a nation where, through liberty, mankind can flourish and worship according to individual conscience. The United States Department of State Collection affirms the fact that the strength of this country comes about through continued renewal of tradition and innovation, through creative people from all nations who come to and are welcomed at these shores, even as newcomers were first welcomed by natives in the past. We are, indeed, a "Nation of nations,"[7] a land of hope—where, as the message on the banner held by the bald eagle of the Great Seal proclaims: E PLURIBUS UNUM.

—*Jonathan L. Fairbanks*

Cat. 110

Edward Dalton Marchant (1806–1887)

Henry Clay

1838

Oil on canvas, 29 ¼ x 24 ¼ in.
Department of State Collection (1972.0026)

For its exceptional quality, this likeness of Henry Clay (1777–1852) deserves an honored place among portraits of American statesmen and politicians. It is startlingly beautiful, embodying the strength of Clay's character, enhanced by a touch of romantic ardor.

The artist Edward Marchant was born in Edgartown, Massachusetts, December 16, 1806, and died in Asbury Park, New Jersey, August 15, 1887. He painted miniature portraits in watercolor as well as full-scale portraits in oil. William Dunlap, the first historian of American art, noted "several portraits of superior merit" by Marchant and concluded: "Of prepossessing manners and undoubted abilities, [Marchant] must succeed in the profession he has chosen."[1] In this canvas, he shows a subtle skill in drawing, composition, and color that supports Dunlap's judgment.[2] The almost frontal pose is softened by the turn of the head, which is in slight contrapposto with the sloping design of the shirtfront. The clothing is fluidly drawn and provides an elegant pedestal for the splendid head.

Stability combines with animation in the characterization of Clay's head; the pupils of the intelligent eyes are picked out with strong highlights, the high complexion is vital but not florid, and the compressed lips show a characteristic slight pull toward the left side of his face. Marchant's tonal skill is evident in the costume and in the masterly transition between figure and background.

This portrait was purchased by Congress from the artist's widow and daughter on September 29, 1890, and was accompanied by a letter from the daughter, Adeline B. Marchant:

> While passing the summer of 1838 in Cincinnati, Mr. Marchant, who was an intense admirer of Mr. Clay, conceived the idea of adding his portrait to a collection he was engaged in making for himself, of the distinguished men of our own country. Accordingly . . . he went to Ashland [Clay's home, near Lexington, Kentucky], where he was kindly received by Mr. Clay, who at once acceded to his request, & insisted upon his making his home with him during the progress of the picture. After completing the head, &c. which occupied about ten days, he returned to Cincinnati where he finished the drapery. The picture was seen by a number of persons at Mr. Clay's own house, and was applauded without a dissenting voice, Mrs. Clay actually shedding tears over it. She was anxious to retain it, but Mr. Marchant felt that he must have the original, and offered to make her a copy, but this she refused, saying that it was the best ever painted of him, & she was afraid the copy would not suit her as well.[3]

Many portraits were made of the "great pacificator," but none is stronger than this.

—*William Kloss*

Cat. 111
Fitz Hugh Lane (1804–1865)

View of Boston Harbor

1852

Oil on canvas, 22 ¹/₂ x 34 ³/₄ in.
Funds donated by Miss Elizabeth Cheney (1974.0023)

Fitz Hugh Lane produced a significant group of paintings of Boston harbor in the early 1850s, and they mark his attainment of full artistic maturity. The majority embody a poetic sense of suspended time, although *View of Boston Harbor* is an exception. The drama of sky and water and the activity of the shipping relate it to seventeenth-century Dutch marine paintings, especially those of the younger Willem van de Velde.

The composition is not unique in Lane's oeuvre. In a painting of New York Harbor also from the 1850s (private collection), the two largest vessels and the small foreground sailboat are nearly identical.[1] Using his own drawings as reference, he economically repeated the design and position of ships in various compositions, although he was careful not to abuse this practice.

Despite the relative activity in the painting, *View of Boston Harbor* has a unity of tone that imparts a hushed note to the scene. Moreover, the commanding rhythms of the ocean swells are full, easy, and regular. The great clipper ship at right center is marked by animated rigging: taut lines contrast with free curving ones. The rigging, remarkably well preserved, has a crispness and clarity all the more impressive for being painted freehand with a fine brush.[2] Within the open center of the picture, Lane frames the distant but distinctive dome of Charles Bulfinch's State House, a feature of many of his Boston Harbor paintings.

In the development of a coherent space, Lane uses alternating bands of shadow and light on the water, a favorite device of Robert Salmon, his most important predecessor in American marine painting. Lane goes beyond Salmon, however, to develop a more varied perspective, which includes his skillful variation of the angle of view of his many vessels and their placement in space.

Many details delight and instruct the observer: for instance, the wit of Lane's signature, inscribed in a concave arc that echoes the trough of the wave, or the steamer glimpsed in the far right background. The fact that in 1852 such vessels were far more prominent in Boston Harbor than in his painting of it suggests that Lane shared the common sentiment that the progress represented by steam power on land or on water threatened the ordained harmony between man and nature typified by majestic wind-powered ships.

—*William Kloss*

Cat. 112
Unidentified artist

John Watson Foster

ca. 1866–70

Oil on canvas, 44 x 37 in.
Estate of Allen Dulles (1975.0001)

The diplomatic career of John Watson Foster (1836–1917) consisted of several appointments during the 1870s and 1880s, followed by service as secretary of state. President Ulysses S. Grant made him minister to Mexico in 1873, an appointment renewed by President Rutherford B. Hayes. He was transferred to Russia in 1880–81, then retired to private life and a legal career in Washington, D.C., representing foreign legations in United States courts. In 1883 President Chester A. Arthur appointed him minister to Spain, with whose government he negotiated a significant commercial treaty that was opposed and finally refused by the Senate in 1885. Unsuccessful in his efforts to revive the treaty, Foster was recalled.[1] He served as secretary of state during the last two years of the Benjamin Harrison administration (1892–93). His grandson John Foster Dulles was to become a more prominent secretary of state under President Dwight D. Eisenhower.

The handsome, properly serious young man was probably painted just following his Civil War service, when he had become editor of the Evansville, Indiana, *Daily Journal*, or at the end of the 1860s, when he was postmaster of that city. This is suggested by his apparent age and by the certainty that any portrait painted during his late twenties would have shown him in military uniform. John Foster was born in Pike County, Indiana, on March 2, 1836, graduated from Indiana State University in 1855, attended Harvard Law School for a year, was admitted to the bar, and opened a law practice in Evansville. At the outset of the Civil War he entered Union service as a major in the Twenty-fifth Indiana Infantry. Often promoted, he served throughout the war in the western armies under Generals Grant and Sherman. He was commander of the cavalry brigade that entered Knoxville in early September 1863, in advance of General Burnside's Army of the Ohio, an often overlooked but quite significant tactical victory for the Union. Foster's distinguished service was surely a factor in his first diplomatic appointment.

The artist is unknown. Probably an Indiana painter, he continues in the old

American tradition of folk artists whose training was rudimentary but whose strengths were an inherent instinct for design and structure. At the State Department the Foster portrait hangs among many official portraits by more technically competent artists, yet it stands out for its forcefulness. With a minimum of naturalistic detail, the artist has grasped the simple, sure structure of the head. Yet it is not a generalized portrait. The large chin, full lips, long nose, and introspective pale eyes are con-

vincing signs of an accurate likeness. He skillfully paints the black against black of the clothes, disposing the highlights in the waistcoat with intuitive rhythm. Uncomfortable with accessories or with depicting space beyond the figure, he simply floats a dim column in a nebulous background and uses the corner of a table as an excuse for an effective contrasting patch of bright red in the black and white environment.

—*William Kloss*

Plates

China, for export, ca. 1795–1810

Porcelain with overglaze enamels, 7/8 x 9 1/2 (dia.) in.
Gift of Misses Aimée and Rosamond Lamb (1985.0043.001)

Services of Chinese export porcelain personalized simply by the addition of initials or monograms in shields, medallions, or borders were relatively common in the early American market. Such simple individualization satisfied the desire for something special in a manner consistent with the accepted definition of democratic behavior. A few personalized Chinese export porcelain services from the late eighteenth century, however, display armorial or pseudo-armorial decoration, reflecting another aspect of the American democratic attitude—the notion that social standing could be redefined simply by adopting the accoutrements of a higher class even if one were not born into it. American services with heraldic devices in the manner of Old World services include those for James H. Giles of New York (made ca. 1785), the Chase family of Maryland (made about 1795), Elias Boudinot of New Jersey (made about 1790), Charles Manigault of South Carolina (made about 1820), the Clement family of Philadelphia (made about 1800), and the Sargent family of Massachusetts, as seen in this plate and related examples.[1]

Four plates from the Sargent service are preserved in the Diplomatic Reception Rooms, given by descendants of Ignatius Sargent of Gloucester, Massachusetts.[2] In the center of each plate is the Sargent arms, as recorded in the 1682–1683 "Visitation to Gloucestershire": chevron between three dolphins, embowed or. The crest shown here and used by some American Sargents is an eagle rather than the more traditional dolphin. The banner below the armorial bears the motto NEC QUAERERE HONOR EM NEC SPERNERE (neither to seek nor to despise honors). A bookplate belonging to Ignatius Sargent and engraved by Joseph Callender (1751–1821) probably was used as the source for the Chinese decorators to copy.[3]

—*Ellen Paul Denker and Bert R. Denker*

Cat. 115

Attributed to Michael Allison (1773–1855)

Linen press

New York, N.Y., ca. 1800–1810

Mahogany, mahogany veneer; eastern white pine,
yellow poplar, satinwood veneer, 98 x 48 x 21 ³/₄ in.
Funds donated by the Honorable Jefferson Patterson
and Mrs. Patterson (1966.0111)

Of a form called a wardrobe, linen press, clothespress, or press-cupboard-on-chest in documents of the period, this handsome case piece is one of the most striking realizations extant and the only known example of American furniture ornamented with nine American eagles.[1]

This linen press has been attributed to Michael Allison, the prolific New York cabinetmaker. The delicately flared French feet, scalloped skirt, and shimmering matched mahogany veneers are characteristics of Allison's work, as they are of the finest Federal-period New York cabinet shops.

This example is closely related to a linen press at Winterthur also attributed to Allison. Parallel features on both examples include inlaid Prince of Wales feathers on the plinth, inlaid eagles, the highly individualized shape of the skirt, and a scrolled pediment with lacy framework. The fretwork on the Winterthur example— a holdover from an earlier era—is set against a solid background.[2]

While the evidence points to a New York attribution for the Winterthur and Collection's examples, the form and specific decorative elements also relate to a Baltimore linen press with the label of John Shaw (1745–1829) in the Baltimore Museum of Art. This object is distinguished by a scrolled pediment with pierced fretwork.[3] The Collection's linen press is similar to a case piece illustrated by Chippendale and to mid-eighteenth-century English and Irish desk and bookcases with simple bonnet tops and plain, linear facades.[4] Here, the earlier, conservative frontality has been updated with neoclassical ornament: inlaid ovals on the doors, fine stringing on the drawers, and a delicately pierced pediment.

Hepplewhite illustrated four designs for wardrobes with sliding shelves and doors concealing drawers. Conceived in an era when few houses had closets, such wardrobes were a visually appealing solution to a practical problem.

—*Page Talbott*

Cat. 116

Joshua Shaw (1776–1860)[1]

View on the Kiskeminitas

1838

Oil on canvas, 34 ¾ x 48 in.
Funds donated by the Freed Foundation (1983.0003)

Through the publication of *Picturesque Views of American Scenery* in 1820–21, Joshua Shaw provided a major impetus for the Hudson River School, which arose in the mid-1820s with the advent of Thomas Doughty and Thomas Cole. In this book, the first such venture in America, Shaw remarked that every inch of European terrain had been recorded by artists, "while America only, of all the countries of civilized man, is unsung and undescribed." Moreover, he went on, "In no quarter of the globe are the majesty and loveliness of nature more strikingly conspicuous . . . [Here is] every variety of the beautiful and the sublime . . . unsurpassed by any of the boasted scenery of other countries."[2] The words "picturesque" and "sublime" are key to understanding the poetic impulse by which Shaw and those who followed his lead modified their realistic depiction of American landscape.

View on the Kiskeminitas represents the English-born Shaw at his peak. The graceful configuration of trees is reminiscent of Gainsborough and the parklike expanse of land may be indebted to the topographic gouaches and watercolors of Paul Sandby. Above all, the atmospheric effects—an evocative shifting of light, a sense of changeable weather—appear in the paintings of Richard Wilson (1713–1782), the most important influence on Shaw's style. John Ruskin wrote that with "Richard Wilson the history of sincere landscape art founded on a meditative love of nature begins in England."[3] Shaw performed the same office for American landscape art. Here, the clouds and their shadows give a sense of the flow of time, just as the river does. Also English are the detailed yet painterly foliage in the foreground and the tall trees. There the artist used an ingenious technique, pressing a loaded brush against the canvas so that the hairs splay out, to suggest a fan of foliage.

Shaw's panoramic view opens outward from the center of a light-filled clearing. The middle ground is abridged with a broad band of shadow, and the jump from the cows to the cabin behind them is far too abrupt, but this illogical shift in scale unexpectedly heightens the sense of space.

The cattle and trees are pastoral props in other landscapes by Shaw (who assimilated much from the seventeenth-century Dutch painter Aelbert Cuyp).[4]

The subject of this landscape is more complex than it at first appears, as smoke can be seen rising from industrial buildings on the far side of the river. Images of the progress of invention in pre–Civil War landscape paintings are often thought to be ironic. In this instance, however, there is no marked sense of collision between the natural and the manmade realms. The plumes of smoke bend with the lines of the hills and the Kiskeminitas (a tributary of the Allegheny River) and merge unobtrusively with the transient clouds, mingling earth and sky. Joshua Shaw was a product of the Industrial Revolution in England. One of England's great painters, Joseph Wright of Derby (1734–1797), had also dealt with factories in the landscape without irony but with a keen sense of pictorial contrast, as Shaw does here. Himself an inventor (he

received compensation from the American and Russian governments for his invention of the percussion cap and priming devices for firearms), Shaw clearly balances the pastoral part of his painting with details of the busy doings of modern industry. The sense of repose is most pervasive in the undisturbed canal gently clasped by the footbridge and its limpid reflection. Across the river, spanned by an impressive covered bridge, itself a symbol of commerce, are the industrial buildings and the town (possibly Freeport) behind them.

Surprisingly, the industries shown here are not the iron-ore blast furnaces usually associated with the Pittsburgh area. A Pittsburgh city directory of 1826 states:

> On the Conemaugh and Kiskeminitas rivers, about 40 miles from Pittsburgh, there are twenty-five salt manufactories in operation. . . Of all these works now in blast, twenty-four are on the Kiskeminitas, situated within three miles of each other. . . These establishments give employment to at least 400 persons,

and support, including managers, coopers, blacksmiths, colliers, boilers, &C. and their families, from 10 to 1200 souls.[5]

Shaw appreciated the importance of salt as a trading commodity and the local pride in its new abundance. In his harmonious painting, the ingenuity and industry of man in tapping earth's abundance are celebrated, not lamented.[6]

—*William Kloss*

Punch bowl

China, for export, ca. 1780

Porcelain with overglaze polychrome enamels, 6 ¹/₈ x 14 ¹/₂ (dia.) in.
Funds donated by Robert E. Vogel and Barbara Shipley Vogel (1965.0004.003)

This punch bowl celebrates Western trade with China by focusing on the bustling port of Canton (Guangzhou). The decoration here offers a close look at life along the shore of the busy Pearl River, where Western warehouses, traders, and their assistants jammed the limited space allowed them by the Chinese during the half-year when the weather allowed active trading to take place in the Canton hongs.

Although referred to as hongs, warehouses, or factories, these buildings housed all the activities of the foreigners.[1] Offices, large storage rooms, dining areas, and sleeping and living quarters were dispersed throughout the maze of small, two- and three-story buildings that composed a single hong rented by a country or trading company from the Chinese merchant who owned it.[2] Thirteen such hongs lined the wharf, which measured little more than one thousand feet long, although most extended back from the shore promenade by five hundred feet or more. Hongs were rented on an annual basis, but the same quarters were frequently taken year after year by the same lessee, whose nationality was announced by the flag flying in front. This practice helps to date "hong" bowls. Merchants from Denmark, France, Sweden, England, and Holland were longtime traders at Canton in the eighteenth century. The Imperial flag (yellow with double-headed eagle), however, was recorded only between 1779 and 1781, during two seasons when it was said to have been used by a Hungarian-licensed French ship.[3] Moreover, the red and gilt spearhead border around the foot, the elaborate interior border of trellis and hanging flower baskets, and the beautiful floral display painted in the bottom confirm the period of the bowl.

Scenes of the Western trading area at Canton first appeared on punch bowls about 1765 and were painted in one or two panels.[4] Continuous views, as on the Collection's bowl, began to be painted about 1780. As the fashion for punch declined after 1800, paintings of similar port views replaced the "hong" bowls as souvenirs of the China trade.[5]

—*Ellen Paul Denker and Bert R. Denker*

Cat. 118 and 119

Jacob Wood (d. 1850) and Jasper W. Hughes
(firm working 1840–1899)

Pair of goblets

New York, N.Y., ca. 1848

18-karat gold, 5 ³/₈ x 2 ⁷/₈ (dia. foot) in.; weight 6 oz. 9 dwt.
(1970.0086.001), 7 oz. (1970.0086.002)
Gift of Mr. Philip H. Hammerslough

Gold has been used rarely in the United States for domestic objects, although most early craftsmen called themselves goldsmiths because the techniques of working in silver and gold were identical. This pair of gold cups is in the naturalistic manner characteristic of mid-nineteenth-century New York rococo revival silver. The design of broad, curling, embossed, and engraved grapevines with chased leaves and fruit was used on silver marked by a number of New York smiths around 1850.[1]

A beautifully engraved inside-cylindered locomotive appears on one side of each goblet. This type of engine was popular with New England locomotive manufacturers, but the design may have been copied from a printer's line-cut or another readily available print source. This engraving suggests that the cups were made as presentation pieces to commemorate an achievement in the development of railroading. The reserves on the opposite side of each cup lack inscriptions, however, indicating that the presentation was never made.

Jacob Wood and Jasper W. Hughes served their apprenticeships under William Gale and are listed as silversmiths in the partnership of Gale, Wood, and Hughes between 1833 and 1845. Wood and Hughes appear as partners in the New York City directories in 1840, and again between 1845 and 1851, listing themselves as jewelers and makers of silver forks and spoons. This suggests that they worked only in small wares and that the hollowwares they retailed were made by others. The high quality of these extraordinary gold goblets and their great similarity to work by John Chandler Moore, known to have supplied the firms of Marquand, Ball, and Black as well as Tiffany & Co. and others, may indicate that the goblets were actually crafted by Moore. Jacob Wood died in 1850, and the firm continued under Charles Wood, Stephen T. Fraprie, and Jasper W. Hughes until 1856, when Hughes retired. The company took on new partners and remained in business until 1899, when it was purchased by the firm of Graff, Washbourne, and Dunn.[2]

*—Jennifer F. Goldsborough
and Barbara McLean Ward*

Cat. 120
Charles Bird King (1785–1862);
copy of a portrait by Joseph Wood (ca. 1778–1830)

James Madison

1826

Oil on panel, 24 x 19 ½ in.
Funds donated by Mr. and Mrs. David S. Ingalls (1979.0035)

Charles Bird King acknowledged in his inscription on the reverse of this portrait that he had copied it "from Wood."[1] Joseph Wood, an accomplished portraitist (though "his inclinations were for drawing landscapes"), preferred to work in miniature or in cabinet size, using the latter for his portrait of James Madison. Wood's portrait, measuring 9 by 7 inches, painted on wood, and its companion piece, a portrait of Dolley Madison, are now in the Virginia Historical Society, Richmond.[2] Wood depicts Madison seated half-length with hands folded, looking directly at the viewer. It is a very winning study of the man, probing and sensitive. Although King enlarged the format, he wanted only a bust-length portrait and therefore copied only Madison's head, even changing his costume. The features of the president are idealized, and, were it not for the strikingly idiosyncratic drawing of the sitter's right eyelid and brow, Wood's prototype might not be recognizable. The strong characterization of the sitter can be credited more to Wood than to King, who must have generalized his copy of Madison to make it more harmonious with his set of portraits for the marquis de Lafayette.[3]

—*William Kloss*

Cat. 121
Thomas Sully (1783–1872)

James Monroe
1829

Oil on canvas mounted on board, in the original
gilt frame, 19 x 15 in.
Funds donated by Mrs. Thomas Lyle Williams, Jr.,
in memory of her husband (1967.0049)

During his presidency and in his declining
years, James Monroe was widely popular,
particularly in his native Virginia. At the
time of his sitting for this portrait, in June
1829, he was seventy-one years old and also
deeply in debt.[1] While Thomas Sully chose
to emphasize the graceful image of the
public's perception, he also gave a note
of quiet introspection to Monroe's eyes.

Although for most of his life Monroe
looked younger than his age, "he was
severely injured in a fall from his horse
[in 1828] and his health thereafter was quite
poor." Despite his frailty, wrote an observer
at the Virginia Convention in October
1829, "there is a cheerful benevolence about
his face most winning in its effect upon
those whom he addresses."[2]

Perhaps it was this demeanor that confirmed Sully in his decision, habitual in any
case, to emphasize Monroe's suavity over his
debility. It is also possible that Sully painted
the flattering portrait to accord with Monroe's appearance as president. Before being
mounted, the canvas was relined at least
twice. A piece of canvas glued to the back is
inscribed "President Monroe 1820 / relined
1909 New York." The first line, perhaps
copied from the original canvas, may have
been meant to indicate the artist's intention
to subtract the years, a common practice in
portraiture.[3]

—*William Kloss*

Cat. 122

Card table

New York, N.Y., ca. 1810–1815

Mahogany, 29 ³/₄ x 35 ¹/₂ x 17 ¹/₂ in.
(1997.0007)

Washingtonian Benjamin Henry Tayloe (d. 1868) was one of the many who attended the sale of the personal effects of Henry Clay when he moved out of the Decatur House in 1829. In Tayloe's reminiscences, he recounts this experience: "His furniture was handsome. At his sale of it, on his retirement from office, in 1830 [*sic*] I bought, as a reminiscence, the center-table and card-tables of the drawing room."[1]

The Henry Clay Papers further document the sale:

> Sold on account, Henry Clay, Esquire, by P. Mauro and Son, Auctionary, Washington City, February 27, 1829.
>
> Pair of card tables........ $59.00
>
> Pair of card tables........ $40.00[2]

One of these card tables is now in the Collection of the Department of State and documents the taste of one of the most famous secretaries of state, Henry Clay, who served in that position from 1827 to 1829. He was one of three secretaries of state to live in the home built by Benjamin Henry Latrobe for Stephen Decatur, U.S. Naval Commissioner under James Monroe. The other two were Martin Van Buren and Edward Livingston.

An important statesman and famous orator, Clay served as U.S. Senator and Speaker of the House, and was a three-time presidential candidate. He lived most of his life in Lexington, Kentucky. His house, Ashland, built in 1809, was torn down in 1857 to make way for a second house built by his son James Clay. During his frequent stays in Washington, Clay lived first in a house only a few blocks from Decatur House. Some of the furniture used there must surely have made its way to his new residence on Lafayette Square.

The form of Clay's card table, a so-called "trick leg" table on which the two rear legs swing back to support the open top, has been associated with the preeminent New York cabinetmaker Duncan Phyfe since the publication of Charles Over Cornelius's *Furniture Masterpieces of Duncan Phyfe* in 1922.[3] Another early Phyfe scholar, Nancy McClelland, illustrated a number of related examples in *Duncan Phyfe and the English Regency, 1795–1830*, such as a satinwood card table with brass edging and a console table.[4]

Charles F. Montgomery described this form as "among the finest New York card tables" and acknowledged the attribution of such tables to Phyfe, but he demonstrated that these tables were "not exclusively made by Phyfe" by citing *The New-York Revised Prices for Manufacturing Cabinet and Chair Work* for 1810.[5] Customers of any New York cabinetmaker could order:

> A Solid Eliptic Pillar and Claw Card Table
>
> Three feet long, three claws, (as No. 1, in plate)
>
> Two of ditto to turn out with the joint rail, £4 12 0

For example, a similar card table by Phyfe's contemporary, Michael Allison, one of a pair given by the Newcomb family to Lucinda Newcomb and Benjamin Leonard Johnson on their marriage in 1832, is nearly identical to the Collection's example, with a clover-leaf top, leaf-carved vase-shaped support, and carved and reeded legs ending in brass lion's-paw feet.[6]

Certainly, the Clay card table is of New York City origin, in the English style, and made in the shop of an experienced craftsman. Its actual maker is, however, unknown.

—*Page Talbott*

Cat. 123
William Douglas MacLeod (1811–1892)

A Glimpse of the Capitol at Washington

ca. 1844

Oil on canvas, 21 ¾ x 29 ½ in.
Funds donated by Mrs. Nancy S. Reynolds (1969.0034)

This image of a grand if as yet somewhat disproportionate Capitol Building, with few near neighbors of consequence and many acres of pasture, is an authentic record.[1] In 1844 most of the buildings in the immediate neighborhood were boardinghouses and hotels for the use of congressmen. A cluster of houses just east (left) of the Capitol is probably Carroll Row, five Federal town houses built about 1805 on the site now occupied by the Library of Congress.[2]

Charles Bulfinch's Capitol dome, soon to be replaced, looked too tall for its base, but it dominated the skyline in its time. Charles Dickens, arriving in Washington in 1842, had "a beautiful view of the Capitol, which is a fine building of the Corinthian order, placed upon a noble and commanding eminence." He called the rest of Washington "the City of Magnificent Intentions. . . . Spacious avenues, that begin in nothing, and lead nowhere; streets, mile-long, that only want houses, roads and inhabitants. . . . One might fancy the season over, and most of the houses gone out of town for ever with their masters."[3]

Another British visitor, Harriet Martineau, had exclaimed in 1835: "The city itself is unlike any other, that ever was seen, straggling out hither and thither, with a small house or two a quarter of a mile from any other; so that in making calls 'in the city' we had to cross ditches and stiles, and walk alternately on grass and pavements, and strike across a field to reach a street."[4]

Despite its ragged appearance, Washington was witness to stirring events in 1844. In February the accidental explosion of the great cannon on the steam-propelled warship *Princeton* killed many of the official party on board, including the secretaries of navy and state. Three months later Samuel F. B. Morse sent the historic telegraphic message from the Capitol Building to Baltimore: "What hath God wrought." The Whigs rejected "his accidency" President Tyler for renomination, choosing Henry Clay instead. In his last bid for the presidency, Clay narrowly lost to Democrat James K. Polk.

Although his innocent idyll seems at odds with these significant moments,

MacLeod (born in Alexandria, then part of the District of Columbia) was a young man when he painted his "glimpse" and could not have failed to be stirred by the atmosphere of change, even if he preferred to appear detached. MacLeod, after some ten years in New York City, returned to the capital in 1856, and lived to see the city change radically. As sectional tensions grew and the Civil War overwhelmed the country, he was there as a witness, but always at a distance, as a landscape painter.

With the war, the true pastoral note in the national landscape tradition, represented by an easy interaction between man and nature, gradually evaporated and bucolic paintings were replaced by self-conscious landscapes of introspection or heroic vistas of grandeur or apocalypse, confounding Dickens's prediction that "such as it is, it is likely to remain."

Washington became a populous city, which prospered in the Reconstruction era. Between 1874 and 1888, MacLeod was curator of the new Corcoran Gallery of Art, founded on a banking fortune. When he died in 1892 it was in an America transformed by the Industrial Revolution, a country polarized by extremes of wealth and poverty, a society politically reunified but spiritually at war with itself.

—*William Kloss*

Cat. 124

Samuel Child Kirk (1793–1872; working 1815–1872)

Water pitcher

Baltimore, Md., ca. 1840

Silver, 16 ³/₈ x 4 ³/₄ (dia. base) in.; weight 50 oz. 14 dwt.
Gift of Mrs. Charles W. Bunker (1978.0074)

This tall, elegant, and richly ornamented water pitcher reflects Baltimore's repoussé style of the early 1830s, which emerged under the guiding spirits of Samuel Kirk and his competitor, Andrew Ellicott Warner (1786–1870). It also exemplifies the eclecticism of midcentury Baltimore silver, which combines rococo, neoclassical, and late-seventeenth-century high-baroque English silver design elements.

Samuel Kirk and his successors employed this form of pitcher hundreds of times between about 1820 and the mid-twentieth century. It was one of his most popular and influential designs. The rectangular handle with a mask terminal was peculiar to Baltimore. The basic form is also sometimes found with more conventional, tall, C-scroll handles.[1] Since all the repoussé ornamentation was done by hand, these pitchers could easily be individualized in design and decoration for custom orders. Fantastic, miniature chinoiserie buildings and landscapes issuing from large flowers and scrolls were a favorite Baltimore motif of the 1840s and appear from time to time throughout the century.

Kirk was born in Doylestown, Pennsylvania, and apprenticed under James Howell of Philadelphia. His father was not a practicing silversmith, but both he and his wife descended from generations of well-known English silversmiths of the Kirk and Child families. Throughout his long career, Kirk had an uncanny understanding of previous styles of silver, as well as a thorough knowledge of what was being made of silver internationally. Kirk's earliest work is in the Philadelphia Empire style. Perhaps the originator and certainly the disseminator of the ornate Baltimore repoussé style, Kirk was world famous for his brilliance as a designer, his eagerness to adopt technical and artistic innovations, and his genius as a promoter.

Baltimore repoussé silver had an enormous influence on other great American silver firms, such as Gorham Manufacturing Company, Tiffany & Co., and Reed and Barton. Repoussé silver continued to be demanded in Maryland and the rest of the South until World War II; Kirk also made handsome silver in a wide variety of other styles when he had the opportunity.

—*Jennifer F. Goldsborough*

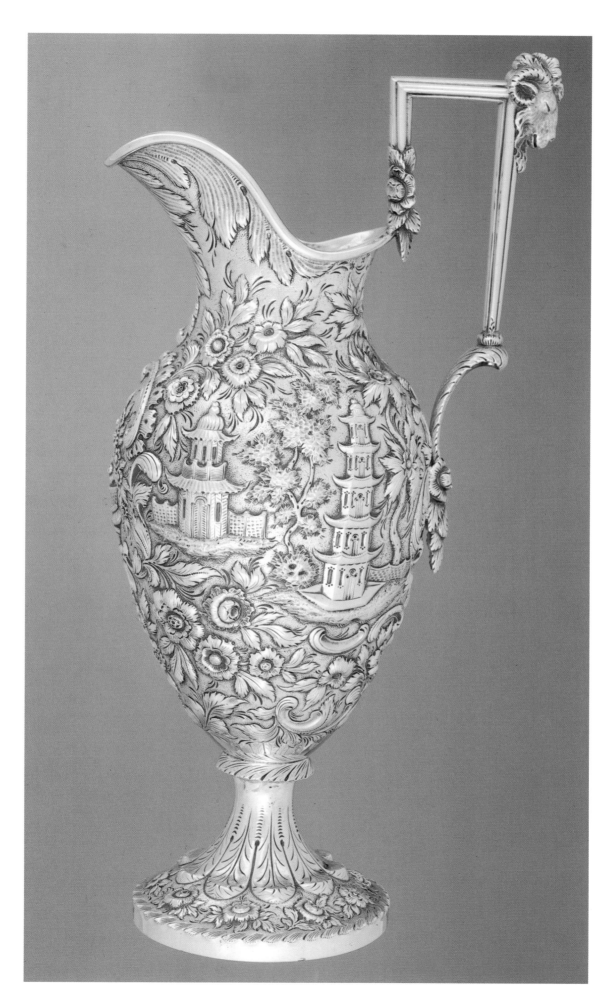

Cat. 125

Severin Roesen (working in America 1848–1872)

A Two-Tiered Still Life with Fruit ("Nature's Bounty")

after 1852

Oil on canvas, mounted on Masonite, 29 ¼ x 44 ¼ in.
Gift of Mrs. Pennington Sefton (1984.0033)

After his first years in New York City (1848–52), Roesen moved to Huntington, Pennsylvania, via Harrisburg, and thence to Williamsport, Pennsylvania, where, so far as we know, he spent the remainder of his life. His patrons there were newly wealthy timber merchants who were quintessentially Victorian in their love of overwhelmingly detailed, relentlessly decorative paintings of cornucopias of fruit. His paintings after 1852 are nearly impossible to date since his style shows little change. Although his Williamsport patrons, many of German descent, commissioned or bought an abundance of Roesen's paintings, his departure from New York cut him off from other artists and his influence was slight. Only in recent decades has his art become widely known.[1]

In the elaborate works typical of his career, Roesen often introduced a two-tiered marble tabletop, not rendering an actual table but conjuring one as an artistic caprice. In the Collection's example, he brought considerable organizational competence to bear on the greengrocer's pile he chose to paint.[2] The two levels of the large rectangle are joined together by the implicit diagonal running from the stem of berries at the lower left through the grape leaf and tendrils at the upper right. In addition, a second compositional form is introduced: a horizontal oval defined by the light within which clusters of white grapes alternate with rounded fruit such as peaches. The bottom of that oval is emphasized by the convex curve of the table, which is then reiterated by the curves of the watermelon slice and the ceramic fruit basket.

This painting is signed, in script, at the lower left center, "S Roesen" (the letters "SR" in the form of a monogram), with a vine tendril underneath. Signing the work with a tendril of the grapevine is a Roesen characteristic, an elegantly self-conscious touch that has undoubtedly helped boost his appeal in the contemporary art market. His name disappears from the Williamsport directories after 1872, the year of his last dated painting. It has been suggested that he died while returning to New York City, but no firm evidence exists.[3]

—*William Kloss*

Cat. 126
Engraved by John Sartain (1808–1897)
after a painting by George Caleb Bingham (1811–1879);
published by Goupil & Co., New York

The County Election

1854

Hand-colored engraving on wove paper, in the original
walnut frame, 33 ½ x 40 in.
Funds donated by Mrs. John Timberlake Gibson
(Cornelius and Anna Cook O'Brien Foundation) (1982.0005)

Following the Compromise of 1850, political giants such as Henry Clay, John C. Calhoun, Daniel Webster, Stephen Douglas, Jefferson Davis, William Seward, and others began adding territory to the United States in present-day Texas, New Mexico, Arizona, Utah, and California. In 1851 the Erie Railroad was the first track between the East Coast and the Great Lakes, and two years later the rails reached Chicago. The Kansas-Nebraska Act of 1854 repealed the Compromise and opened new territories to government by popular sovereignty. Internal civil wars broke out in many states over social, political, and economic issues, not the least of which took place in George Caleb Bingham's Missouri.

The scene for these two pictures is Arrowrock on the Missouri River. As in many American towns, politics were a great passion, and the painter wanted to capture this spirit on canvas and popularize his work through the printed medium. These prints can be seen as glorifying popular sovereignty by showing a broad range of men participating in the process of electioneering and voting. The rich and the poor, the old and the young (Bingham's son is playing in the foreground of each), the practical and the theoretical (Bingham, the artist, is in each), all contribute to make democracy work. Or do these pictures warn viewers of the perils of voting? Each has drunkards, sleepers, and oafs participating in directing the national destiny. The original oil paintings were highly prized in the artist's lifetime. So too were the prints, as evidenced by the care and feeling with which these two were framed and preserved.[1] They stand as telling documents of the American political scene.

—*Donald H. Cresswell*

Cat. 127

Engraved by Louis-Adolphe Gautier (working 1847–1876) after
a painting by George Caleb Bingham (1811–1879); published
by Goupil & Co., New York

Stump Speaking

1856

Hand-colored engraving on wove paper, in the original walnut frame
33 ¹/₂ x 40 in.
Funds donated by the Edmond de Rothchild Foundation (1982.6)

Cat. 128

Alphonse-Léon Nöel (1807-1884),
after William Sidney Mount (1807–1868);
published by Goupil, Vibert, and Company, Paris

The Power of Music

1848 (after the painting of 1847)

Hand-colored lithograph on paper, 14 ¹/₂ x 18 ⁵/₈ in. (image)
Gift of Mr. Stephen Neal Dennis (1994.0018)

The Power of Music is one of the jewels of American art, a painting so touching and embued with such empathy that it has become an icon. From the beginning it was praised by press and public alike and, as one critic wrote, "this picture will insure Mount a permanent reputation."[1] Its appeal needs no explanation. The image of the handsome, aging black man listening with deep pleasure and comprehension to the music emanating from within evokes the same response today that it did when first seen: "We never saw the faculty of listening so exquisitely portrayed as here. . . . He leans his right shoulder against the barn door, . . . and inclines his ear toward the musician; while his eye, looking at nothing, . . . melts with delight at the effect of the ravishing sounds."[2] There are two white men inside the barn with the musician, and they too respond to the music, and the critic just quoted describes their responses, but it is not they who draw and hold the viewer's eye. It is with the black man who listens that we identify.

Part of the collection of the Century Association in New York City for 110 years, the painting is now at the Cleveland Museum of Art. It has been known by several similar titles, but the title by which it is now universally known may have been suggested by the man who commissioned the painting, Charles M. Leupp, who, while traveling in England in 1845 with his friend William Cullen Bryant, had visited William Wordsworth at his estate. Nearly forty years earlier Wordsworth had written a poem that he called "Power of Music," and that his visitors surely knew. Both poem and painting evoke the pervasive life-enhancing effect of music on the human spirit, here specifically the music of the violin: "He fills with his power all their hearts to the brim—Was aught ever heard like his fiddle and him?" This line is representative of Wordsworth's poem, and it is not chauvinistic to observe that Mount's painting is a greater work of art. Although the title is wonderfully apt for the painting, the poem surely could not have inspired it.

Many nineteenth-century American paintings found a second and much wider life in reproductive prints, both engravings and lithographs. A fine print could spread the fame of a painting and its artist literally throughout the country, to tens of thousands of art lovers. In the 1840s the American Art-Union commissioned many paintings that were distributed by lottery while each member received an engraving of the painting. Mount's experiences with the Art-Union were few and unpleasant, so he must have been very pleased when the New York agent of the noted French firm of Goupil, Vibert, and Company, seeing the painting at the National Academy of Design in 1847, sought permission from owner and artist to make a lithograph of *The Power of Music* for international distribution. The painting was sent to Paris where the "celebrated Léon Noël" drew it for the lithograph.[3] The work, perhaps the first American painting published by Goupil, was done with care and sensitivity, and the image was not reversed as often occurs in print reproductions. The American edition of the lithograph appeared in November 1848 in both black-and-white and hand-colored examples. The lithographic image, incidentally, is nearly as large as the painting, giving an unusually good sense of the original.

Many words have been written about the sociopolitical implications of *The Power of Music*, and the outsider position of the black laborer is certainly an intentional allusion to his place in American society, north as well as south. But the further effort to diminish the emotional core of the work by parsing the painting for small details and scanning Mount's diary and letters for evidence of racist bias fails when confronted with the overriding central fact of the painting: the responses of the men, but principally the black man, to the music.

> Never was the power of music more beautifully portrayed than in this rude audience, no longer vulgar, but transfigured. The music has struck the electric cord, and kindled the latent soul that now shines through every feature. To idealize such faces, and such a scene, I conceive to be a great triumph in art.[4]

—*William Kloss*

Cat. 129

John Mix Stanley (1814–1872)

Barter for a Bride

ca. 1854–60

Oil on canvas, 40 x 63 in.
Funds donated by the Morris and Gwendolyn Cafritz
Foundation (1965.0053)

In the fall of 1853 John Mix Stanley began
a six-month stint as an illustrator with the
Pacific Railroad Survey in Washington Territory, led by Isaac I. Stevens, governor of the
Territory. The purpose of the expedition was
to project a northern rail route from St. Paul,
Minnesota, to Puget Sound. The journey
took the survey north of the Oregon Trail
to Fort Union, the region inhabited by the
Blackfoot (or Blackfeet) tribe in what is now
Montana, and northward into Canada. The
Blackfoot Indians had encountered few white
men beyond fur traders (although George
Catlin [1796–1872] had already painted them
in Fort Union in 1832); they had not sent a
delegation to Washington and were considered hostile. *Barter for a Bride*, one of Stanley's
finest surviving works, was probably painted
between 1854 and 1860, after the survey.

The painting represents a courtship ritual
among the Blackfoot. The mounted brave
brings gifts to the chief or his daughter, who
reclines on the hillock. These are borne on two
travois—sledges made of a net between two
poles—pulled by two horses. In the far distance, beneath an atmospheric sky, is the Great
Falls of the Missouri. The family group around
the chief is depicted with both informality and
dignity. Within the pyramidal group, Stanley
paints closely observed facial types and expressions, probably based on his use of the
daguerreotype to record his Indian sitters.[2]
The attitude of the young girl seems rather
blasé to the modern eye, although it is doubtful
that Stanley intended to be humorous.

This fine achievement makes the loss of
many of Stanley's Indian paintings especially
poignant. On January 24, 1865, approximately
150 of his canvases, on display in the Smithsonian "Castle" while awaiting a congressional
decision on their proposed purchase, were
destroyed in a fire that swept the building.[3]
Barter for a Bride, a painting later than those
lost to the fire, has additional significance for
the Department of State's Collection: the
artist was the grandfather of Mrs. Dean
(Alice Stanley) Acheson, wife of the secretary
of state (1949–53) under President Truman.
Mrs. Acheson wrote a book on Stanley.

—*William Kloss*

Cat. 130

From a drawing by Francis F. Palmer (ca. 1812–1876);
published by Currier & Ives, New York (active 1834–1907)

The Rocky Mountains
Emigrants Crossing the Plains

1866

Hand-colored stone lithograph on paper, 21 x 27 in.
Gift of Elizabeth May Bechtel (1971.0155)

The printing firm of Currier & Ives billed itself as "printmakers to the American people," and ever since collectors and scholars have also used that label to describe their work. Currier & Ives issued two kinds of prints: "rush" prints that were pictorial reporting on current events, often sold as newspaper extras, and stock prints intended for decoration. The rush prints were quickly replaced by other hard news, but the aesthetically pleasing and inspirational stock prints were produced for many years after their copyrighted, first appearance. These latter prints continued to inform and impress Americans for a long time.

This print showing immigrants crossing the plains with the Rocky Mountains in the distance was issued one year after the Civil War and was sold for the rest of the century. The end of hostilities enabled great resources to be turned toward occupying western lands. Some Indian tribes had initiated uprisings in hopes that the United States and Confederate States governments could not divert military resources to the West, but those plans were dashed when the war was over.

Francis F. Palmer of Brooklyn, New York, drew this picture for Currier & Ives to express an idealized image of the multitude of Americans (in a wagon train stretching as far as the eye can see) marching through rivers and woods and over plains and mountains to build farms and

cities. Outnumbered and looking on passively are two Indian men on horses. The scene reflects the history of the West and how Americans saw it then and subsequently.

—*Donald H. Cresswell*

Cat. 131

From a drawing by Francis F. Palmer (ca. 1812–1876);
published by Currier & Ives, New York (active 1834–1907)

Across the Continent. "Westward the Course of Empire Takes Its Way."
1868

Hand-colored stone lithograph on paper, 21 x 28 in.
Gift of Elizabeth Hay Bechtel (1971.0156)

The Rocky Mountains (cat. no. 130) had been circulating for two years when this strong and vivacious image was issued as a companion piece. Prior to the Civil War, development of a transcontinental railroad had been delayed due to a government stalemate over which route would be completed first, north or south. With the South defeated, the route through the northern part of the midcontinent was cleared through legislation and work began. In 1865 the decision was made to establish a race between the Union Pacific Railroad, coming from Omaha, Nebraska, and the Central Pacific, leaving Sacramento, California. Each was to lay as much track in as little time as possible and meet in the center.

Huge resources and tens of thousands of people were involved in the financing and the construction, which was completed in 1869.

Currier & Ives turned to one of their favorite and most popular artists, Francis F. Palmer, once again, to provide an image of the western movement. A long train heads west with engine smoking; it is labeled "Through Line / New York / San Francisco." Solid and symmetrical buildings, one a school, are neatly arranged near the track. Industrious men clear the land with axe and shovel, children play in the schoolyard, other children, with their parents, wave to the train that is responsible for their prosperity. In the background to the left is a

panorama of the Great Plains, to the right the majestic mountains. In the woods and toward the right margin are two Indian nomads on horses. The scene reflects the new and greater technology found in an idealized America.

—*Donald H. Creswell*

Cat. 132
Frederic Remington (1861–1909)

Our Elk Outfit at the Ford

1887–88

Oil on fiberboard, 15 x 23 in.
Gift of Mr. and Mrs. John A. Hill (1979.0068)

In 1888 *Century Magazine* accepted a series of articles written by Theodore Roosevelt describing his experiences as a rancher in the Dakota Territory. He had just seen some of Frederic Remington's first illustrations of western life and insisted that the artist be engaged to illustrate his articles. Both men, who had not yet met, had recently failed in their respective ranching endeavors, the victims of bad weather and uncertain markets. Retaining an insatiable appetite for the West, Roosevelt and Remington recorded their experiences with respect, even if through rose-colored glasses. In retrospect, they seemed destined for this collaboration.

Our Elk Outfit at the Ford was an illustration for Roosevelt's article "The Ranchman's Rifle on Crag and Prairie," published in *Century* in June 1888; it later became chapter five of the book in which the reprinted articles were collected. Roosevelt wrote of hunting with his characteristic zest, of "the keen pleasure and strong excitement of the chase" and the hunter's prowess, without which "he would almost always be sadly stinted for fresh meat." *Our Elk Outfit* illustrates his third paragraph:

> A small band of elk yet linger round a great patch of prairie and Bad Lands some thirty-five miles off. . . . Once last season, when we were sorely in need of meat for smoking and drying, we went after them again. . . . My two hunting horses, Manitou and Sorrel Joe, were at home. The former I rode myself, and on the latter I mounted one of my men who was a particularly good hand at finding and following game. With much difficulty we got together a scrub wagon team of four as unkempt, dejected, and vicious-looking broncos as ever stuck fast in a quicksand or balked in pulling up a steep pitch. . . . We got out to the hunting-ground and back in safety; but as the river was high and the horses were weak, we came within an ace of being swamped at one crossing.[1]

When drawing or painting images to be reproduced in books or journals, artists habitually worked in monochrome, as Remington did here, in order to ease the transition to the publishing medium, which might be wood engraving or photogravure.

Were it not for the original context of the illustration, one might not recognize Roosevelt as the second horseman. This is an early moment in developing Roosevelt's image as an intrepid outdoorsman and frontiersman. Remington and Roosevelt became lifelong friends from this first collaboration, and Roosevelt praised Remington's writings as well as his painting and drawing, implicitly comparing him to Rudyard Kipling—not without justification.[2] The great popularity of the *Century* series was a major factor in the "sudden and extraordinary" success of Remington as an illustrator.[3]

—*William Kloss*

Cat. 133
Thomas Moran (1837–1926)

The Cliffs of Green River, Wyoming

1900

Oil on canvas, 20 ¼ x 30 ¼ in.
(1987.0026)

In June 1871 Thomas Moran traveled on the Union Pacific Railroad as far as Corinne, Utah. He continued north by horse and coach to join Dr. Ferdinand V. Hayden's United States Geological Survey expedition near Virginia City, Montana, from which they would enter Yellowstone. But Moran first encountered the spectacular cliffs along the Green River in southwestern Wyoming, and they made a lifelong impression upon him.[1] He sketched the cliffs then and on later trips, and from the sketches he made more than thirty paintings during the next forty years.[2]

Moran was and is celebrated for capturing this sublime western landscape. Rising dramatically from the desolate plain, the cliffs, as John Wesley Powell wrote in 1875, "are all very soft and friable, and are strangely carved by the rains and streams. The fantastic rain-sculpture imitates architectural forms, and suggests rude and weird statuary.[3] The subject became Moran's bread-and-butter topic; not surprisingly, his many versions vary in quality as well as in size and ambition. The Collection's painting is traditional and conservative in its presentation of the diagonally receding cliffs (Moran clung to this viewpoint religiously) and in its shadowed proscenium-like foreground.

The light, however, dramatically striking the trail on which the dozen or so Indians ride, quickens the pace of our entry into the painting. By 1900, when he executed this work, Moran had become a more atmospheric painter, giving softness to the shadows of trees, the clouds of dust rising around the horses, the reflections on the water, and the rocky cliffs. There is very little impasto in the Collection's canvas, although Moran's brushwork is loose and painterly. Indeed, the whole surface quality is muted and mellow, and it induces a mood of reverie. Compared with many similar Morans, the cliffs are pulled closer to the viewer, and the river is given greater prominence.

The somewhat dreamy treatment of the scene may be fairly attributed to Moran's remoteness from the actual motif (he had not revisited the Green River since 1879), his increasing aestheticism as he reached fame and old age, and the irreversible changes in the West itself. The immigrant English painter had witnessed the end of the Old West, and, in 1916, he retired to a California where the gold rush was remote history.[4]

—*William Kloss*

Cat. 134

Cyrus Edwin Dallin (1861–1944)

Appeal to the Great Spirit

ca. 1916–1920

Bronze, 21 5/16 x 21 9/16 x 14 5/8 in.
Gift of Mr. Philip L. Poe (1965.0046)

Dallin was born in Springville, Utah Territory, which his parents had helped found.[1] His playmates were Indian boys from nearby encampments; he later recalled that he often modeled little figures of animals from clay from along the riverbanks with them. When he determined to make sculpture his life's work, he went east for instruction, first in Boston and, in 1888, in Paris. While studying with Henri-Michel Chapu at the Académie Julian, he was taught to depict mythological subjects in the classical mode, but all of that was discarded when Buffalo Bill's Wild West Show visited Paris in 1889, captivating the French who thronged to see it. The sight of an Indian once again so thrilled Dallin that it set him on the course of his most important work: the ennobling of the Indian in bronze monuments.

Success came immediately when he created the first of four great Indian equestrian statues, the much-praised *Signal for Peace*, modeled in Paris. A few years later came the somber but dramatic *Medicine Man* (1900), described by Dallin as gravely warning his people about the intrusions of the whites into their lands.[2] The third of the series, *The Protest*, representing the Indians' decision to take to the warpath, was shown at the St. Louis Exposition of 1904, but it was never put into permanent material.

The final statue in the series, *Appeal to the Great Spirit*, was modeled in Dallin's Boston studio in 1907–08. The plaster version was shown to great acclaim at the National Sculpture Society's exhibition of 1908 in Baltimore and the following year at the annual Salon in Paris, where it was awarded a gold medal. It was cast in bronze in Paris and, in 1912, was erected in front of the Museum of Fine Arts, Boston.

Dallin respected the Native American; his series is a tragic tale, sympathetically told. In *Appeal to the Great Spirit*, the noble Ute warrior—after the attempt at peaceful coexistence failed and after defeat in battle—casts his eyes to the heavens and raises his arms in supplication to the Great Spirit to save his people and their way of life from extinction. There is a strong, bold naturalism in the rendering of the muscular, nearly nude figure of the solemn chieftain. He sits upon a pony of exactly the same type photographed during John Wesley Powell's exploring expedition through Ute territory in 1873–74.[4] The authenticity of details such as the horse and warbonnet has been verified by ethnologists who have studied the history of the Ute peoples.

Dallin's contract with the MFA gave him the right to make and sell reproductions of *Appeal* so long as they did not exceed thirty inches in height. The sculptor knew he had a work of enormous popularity and, in 1915, he signed an agreement with the firm of P. P. Caproni, a Boston manufacturer of plaster reproductions. Caproni produced and marketed small-scale versions of this and other of Dallin's Indian subjects by the thousands.[5] In 1916 Dallin completed a contract with Gorham Manufacturing Company of Providence, Rhode Island, to make bronze replicas in three sizes—one less than nine inches in height, one slightly over twenty inches, and the third about thirty-seven inches high. The version in the Collection is of the middle size, one of 109 copies cast by Gorham.[6] The casting is of an especially fine quality and has a rich brown patina. The date "1913," inscribed on the base, refers to the year in which Dallin modeled the original of this size; the Collection's version was probably cast within a few years of the date Dallin entered into the contract with the Gorham foundry, about 1916–20.

—*Wayne Craven*

Notes

Opposite: Detail of map of Virginia, 1612–24 (see page 44)

Introduction, p. 22

1. See Crane Brinton, *The Shaping of the Modern Mind* (New York: New American Library, 1953), 112–18.
2. Klapthor 1999, 20–25.
3. For example, it is worth noting that silversmith George Christian Gebelein (1878–1945) of Boston was proud to trace the lineage of his learning through master-apprenticeship relationships extending back five generations to the patriot Paul Revere. One author used the life and work of Revere as a segue for introducing the work of two other extraordinary craftsmen of Boston who practiced their arts in the twentieth century: wood-carver John Kirchmayer (1860–1930) and master ironsmith Frank Koralewsky (active ca. 1900–1930). Both brought training and skills from Germany to this country. See Katharine Gibson, *The Goldsmith of Florence: A Book of Great Craftsmen* (New York: The Macmillan Company, 1929), 150–205.
4. Allan Greenberg, "The Diplomatic Reception Rooms of Edward Vason Jones," *Antiques* 132, no. 1 (July 1987): 122–31.
5. Ibid., 125–26.
6. Greenberg, "Diplomatic Reception Rooms of Jones," 130.
7. Frederick D. Nichols, "Rooms Architecturally Redesigned by John Blatteau and Walter M. Macomber," *Antiques* 132, no. 1 (July 1987):144–45.
8. George L. Hersey, "Allan Greenberg and the Classical Game," *Architectural Record* (October 1985):160–61.
9. Paul Goldberger, "Allan Greenberg's Rooms in the Department of State, "*Antiques* 132, no. 1 (July 1987): 132–43. Note the superb photographs by Richard Cheek. See also Geoffrey Scott, *The Architecture of Humanism: A Study in the History of Taste* (1914; reprint, New York: Norton, 1999).
10. *Benjamin Franklin's Autobiography* (New York: Rinehart & Co., 1948), 35.
11. *Fruits of a Father's Love: Being the Advice of William Penn to His Children* was published in Philadelphia as early as 1727 by Andrew Bradford. The passage cited is quoted from a later edition bound with Penn's *Fruits of Solitude* (Philadelphia: Benjamin Johnson, 1792), 24.
12. Stenton is preserved as a historic house with much of its content intact. See Philip D. Zimmerman, "Eighteenth-Century Philadelphia Case Furniture at Stenton," *Antiques* 161, no. 5 (May 2002): 94–101. An elegant upholstered easy chair made in Philadelphia and owned by Logan is illustrated in Jack L. Lindsey, "Pondering the Balance: The Decorative Arts of the Delaware Valley, 1680–1756," in *Worldly Goods: The Arts of Early Pennsylvania, 1680–1758* (Philadelphia: Philadelphia Museum of Art, 1999), 74, fig. 105.
13. Quoted in Lindsey, "Pondering the Balance," 76.

Charting the New World: Views and Visions of America

Introduction, p. 38

1. Hugh Honour, *The New Golden Land: Charting the New World Views and Visions of America, European Images of America from the Discoveries to the Present Time* (New York: Pantheon Books, 1975), 18–28.
2. West's profound influence on aspiring American painters is superbly documented in Evans.

Cat. 1

1. Cumming 1966, 8. See also Cumming 1958, pl. 14, 122–23.
2. John White's watercolors are now in the British Library. See Hulton and Quinn for White's American drawings.

Cat. 2

1. For the best list of states and derivatives of the map, see Verner, passim.
2. Morrison et al., 11–12.

Cat. 3

1. Schwartz and Ehrenberg, 140.
2. Ronald Vere Tooley, "California as an Island," in *The Mapping of America* (London: Holland Press, 1980), 130.

Cat. 4

1. Little, ix: "As has been recounted, in a letter to the editors reportedly printed in a Boston newspaper of the 1870s, he 'took refuge' on the ship while she was lying at Naples. This reminiscence must have been written by Elias Hasket Derby III, who as a boy had known Corné . . ."
2. Ibid., 8, 10. At least eight such paintings have survived, inscribed "Naples 1799."
3. Wilmerding *Marine Painting*, 70.
4. Little, xiv, reported that Corné's gravestone in Newport's "Old Cemetary" bears an "inscription which records his death on 10 July 1845, age ninety-three, proving that his year of birth may definitely be accepted as 1752." It is repeated here because later publications have sometimes given different dates, including ca. 1752.
5. See Crossman and Strickland, 777–78.

Cat. 5

1. Kathryn C. Buhler, *Mount Vernon Silver* (Mount Vernon, Va.: The Mount Vernon Ladies' Association of the Union, 1957), 50.
2. Ibid., 49.
3. Ibid., 50.
4. Ibid., 71–72.

Cat. 6

1. The name derives from the fact that Stuart willed the original life portrait to the Boston Athenaeum, where it remained until its joint purchase by the Museum of Fine Arts, Boston, and the National Portrait Gallery, Washington, D.C.
2. John Dowling Herbert, quoted in William T. Whitely, *Gilbert Stuart* (Cambridge, Mass., 1932), 85; see also Ellen G. Miles, *American Paintings of the Eighteenth Century* (Washington, D.C.: National Gallery of Art, 1995), 161–62.
3. Sigma [pseudonym], "The Character and Personal Appearance of Washington," *National Intelligencer*, February 1847, quoted in Ellen G. Miles, *George and Martha Washington: Portraits from the Presidential Years* (Washington, D.C.: Smithsonian Institution, National Portrait Gallery, 1999), 46.

Cat. 7

1. See Allen Staley, *Benjamin West—American Painter at the English Court* (Baltimore: Baltimore Museum of Art, 1989), 59.
2. Staley, *Benjamin West*, 62.
3. It is hard to explain the close color correspondence between West's original painting and the Collection's small copy after the engraving. Perhaps our artist was copying an engraving that had been accurately hand-colored after the original, for if he had seen the original he surely would not have reversed his copy.
4. Von Erffa and Staley, 207, cat. no. 85.

Cat. 8

1. The painting is signed at the lower right, "Ferd Richardt," and is also inscribed on protective cardboard backing "Wax Relined/ By Kim Clark/ Rockport, Ma./1988."
2. Adamson, 43–5, figs. 33–4, cat. nos. 162–63. "Conceived as a complementary pair," the Vanderlyns raise the possibility that this Richardt also has a mate.
3. Ibid., 151, cat. no. 144, illustrated in color as the frontispiece. It measures 56 ¹/₈ by 35 ³/₈ in.

Cat. 9

1. See Philip M. Isaacson, *The American Eagle* (Boston: New York Graphic Society, 1975).
2. Franklin's oft-quoted comments in a letter to Sarah Bache, January 26, 1784, are reprinted in Isaacson, *American Eagle*, 43.
3. Related eagles are published in Robert Bishop, *American Folk Sculpture* (New York: E. P. Dutton, 1974), 173, fig. 314, and Isaacson, *American Eagle*, 105, fig. 105. Although Bishop refers to an "early" style of Bellamy eagles, it is generally thought that his style did not waver. See Isaacson, *American Eagle*, ch. 8, esp. 116, and Yvonne Brault Smith, *John Haley Bellamy, Carver of Eagles*, Portsmouth Marine Society, publication 1 (Hampton, N.H.: Peter E. Randall, 1982), ch. 7 and passim.
4. In 1863 West Virginia was the thirty-fifth state to enter the Union, followed in 1864 by Nevada. Although the number of stars depicted in inlays and other ornament is sometimes used to date objects, the thirty-five stars here seem to be insufficient evidence on which to date this object.

Cat. 10

1. Subsequently it has been treated in several published articles. See the citations in Conger and Rollins, *Treasures of State*, cat. no. 13.
2. The object is documented through numerous inscriptions, including, all in pencil in the same hand, "Do Sprage Benj. Frothingham" on the rear surface of the back of the upper drawer of the lower case ("Do" is an archaic form of "Dr."; see Randall 1974, 248); "Benj. Frothingham" on the bottoms of two upper left desk interior drawers; "Do Sprage 1753" on the side of the inner left secret document drawer; "BF 1753" on the bottom of the upper left letter drawer; "TN jr" on the back of the upper left letter drawer. For additional and later inscriptions, see Conger and Rollins, *Treasures of State*, cat. no. 13.

   Only a documented desk attributed to James McMillian, undated, might have been made earlier. See Vincent, 148.
3. See Chippendale, pl. cxxxv, illustrating a tall-case clock with bombé lower case and identically shaped feet.
4. Only two bombé objects made in early-nineteenth-century Boston are known: a desk and bookcase owned by the John Hancock Mutual Life Insurance Company, Boston, and a tall-case clock in a private collection.
5. Hunnewell, 65.
6. Ibid., 164.
7. Suffolk County Probate Records, docket 8671, 134, October 15, 1765.
8. Two other Boston bombé desk and bookcases with waist moldings are known: one in Bayou Bend, the other in an advertisement, *Antiques* 50, no. 5 (November 1971): 650, 651.

   The molding of the Collection's example was restored by William Young; the shape was based on

the related example at Bayou Bend (acc. no. B69.363); Michael Brown assisted in the research. The finials and their plinths are also restored; they are based on a blockfront bookcase at Winterthur (acc. no. 60.1134), after a recommendation from Brock Jobe and with assistance from Greg Landrey and Michael Podmaniczky. The Collection is also indebted to Nancy Richards, Philip Zimmerman, Robert Trent, and Charles Hummel for their help in this project.
9. Pictured in Morse 1902, 134–36 (location unknown).

Cat. 11

1. Peter Marzio, *The Democratic Art: Chromolithography, 1840–1900* (Boston: David R. Godine, 1979), 184–85.
2. Archibald Willard, quoted in Willard F. Gordon, "*The Spirit of '76*," *An American Portrait* (Fallbrook, Calif.: Quail Hill Associates, 1976), 25.
3. Thomas H. Pauly, "In Search of 'The Spirit of '76,'" *American Quarterly* 28, no. 4 (fall 1976): 457.
4. Ibid., 458.

The Look of Colonial America: Commerce and Crafts, Artisans and Patrons

Introduction, p. 58

1. Falino, 152–82.
2. Phillip M. Johnston, "The William and Mary Style in America," in *Courts and Colonies* (Seattle and London: University of Washington Press, 1988), 76–77.
3. As quoted by Heckscher and Bowman, 153.
4. Kevin M. Sweeney, "High-Style Vernacular: Lifestyles of the Colonial Elite," in Cary Carson, Ronald Hoffman, and Peter J. Albert, eds., *Of Consuming Interests: The Style of Life in the Eighteenth Century*, (Charlottesville: University Press of Virginia for the United States Capitol Historical Society, 1994), 24–25.
5. As quoted in Daniel J. Boorstin, *The Americans: The Colonial Experience* (New York: Random House, 1958), 156.
6. See "A Nation United" in this catalogue for more examples of furniture made in the South in the State Department Collection. For recent scholarship, see Ronald Hurst and Jonathan Prown, *Southern Furniture, 1680–1830: The Colonial Williamsburg Collection* (New York: Colonial Williamsburg Foundation in association with Harry N. Abrams, 1997); Francis J. Puig and Michael Conforti, eds., *The American Craftsman and the European Tradition, 1620–1820* (Hanover, N.H.: University Press of New England for the Minneapolis Institute of Arts, 1989); Heckscher and Bowman; and the annual journal *American Furniture*, published since 1993 by the Chipstone Foundation and distributed by the University Press of New England, Hanover, N.H., and London.
7. See Heckscher and Bowman.
8. "Philadelphia Furniture, 1760–90: Native-Born and London-Trained Craftsmen," in Puig and Conforti, *American Craftsman and the European Tradition*, 92–101.
9. See Wainwright.
10. See Janice G. Schimmelman, "A Checklist of European Treatises on Art and Essays on Aesthetics Available in America Through 1815," *Proceedings of*

the American Antiquarian Society 93, part 1 (1983): 95–195. For Jefferson's correspondence with Robert Skipwith, see *Thomas Jefferson: Writings* (New York: The Library of America, Penguin Books, 1984), 740–45.
11. Edmund Burk [sic], *A Philosophical Inquiry into the Origin of Our Ideas of the Sublime and Beautiful. With An Introductory Discourse Concerning Taste, And Several Other Additions* (Philadelphia: J. Watts, 1806).

Cat. 12

1. Forman 1983, 167–70.
2. Kirk 1982, nos. 819–30.
3. The full set is illustrated and discussed in Conger and Rollins, *Treasures of State*, cat. no. 8.
4. An armchair with simple piercing is at Bayou Bend (Warren 1975, no. 48), and a side chair with identical piercing is at Williamsburg. Side chairs with more elaborate piercing are illustrated in an advertisement, H. & R. Sandor, Inc., *Antiques* 94, no. 2 (August 1968): 151, and in Sack *Collection*, 5: 1289.
5. Kirk 1982, 259, nos. 890–92.
6. Gershenson 1967, 639.

Cat. 13

1. This high chest has been published in Schiffer and Schiffer, no. 141.
2. Hornor 1935, pl. 62; Rollins, 1104, pl. 3.
3. The Savery high chest is in the collection of H. Richard Dietrich, Jr., of Philadelphia (*Philadelphia: Three Centuries*, cat. no. 75); the Tufft dressing table is in the Philadelphia Museum of Art (Woodhouse, 292–93).
4. Schiffer and Schiffer, 265–66.

Cat. 14

1. Gottesman 1938, 134.
2. See Warren 1975, cat. no. 95, for a fifth settee that is attributed to either New York City or Boston.
3. For the Beekman chair, see Downs 1952, cat. no. 106; for a discussion of the New York Queen Anne chair of this type, see Conger and Rollins, *Treasures of State*, cat. no. 11.
4. Macquoid, 3:98, fig. 37, and pl. VII.
5. Heckscher 1985, no. 82.
6. Anne Grant, *Memoirs of an American Lady* (1832; reprint, New York: Dodd, Mead & Co., 1901), 85.
7. A portrait of Beekman of ca. 1767 by Abraham Delanoy (New-York Historical Society) depicts him seated on a damask-covered easy chair similar in style to the settee. For a full history of the family, see Philip L. White, *The Beekmans of New York in Politics and Commerce, 1647–1877* (New York: New-York Historical Society, 1956).

Cat. 15

1. For references to objects with similar carving, see Ward 1988a, cat. no. 112.
2. See Kirk 1982, nos. 1267–1357, for a large group of related tables; see esp. no. 1273 (a seventeenth-century Japanese table derived from sixteenth-century Chinese prototypes).
3. Jack Lindsey, *Worldly Goods: The Arts of Early Pennsylvania, 1680–1758* (Philadelphia: Philadelphia Museum of Art, 1999), 151–52. For related Irish work, see Gerald A. Kenyon, *The Collection of Irish Furniture at Malahide Castle* (Dublin: By the author, 1994), and the Knight of Glin, *Irish Furniture* (Dublin: Eason & Son, 1978).
4. Luke Beckerdite, "An Identity Crisis: Philadelphia and Baltimore Furniture Styles of the Mid-Eighteenth Century," in Catherine E. Hutchins, ed.,

Shaping a National Identity: The Philadelphia Experience, 1750–1800 (Winterthur, Del. Henry Francis du Pont Winterthur Museum, 1994), 243–81; fig. 27. For a similar table attributed to a different hand, see *Philadelphia: Three Centuries*, cat. no. 101.

Cat. 16

1. One maverick example has four claw-and-ball feet and other features quite separate from the rest of the group; see Warren 1975, 60, cat. no. 115.
2. Rodriguez Roque, 38–39, cat. no. 17.
3. Ott, 98–99, cat. no. 63; Montgomery and Kane, 148–49, cat. no. 97; and Moses, 41, nos. 1.25 and 1.25a.
4. Moses, 42, nos. 1.26 and 24; and Ott, 100–101, cat. no. 64.
5. Ott, 102–103, no. 65; Rodriguez Roque, 40–41, cat. no. 18; and Carpenter 1954, 88, cat. no. 60.
6. Moses identifies the dressing table's characteristic foot as the documented work of John Goddard (Moses, 210).

Cat. 17

1. The other three clocks are at Winterthur, the Metropolitan Museum of Art, and in the collection of Eric M. Wunsch of New York City. For their help on these related examples, sincere thanks go to Robert F. Trent, Morrison H. Heckscher, Eric M. Wunsch, Richard L. Champlin, Robert Emlen, Elliot Caldwell, and Linda Eppich.
2. Heckscher 1985, 294–95.
3. Ibid., 294–95.
4. The author is grateful to Donald L. Fennimore of Winterthur for his review of the brass fret and his reference to an English hardware catalogue of ca. 1783–89 at Winterthur citing "pierced brass frets for clock bonnets" for sale.
5. Originally, two long arched voids were cut into the lower portion of the pediment, allowing the sound of the bell to penetrate through the paper and fret. For the same reason, the other three clocks are pierced with a series of holes approximately three quarters of an inch in diameter.
6. Many conservators worked on various aspects of the clock's treatment, including Robert Mussey, David Mitchell, Georgett Rudes, Edward LaFond, Marylou Davis, Gene Farrell, and Henry Lie. The original finial did not survive; a reproduction of an eighteenth-century finial original to the Wady clock in the Wunsch collection has been used to suggest an original treatment.

Cat. 18

1. Monkhouse and Michie, 85, no. 31.
2. The labeled Edmund Townsend bureau table is at the Museum of Fine Arts, Boston. See Hipkiss, cat. no. 38.
3. Moses, pl. 20.
4. Ibid., 252, 263, fig. 6.11.
5. Monkhouse and Michie, 84, no. 30.

Cat. 19

1. Brock Jobe, ed., *Portsmouth Furniture: Masterworks from the New Hampshire Seacoast* (Boston: Society for the Preservation of New England Antiquities, 1993), cat. no. 49; see also cat. no. 48. The table is also catalogued in Conger and Rollins, *Treasures of State*, cat. no. 61.
2. Chippendale, pl. LI, offers a precedent for the Collection's table, but it is far too elaborate to have served as the immediate source. For related English and Irish tables, see: Macquoid 3:235; advertisement, *Antiques* 86, no. 6 (December 1964): 693; Hinckley, 205, 207, figs. 374, 378; DAPC, 59.1933;

Robert Wemyss Symonds Collection of Photographs, Winterthur.
3. The tables are located at the Department of State; the Warner House in Portsmouth (Jane C. Giffen, "The Moffatt-Ladd House at Portsmouth, New Hampshire, Pt. 1," *Connoisseur* 171 [October 1970]: 117); Strawbery Banke Museum (Lockwood, 2:209–10, fig. 738); the Metropolitan Museum of Art (Heckscher 1985, no. 118); Carnegie Museum (Jobe and Kaye, figs. I–36); Brooklyn Museum (*Girl Scouts*, no. 653); and Los Angeles County Museum of Art.
4. Members of the Wendell family donated the table to Strawbery Banke Museum in 1988 and the stand to the Warner House in 1989. The table is discussed in n. 3; for an illustration of the stand, see Biddle 1963, no. 84.
5. Now in the Warner House; see n. 3.
6. William Whipple, inventory, taken November 15, 1788, docket 5176, Rockingham County Probate Records, Rockingham County Courthouse, Exeter, N.H.
7. "This Table belongs to Mary Anderson [?] Poore of . . . [?], Greenwood [or Greenland], Maine" is written in pencil on a paper label pasted beneath the top.

Cat. 20

1. The Collection's chair is published in Fitzgerald 1982, 63. See Prown 1966, 1: fig. 93 (for Bours); Jobe and Kaye, 362 (for Wyllis); and Cummings 1964, 253, 255–56.
2. Compare, for example, Ott, no. 20.
3. For examples of chairs with these options, see Sack *Collection*, 4: 1013 and 7: 1743; and Bernard & S. Dean Levy, New York, *Catalogue* 5 (spring 1986), 65.

Cat. 21

1. Published in Fairbanks and Bates, 178; *Paul Revere's Boston*, 76–77; Sack 1987, 163; Sack 1950, 100; Sack 1989, 1186. E. G. Nicholson of Hampton Falls, N. H., kindly provided funding for part of the research on this piece. For research assistance, the author thanks Milo Naeve, Thomas Michie, Morrison H. Heckscher, Brock Jobe, Michael Podmaniczky, Greg Landrey, Ron Bourgeault, and the Dietrich American Foundation.
2. The hardware was regilt in Paris in 1989 (after the photograph was taken). The pattern was popular in London at the time the chest was made. See anonymous Birmingham catalogue, ca. 1770, at Winterthur: TS 573 M58e, pl 32, no. 568, and TS 573 M58g, pl. 71, no. 1579, and pl. 46, no. 568.
3. The Dietrich American Foundation, Philadelphia, on loan to the Metropolitan Museum of Art; the Art Institute of Chicago (acc. no 1979.499); private collection, Sotheby's, New York, sale 5500, October 25, 1986, lot 28; collection of Julian Wood Glass, Jr., illustrated in Sack 1989, 1178–79; also illustrated in an advertisement by Joe Kindig, *Antiques* 39, no. 3 (March 1941): frontispiece; private collection; Rhode Island School of Design; Winterthur (acc. no. 59.1881); Sotheby's, New York, sale 5680, January 28–30, 1988, lot 1909; Museum of Fine Arts, Boston; illustrated in *American Collector* 3 (October 18, 1934). The first five are evidently products of the same shop.

Desks and desk and bookcases probably by the same shop as the first five cited above are the "Dawes" desk and bookcase at Bayou Bend; the "Barrell" family desk and bookcase (with major

alterations) and the "Brinley" desk-and-bookcase at Winterthur; the desk at the Groton School, Groton, Mass.; the desk and bookcase at Rhode Island School of Design (with major alterations to the pediment, cornice, and interior); the two-part desk formerly in the Dietrich American Foundation collection and previously displayed at the Huntington Museum and Library, Pasadena.
4. "Records of the Church in Brattle Square, Boston," in Richard D. Pierce, ed., *Publications of the Colonial Society of Massachusetts* (Boston: Colonial Society of Massachusetts, 1961), 39–41. The pulpit is illustrated and discussed in Robert Mussey and Anne Rogers Haley, "John Cogswell and Boston Bombé Furniture: Thirty-Five Years of Revolution in Politics and Design," *American Furniture* 1994 (Milwaukee, Wis.: Chipstone Foundation, 1994), 74–77.
5. Frederick C. Detweiler, "Thomas Dawes' Church in Brattle Square," *Old-Time New England* 69, nos. 3–4 (1979): 1–17. John Hancock personally commissioned and purchased the pulpit and supervised its construction and installation by the joiner Thomas Crafts, Jr., or his father, Thomas Crafts.
6. Malcolm Storer, *Annals of the Storer Family* (Boston: Wright & Potter, 1927), 49.
7. Suffolk County Probate Records, docket 22829, vol. 105:37, 202. His estate inventory does not include an entry for a "swel'd," "ogee," or "commode" chest, believed to be the eighteenth-century terms for the bombé form, but does make reference to both a "bureau" and a "case of drawers." It is not possible to say if either reference identifies this chest, and no further sources link the chest more firmly to Storer.
8. See Mussey and Haley, "John Cogswell," for a full discussion of Cogswell's life and bombé furniture.
9. Gilbert Vincent, "The Bombé Furniture of Boston," in Whitehill, 140–44.

Cat. 22

1. Hurd made several tankards for New England Congregational churches for use in the communion service. One example, in the collection of the First Church of Christ in Deerfield, Mass., is nearly identical to this one. For more on the use of tankards in the communion service, see Ward 1988, 1–24; Flynt and Fales, 47–48.
2. Ward 1983, 261.
3. French, 3–27, 57–66, 143–46.
4. Ward 1989, 72–76; French, 3–13. In the Boston court records there is a deposition that helps to explain Hurd's predicament. In 1743 Hurd had borrowed "Gold Dust and Silver and Paper" from one Benjamin Bourne at 30 percent interest. When Bourne came to collect, however, Hurd calculated that he was being charged 34 percent interest. Bourne, aware of the high rate of inflation, had tied his interest rate to the price of molasses so that it would keep up with rising costs. Hurd protested that he could not pay Bourne the total debt right away but could only pay the "Least Note which was for 476:18:0 old Tenor," because if he paid both notes he would not be able to pay for "a Large Quantity of Silver which he had bargain'd for." Hurd was, therefore, forced to sign a new note, again at the rate of 34 percent interest. See Suffolk Court Files 62302, Colonial Court Record Series, Commonwealth of Massachusetts Archives, Boston, Mass.
5. On the importance of the engravers in the Hurd shop, including Jacob's talented son Nathaniel, see

Ward 1983, 245–335. On the shop performing services for smaller firms, see Greene, 47 and 48. A resoldered thumbpiece accounts for the difference between the original weight scratched underneath the base ("27 oz. 6 dwt./ £12-5-6") and the present weight of the object. The initials engraved on the front, "IP," remain unidentified.

Cat. 23

1. Belden 1983, 19–23, 208.
2. Dr. Alexander Hamilton, *Itinerarium*, ed. Albert Bushnell Hart (1907, reprint New York: Arno Press, 1971), 132.
3. Cary Carson, "The Consumer Revolution in America: Why Demand?" in Cary Carson, Ronald Hoffman, and Peter J. Albert, eds., *Of Consuming Interests: The Style of Life in the Eighteenth Century*, (Charlottesville: University Press of Virginia for the United States Capitol Historical Society, 1994), 600.
4. Kane 1998, 598–615 (Barbara M. Ward entry on Jacob Hurd).
5. Kathryn C. Buhler, manuscript notes, Department of the Art of the Americas, Museum of Fine Arts, Boston.

Cat. 24

1. The English chairs owned in Newbury are discussed in Jobe and Kaye, cat. no. 130.
2. Quoted in Montgomery 1966, cat. no. 11.
3. Compare, for example, another chair in the Department of State Collection (74.89, a gift of the family of Mrs. Janet Barker Hope). For simplified versions, see Randall 1965, cat. nos. 156–57.
4. Montgomery 1966, cat. no. 12.

Cat. 25

1. Miller 1957, no. 43.
2. Downs 1952, no. 84; Bernard & S. Dean Levy, *Opulence and Splendor: The New York Chair, 1690–1830* (New York: Bernard & S. Dean Levy, 1984), 21.
3. Among John Singleton Copley's well-known portraits of Bostonians, the two with easy chairs depict Mrs. Michael Gill and Mrs. John Powell, both in old age. In New York City, Abraham Delanoy painted Dr. William Beekman at age eighty-three in a silk damask–upholstered easy chair (New-York Historical Society).

Cat. 26

1. Rosenbaum, 25–41. See also Barquist 2001; no tulip-shaped tankard by Myers was included in this exhibition.
2. Ibid., 41–49.
3. Ibid., 131–34. For a related Philadelphia example, see Fales *Joseph Richardson and Family*, 118.

Cat. 27

1. Heckscher 1973.
2. See DAB, s.v. "Richard Varick"; *Catalogue of American Portraits*, 2:840; Smith 1972, 56–57; Patterson, 72, 87, 93, 223.

Cat. 28

1. Advertisement, *Antiques* 97, no. 5 (May 1970): 692.
2. In the New-York Historical Society (acc. no. 1956.135), and illustrated in an advertisement, *Antiques* 78, no. 5 (November 1960): 408. A large collection of Verplanck's furniture is at the Metropolitan Museum of Art (see Heckscher 1985, figs. 24, 68, 75, 82, 92, 93, 105, 125).
3. Illustrated in an advertisement, *Antiques* 80, no. 1 (July 1961): 20.
4. See Macquoid and Edwards, 1:figs. 79, 81. For similar examples, see Downs 1952, cat. nos. 26, 52 (the correct line of inheritance appears in Heckscher

1985, cat. no. 146); and a pair in the Schuyler Mansion, Albany, owned by the New York State park system.
5. Illustrated in Bernard & S. Dean Levy, New York, *Catalogue* 6 (January 6, 1988): 111.
6. The "E S Conkling" inscribed in black paint on the rear rail of the armchair probably refers to Enos S. Conkling, who appears in the *New York Directory* in 1832 as a merchant living in Manhattan. After changing occupations and living quarters several times, he is listed as a jeweler on Broadway in 1853. He moved his residence to Brooklyn in 1858 and remained listed as a jeweler in Manhattan until 1863, when he disappeared from the directory. As the word "Brooklyn" inscribed on the side chair is written in the same hand, Conkling's ownership must have extended over a portion of his residence in Brooklyn, from 1858 to 1863.

Cat. 29

1. *Philadelphia: Three Centuries*, 19, 30.

Cat. 30

1. Contemporary silversmiths, such as Joseph Richardson (1711–1784), to whom Syng is frequently compared, often employed a simple, tubular socket to affix the lower end of teapot handles.
2. Buhler and Hood, 2:180.
3. Joseph Richardson, Sr., used a similar scrolled leaf mark between 1750 and 1775, and Martha Gandy Fales has posited that the two silversmiths may have applied the device as an informal assay mark when the city of Philadelphia refused to grant the petition by local silversmiths to establish a city assay office; see Fales, *Joseph Richardson and Family*, 72–73.

Cat. 31

1. Warren 1976, n.p.; Hindes, 302–304; Prime 1929, 1:98.
2. These two coffeepots are illustrated in Warren 1976, nos. 25, 26.
3. Woodcock made pieces to fill out tea and coffee services by the Richardsons; see Warren 1976, fig. 4 and nos. 11, 13. The Department of State's coffeepot appears as no. 24 in the Warren catalogue. The initials engraved on the side of the pot are there identified as "TMR" but are now interpreted as "MR." Humphreys made a very similar coffeepot with nearly identical finial and spout, now at Historic Deerfield (see Flynt and Fales, 93).

Cat. 32

1. Conger and Rollins, *Treasures of State*, cat. no. 23. These chairs were exhibited in the Girl Scouts loan exhibition (see *Girl Scouts*, no. 648), and are illustrated in *Antiques* 123, no. 5 (May 1983): 879.
2. See Flanigan, no. 8.
3. See Hummel 1976, 67–68.
4. See Conger and Rollins, *Treasures of State*, cat. nos. 18–19. This attribution was first proposed, in conversation with the author, by Alan Miller and Luke Beckerdite.
5. Advertisement, *Antiques* 132, no. 5 (November 1987): 857. Although it is possible that Miss Parsons had inherited these chairs from their original owners, she was well known as a collector in her own right, and the chairs were exhibited at the Philadelphia Museum of Art from 1928 to 1936. Her collection was gradually dispersed in several auctions in the 1930s.

Cat. 33

1. Weil, 183.

2. Thomas Chippendale recommended that armchairs of this type be "covered with Spanish Leather, or Damask, & c. and nailed with Brass Nails" (Chippendale, 4). Manuscript designs for French chairs with tufted upholstery survive by William and John Linnell (Hayward and Kirkham, 2: no. 40) and an unknown English designer (Thornton 1987, 36). Mid-eighteenth-century English armchairs retaining their original tufted upholstery include a set upholstered in silk damask made for Corsham Court between 1765 and 1769 (Fowler and Cornforth, 156) and a pair by the Linnells with leather upholstery made for Osterley Park in 1767 (Hayward and Kirkham, 2: no. 69).
3. A photograph of this chair frame without upholstery was reproduced in an advertisement for John S. Walton, New York, in *Antiques* 98, no. 4 (October 1970): 476. The pine strip at the bottom of the back frame was added by a later upholsterer to compensate for the high placement of the original bottom member.
4. An extremely rare variation of this form included an opening between the back and seat and carving on the exposed portion of the stiles; a Philadelphia armchair of this type is at Winterthur (Hummel 1976, 60).

Cat. 34

1. For the sofa, see Shepherd, 6–8, and *Philadelphia: Three Centuries*, cat. no. 79; for the armchairs, see Conger and Rollins, *Treasures of State*, 138–39, cat. no. 55. Other sofas of this type descended in the Ferris family of Wilmington, Del. and the Burd and Fisher-Wharton families of Philadelphia; the last example is also in the Diplomatic Reception Rooms. Examples more closely related in their design to the present sofa, in the Metropolitan Museum of Art and at Bayou Bend, lack firm provenances but have secondary woods that suggest origins in Philadelphia. In addition to the Affleck-Penn suite cited above, documented examples include the case made by John Folwell in 1771 for David Rittenhouse's orrery and furniture made in 1783 by Thomas Tufft for the Logan family.
2. Hornor 1935, 189, pls. 272–73.
3. The use of these elements is documented in designs by Thomas Chippendale as well as by English sofas that retain their original upholstery; see Chippendale, pl. XXIX, and a set made in 1765–69 for the Picture Gallery at Corsham Court in Wiltshire, pictured in John Kenworthy-Browne, *Chippendale and His Contemporaries* (London: Orbis Publishing, 1975), 28, pls. 21 and 22.
4. Elizabeth Lahikainen and Associates, "Upholstery Conservation Treatment Report EL-176-95," Curator's files, U.S. Department of State.
5. According to a furniture price list published in Philadelphia in 1772, the frame of a similar mahogany sofa with Marlborough Feet . . . with bases cost £5, but the upholstery would have added as much as £10 to £20 to the total cost. Weil, 184; Hornor 1935, 150–53.
6. Hornor 1935, 152.

Cat. 35

1. *Pennsylvania Gazette*, May 18, 1738, as cited by Prime 1932, 163.
2. Hornor 1935, 143.
3. Ince and Mayhew, pl. 13, illustrates "Claw Tables" with tilting tops, but the bases are unlike those found on American tables.
4. Weil, 187. The Collection's table was owned by Dr.

James Hutchinson (1752–1793) of Philadelphia, who may have inherited it from a relative in the Howell family. Hornor called it the "Howell-Hutchinson-Fox-Lukens" table in 1935, when it was owned by Dr. and Mrs. George T. Lukens (see Hornor 1935, 142, pl. 222). It descended to their son, John Brockie Lukens of Lafayette Hill, Pa.

5. Cited in Prime 1929, 185.
6. See Conger and Rollins, *Treasures of State*, cat. no. 85.
7. I am indebted to Luke Beckerdite and Alan Miller for this observation, and particularly to Luke Beckerdite for sharing his extensive research on this carver's techniques and individual production.
8. Hornor 1935, pl. 223.

Cat. 36
1. Barquist, 294–97; see also 308–10.

Cat. 37
1. See McElroy 1970, 51–54, for documentary references to chests of drawers prior to 1730. A Philadelphia high chest in the Chippendale style, dated 1753 and signed by its makers, Henry Cliffton and Thomas Carteret, is illustrated in Sack 1988, 1125.
2. Montgomery "Regional Preferences," 60.
3. Weil, 181.
4. The related high chests are at Yale (Ward 1988a, cat. no. 147) and Winterthur (Downs 1952, cat. no. 197); and illustrated in Hornor 1935, pl. 141. The double chest descended in the Richardson family of Wilmington and is privately owned.
5. I am indebted to Luke Beckerdite for sharing his research on this individual, whom he calls the "Garvan carver."
6. Hornor 1935, pl. 141. The Delaveau high chest has a peanut-shaped cabochon carved on its skirt similar to the one on the chest in the Collection.

Cat. 38 and 39
1. See Conger and Rollins, *Treasures of State*, cat. no. 36. For the Hopkins piece, see Elder and Stokes, 30. The Baltimore Museum of Art also owns an armchair descended from Governor Robert Bowie of Maryland that is nearly identical to the Key chairs; see Elder and Stokes, cat. no. 15. Like the chairs, the high chest would probably be attributed to Philadelphia were it not for the label. For a further discussion of both this problem and Hopkins, see Weidman 1984, 46, and Beckerdite 1986, 21–64.
2. Hornor 1935, pls. 102, 103, 157, and 159.
3. *Maryland Gazette* (Annapolis), April 9, 1767.
4. This group of chairs in the Department of State Collection was brought together through the kind efforts of William Wightman Phillips. Inscriptions on the two chairs support this history of ownership. For a complete discussion of provenance, see Conger and Rollins, *Treasure of State*, cat. no. 36.

Cat. 40
1. The other five chairs in the Collection are 65.55.1–5, gift of Mrs. Frank Hollowbush; see Conger and Rollins, *Treasures of State*, cat. no. 38. See also Smith 1970, 772; Fairbanks and Bates, 155.
2. For New York examples, see Downs 1952, cat. no. 52.
3. See Heckscher 1985, cat. nos. 27–29; Kirk 1982, 266, no. 934.
4. The so-called Penn family chairs are illustrated in Hornor 1935, pl. 335. For other variants with different amounts of carved ornament, see Hornor 1935, pls. 333–34.

Cat. 41
1. Published in Conger and Rollins, *Treasures of State*, cat. no. 17. See also Sack *Collection*, 3: 616–17; *Antiques* 96, no. 6 (December 1969): inside cover; Sack 1987, 162. Another set of Loockerman chairs is in the Collection; see Conger and Rollins, *Treasures of State*, cat. no. 77. Other Loockerman furniture is in the collection of the Philadelphia Museum of Art (see *Philadelphia: Three Centuries*, cat. no. 101, for a table). Others were sold at Sotheby's, New York, sale 5295, February 2, 1985. See also Philip D. Zimmerman, "Queen Anne and Chippendale Chairs in Delaware," *Antiques* 160, no. 3 (September 2001): 331–39, for a discussion of five sets of Loockerman chairs, including the Collection's chairs, from both Philadelphia and Delaware.
2. Weil, 182.
3. For examples with minor variations, see Monkhouse and Michie, cat. nos. 110–111; *Antiques* 107, no. 4 (April 1975): 626; and Anderson Galleries, New York, Jacob Paxson Temple Collection, sale 1626, January 23–28, 1922, lot 1661.
4. The Hollingsworth-Morris chair is illustrated in Hornor 1935, pl. 220.
5. See Heckscher 1985, cat. no. 48, for an identical chair. Compare the Wistar family armchair, illustrated in Hornor 1935, pl. 154.

Cat. 42
1. Quoted in Edmund S. Morgan, ed., *Prologue to Revolution: Sources and Documents on the Stamp Act Crisis, 1764–1766* (New York: W. W. Norton, 1973), 136.
2. Howard, 1974, 404–405.
3. *Dictionary of National Biography* (London: Oxford University Press, 1937), s.v. "William Pitt," vol. 15, 1240–1253.

Cat. 43
1. The provenance remains problematic. The painting is identical with no. 867 in Park, 2:777, and 4:541 (ill.), although there is a slight discrepancy in the stated dimensions. No. 867 is a study of the head, as described in this text, for Park, no. 865, the large half-length figure that in 1919 passed from the Van Rensselaer family to the Thomas B. Clarke Collection in New York. A letter from M. Knoedler & Co., New York, to Robert L. Clarkson (May 20, 1936) makes it appear that the Department of State's head also belonged to T. B. Clarke, although its prior provenance as given by Park is not that of the finished portrait (no. 865).
2. DAB, s.v. "Stephen Van Rensselaer."

The Road to Independence: Statesmen and Diplomats

Introduction, p. 98
1. Daniel J. Boorstin, *The Americans: The Colonial Experience* (New York: Random House, 1958), 155–58.
2. For the meaning of Copley's famous portrait of Revere and his Liberty Bowl, see Jonathan L. Fairbanks, "Paul Revere and 1768: His Portrait and the Liberty Bowl," in Jeannine Falino and Gerald W. R. Ward, eds., *New England Silver and Silversmithing, 1620–1815* (Boston: Colonial Society of Massachusetts, 2001), 135–51. For an

account of the massacre, see Hiller B. Zobel, *The Boston Massacre* (New York: Norton, 1970).
3. For Lexington and Concord, see David Hackett Fischer, *Paul Revere's Ride* (New York: Oxford University Press, 1994).
4. A chronological list of the secretaries of state is recorded in Conger and Rollins, *Treasures of State*, 480–81.
5. Richard Brookhiser, *Founding Father: Rediscovering George Washington* (New York: Simon & Schuster, 1996), 103.
6. Conger and Rollins, *Treasures of State*, cat. no. 100.
7. Frank H. Sommer, "Emblem and Device: The Origin of the Great Seal of the United States," *Art Quarterly* 24, no. 1 (spring 1961): 57–79.
8. Thomas Jefferson to Martha Jefferson, 1783, in *The Jeffersonian Cyclopedia*, John P. Foley ed. (New York: Funk & Wagnalls, 1900), 264. See also Susan R. Stein, *The Worlds of Thomas Jefferson at Monticello* (New York: Harry N. Abrams, 1993), 39.
9. *Jeffersonian Cyclopedia*, 528.
10. Samuel Adams to John Adams, 1785 in Falino, 152.

Cat. 44
1. The standard reference is Brigham.
2. Morison, 199–201, is the source from which this summary of the event is drawn. Interestingly, Paul Revere also drew a plan of King Street and vicinity that was used in the trial of the British soldiers (see Andrews, 98).
3. Brigham, 52–53.
4. Bialostocki, 211–18, esp. 215–16.

Cat. 45
1. Despite its continuous exhibition history it was doubted by Fiske Kimball in 1944 ("The Life Portraits of Jefferson and Their Replicas," *Proceedings of the American Philosophical Society* 88 [1944]: 497–534) whose opinion was followed by Charles Coleman Sellers. The doubts were misplaced, as a 1952 restoration of the painting by Elizabeth Jones of the Fogg Art Museum, removing distorting overpainting by earlier restorers, stunningly revealed. See Alfred L. Bush, *The Life Portraits of Thomas Jefferson* (Charlottesville:: University Press of Virginia, 1987), 19–21.
2. Bush, *Life Portraits*, 19; C. W. Peale, diary of 1818, cited in a report on the painting by Anne Clapp (January 28, 1962).
3. Sarah Miriam Peale copied some of her uncle's portraits. One suggestive comparison is her copy (ca. 1830) of Charles's portrait of *General Otho Holland Williams* (1782). For CWP's original, see Edgar P. Richardson et al., *Charles Willson Peale and His World* (New York: Harry N. Abrams, 1982), 61; for Sarah's copy, see *Four Generations of Commissions: The Peale Collection of the Maryland Historical Society* (Baltimore: Maryland Historical Society, 1975), 106, no. 87.

Cat. 46
1. Ralston, 271–73.
2. For more information on the Niderviller factory, see Tilmans, 125–26, and *Porcelainiers*, 248–49ff.

Cat. 47
1. *Robert Hooper* descended in the family until 1980; it is now in the Pennsylvania Academy of the Fine Arts. *Hannah White Hooper* is in the New York Public Library (Lenox Collection). See Prown 1966, 1: 219.
2. Ibid., 1: 172.
3. Copley also painted miniatures in oil on copper, usually of larger dimensions. There are about

twenty-two examples. These inventories are based on Prown's catalogue; see his no. 1. See also Theresa Fairbanks, "Gold Discovered: John Singleton Copley's Portrait Miniatures on Copper," *Yale University Art Gallery Bulletin* (1999): 75–91.

Cat. 48

1. The painting is signed at the lower right, "JS Copley"; and inscribed on the reverse, "Frances Montresor/ nee Tucker/ Born 1744–died 1826/ PINXIT Copley." Jules D. Prown first discovered Copley's signature in the much-darkened area to the right of the sitter's shoulder: He also discerned a date, of which only the second digit was legible—"7"—and which is no longer apparent. Prown further noted that the Frick Art Reference Library records the date as 1778, which "may have been based on an earlier observation of the picture when the varnish was more transparent." Prown, letter to Clement E. Conger, January 31, 1984, Curatorial Files, Diplomatic Reception Rooms.
2. DAB, s.v. "John Montresor."
3. Reproduced in Prown 1966, fig. 295. Ibid., 233, gives the provenance of John Montresor's portrait. Since it was owned by the London branch of Howard Young Galleries by about 1934, we may assume that both portraits descended through the Montresor family to Mrs. Joan (Montresor) Read.
4. In Penny, 289. For a brilliant, full-length example of this fashion, see Reynolds's *Lady Worsley* in Penny, 289 and 144.
5. Recent, thorough conservation of the painting was revealing. In addition to the flattened impasto caused by glue lining the original linen canvas, it was observed that Copley might have covered most of his white ground layer with bituminous black paint. The inevitable deterioration of the bituminous paint resulted in the cracking and separation of the paint layer, as well as the wrinkling (or curdling) of the surface, and this led to some drastic early restorations. In particular, the hat was a problem. It was suggested that Copley had originally painted it with dark bituminous colors, merely adding the lighter shades of the ribbons and highlights. When the paint deteriorated, the original design of the hat would have been difficult to perceive. A restorer, in addition to overpainting the damage with black paint, apparently disapproved of the lowering hairstyle, altering it by enlarging the hat so that it covered the forehead and most of the hair. An enormous hat was created. This overpaint was removed (conservator's report, July 23, 1984, Curatorial Files, Diplomatic Reception Rooms).

Cat. 49

1. Francis S. Drake, *Memorials of the Society of the Cincinnati of Massachusetts* (Boston: Society of the Cincinnati of Massachusetts, 1873), 8.
2. Drake, *Society of the Cincinnati*, 11–12.
3. Martha Gandy Fales, *Jewelry in America, 1600–1900* (Woodbridge, Suffolk, England: Antique Collectors' Club, 1995), 132–34. The French officers presented George Washington with a unique example of the badge set with diamonds, rubies, and emeralds, which is now owned by the Museum of Society of the Cincinnati, Anderson House, Washington, D.C.
4. Drake, *Society of the Cincinnati; American National Biography* (New York: Oxford University Press, 1999), s.v. "Timothy Pickering"; and information supplied by Emily Schultz of the Museum of The Society of the Cincinnati.

Cat. 50

1. "An Account of a Visit Made to Washington at Mt. Vernon, by an English Gentleman, in 1785. From the Diary of John Hunter," *Pennsylvania Magazine of History and Biography* 17 (1893): 76–81, quoted in Detweiler 1982, 81.
2. For additional examples in the Collection, see Conger and Rollins, *Treasures of State*, cat. no. 160.
3. Shaw's difficulties in procuring the earliest Cincinnati design are discussed in Conger and Rollins, *Treasures of State*, 89 –95. For the later set, see Conger and Rollins, *Treasures of State*, cat. no. 161.
4. Washington's Cincinnati service was passed on by Mrs. Washington to her grandson, George Washington Parke Custis, who used the service at Arlington House. Following the Civil War, the china that remained in the government's possession (after damage and pilfering during removal from Arlington House by Union troops) was released by order of President William McKinley to Mary Custis Lee, the daughter of General Robert E. Lee, and Mary Anna Randolph Custis. There is also evidence that some pieces were given away as gifts by descendants of Mrs. Washington. In 1928 Henry Francis du Pont acquired the more than sixty pieces remaining in the possession of the descendants of Mary Custis Lee. Most other examples from the service have as yet unknown provenances. For a discussion of the argument that there was more than one service with the trumpeting angel bearing the Cincinnati badge, see Conger and Rollins, *Treasures of State*, 95–96. Feller, 762, and Templeman, 758–59, suggest that Henry Lee bought a second service with identical decoration.

Cat. 51

1. E. McSherry Fowble, *Two Centuries of Prints in America, 1680–1880* (Charlottesville: University Press of Virginia for the Henry Francis du Pont Winterthur Museum, 1987), 267; General Edward Erskine Hume, "The Diplomas of the Society of the Cincinnati," *Americana* 29, no. 1 (January 1935): 19–20, 41–43. I wish to thank Emily Schultz of the Museum of The Society of the Cincinnati Headquarters, Anderson House, Washington, D.C., for making this source available to me.
2. Francis S. Drake, *Memorials of the Society of the Cincinnati of Massachusetts* (Boston: Society of the Cincinnati of Massachusetts, 1873), 11–12.
3. Drake, *Society of the Cincinnati*, 8–13.
4. M. Prevost and Roman D'Amat, eds., *Dictionnaire de Biographie Français* (Paris: Librarie Letouzey et Ane, 1959), 8:1226–27; Asa Nird Gardiner, *The Order of the Cincinnati in France, Its Organization and History* (n.p.: Rhode Island State Society of the Cincinnati, 1905), 78. I wish to thank Emily Schultz for making the Gardiner work available to me.

Cat. 52

1. Paul D. Schweizer, "The 'Strong and Striking' Likenesses of William J. Weaver (c. 1759–1817): An Introduction," in *Journal of Early Southern Decorative Arts* 17, no. 2 November 1992): 1–36; and Schweizer, "William J. Weaver's Secret Art of Multiplying Pictures," in *Painting and Portrait Making in the American Northeast*, Dublin Seminar for New England Folklife, Annual Proceedings, 1994 (Boston: Boston University, 1995), 151–66.
2. William Dunlap, *History of the Rise and Progress of the Arts of Design in the United States* (1834; reprint, New York: Dover Publications, 1969), 2: part 1, 64.

3. Schweizer, "William J. Weaver's Secret Art," 159. The author suggests that all the extant versions of Weaver's *Hamilton* must be posthumous since there should be the two stars of a major general, his rank from 1798, on his epaulet, and that if alive "Hamilton probably never would have allowed" a portrait with one star. How Hamilton could have prevented it is unclear, but in any case Weaver is alluding to Hamilton's significant Revolutionary War service.

Cat. 54

1. For a general treatment of Indian trade silver and silver made by Indians from reused trade objects, see Fredrickson and Gibb.
2. See Prucha, 73–88; *Philadelphia: Three Centuries*, 163–64.
3. The portrait is reproduced in Warren et al., 105.
4. Fales *Joseph Richardson and Family*, 159.
5. Ibid., 140–41, 159–62, 297, 306–307.

Cat. 55

1. The seal is marked on the back "PBIWB" in block letters within a small rectangle with a leopard head, a lion rampant, and the date letter "N" for 1808–1809. Sincere thanks go to Milton Gustafson at the National Archives for researching the design of the seal.

Cat. 56

1. Brown 1978, 140–41.
2. Ibid., pl. I, 139, and pl. III, 138.

Cat. 57

1. A later paper label pasted to the underside of the writing surface notes the descent of the desk: "This writing Desk I / give to Horace Appleton / E. Adams / [torn] 1842."
2. See Charles Francis Adams, ed., *Memoirs of John Quincy Adams, Comprising Portions of His Dairy from 1795 to 1848* (Philadelphia: J. B. Lippincott and Co., 1974), 1:1677, and Paul C. Nagel, *John Quincy Adams: A Public Life, A Private Life* (New York: Alfred A. Knopf, 1997), 92–98.
3. The Jefferson desk is owned jointly by the Diplomatic Reception Rooms and the Thomas Jefferson Memorial Foundation, Inc. See Conger and Rollins, *Treasures of State*, cat. no. 94.

Cat. 58

1. Howard C. Rice, Jr., *Thomas Jefferson's Paris* (Princeton: Princeton University Press, 1976), 67.

Cat. 59

1. Harold D. Langley, "Early Diplomatic Couriers," *American Foreign Service Journal* (October 1971): 6–10.
2. Kohn, 60, 63, and passim.
3. Ibid., 106. See also DAB, s.v. "Josiah Harmar."
4. The miniature is signed with initials at the right, "RP," and inscribed in ink on a paper backing (partly obliterated): "Genr . . . [H]armar/painted/ by/Raphael Peale." However, the inscription is not autographic. The artist and his family always spelled his first name "Raphaelle," whether on his paintings, including miniatures, or in correspondence. His contemporaries often did not, and this old inscription, in script, may be attributable to Harmar or a member of his family.
5. Cikovsky, 24; and Sellers 1969, 291.
6. Elam, 94, figs. 117, 120, 121.

Cat. 60

1. Fairman 1927, 85–86. Ary Scheffer was born in Dordrecht when Holland was a new French department under control of the French revolutionary army, and thus he was French under civil law.

2. Very little information exists on Adolphe Phalipon. Neither birth nor death dates are recorded in biographical dictionaries of artists. The only evidence we have that he studied or apprenticed with Scheffer is Phalipon's own entry in the 1879 Salon catalogue, two decades after Scheffer's death and when he himself was an old man: "né à Paris, élève de Scheffer." The primary biographical notice is in Emile Bellier de la Chavignerie and Louis Auvray, *Dictionnaire général des artistes de l'école française* (Paris, 1882, 1885; reprint New York and London: Garland Publishing, 1979), vol. 3. There are three listings that are surely all for the same man. In addition, there is an entry for "Phalipon (Mme), née Louise Vincent," a painter of still lifes and portraits who probably became his wife (in the 1848 Salon catalogue they are recorded at the same address, 2, rue des Beaux-Arts).

Cat. 61

1. Susan Benjamin, *English Enamel Boxes from the Eighteenth Century to the Twentieth Century* (London: Orbis Publishing, 1978), 51–94; see also Nina Fletcher Little, *Neat & Tidy: Boxes and Their Contents Used in Early American Households* (1980; reprint, Hanover, N.H.: University Press of New England, 2001), 93.
2. Simon P. Newman, *Parades and the Politics of the Street: Festive Culture in the Early American Republic* (Philadelphia: University of Pennsylvania Press, 1997), 83–119; and Len Travers, *Celebrating the Fourth: Independence Day and the Rites of Nationalism in the Early Republic* (Amherst: University of Massachusetts Press, 1997), 69–106.
3. David McCullough, *John Adams* (New York: Simon & Schuster, 2001), 645.

A Nation United:
Neoclassicism in the Federal Era

Introduction, p. 126

1. Although it can be demonstrated that certain types of ornament now called "neoclassical" (having been derived from ancient models) were adopted by craftsmen in this country by the late 1760s, such evidence is the exception rather than the rule. These early objects tend to reflect the use of fragmentary neoclassical details rather than reflecting a cohesive treatment of the new style as a whole.
2. Richard L. Bushman, *The Refinement of America: Persons, Houses, Cities* (New York: Alfred A. Knopf, 1992), esp. 72–73.
3. *Philadelphia: Three Centuries*, cat. no. 102.
4. See Graham Hood, "Early Neoclassicism in America," *Antiques* 140, no. 6 (December 1991): 978–85.
5. See Barbara McLean Ward, "Women's Property and Family Continuity in Eighteenth-Century Connecticut," in Peter Benes, ed., *Early American Probate Inventories* (Boston: Boston University, 1988), 74–85.
6. Anne E. Bentley, "The Columbia-Washington Medal," *Proceedings of the Massachusetts Historical Society* 101 (1989): 120–27. For the Shaw service, see also Conger and Rollins, *Treasures of State*, cat. no. 161.
7. Lord Chesterfield's writings were well appreciated in the United States. It was the objective of the editor of an edition of his work published in

Carlisle, Pennsylvania, in 1809 to lay Chesterfield's instruction before every class of youth.
8. Bushman, *Refinement of America*, xviii–xix.
9. Graham Hood, *Bonnin and Morris of Philadelphia: The First American Porcelain Factory, 1770–1772* (Chapel Hill: University of North Carolina Press for the Institute of Early American History and Culture, Williamsburg, Virginia, 1972).
10. Jonathan L. Fairbanks and Rebecca Ann Gay Reynolds, "The Art of Forest Hills Cemetery," *Antiques* 154, no. 5 (November 1998): 697–703, illus. 698.
11. Richard H. Saunders, *Horatio Greenough: An American Sculptor's Drawings* (Middlebury, Vt.: Middlebury College Museum of Art, 1999), 86.

Cat. 62

1. Mary L. Booth, *History of the City of New York* (New York: W.R.C. Clark & Meeker, 1860), 490. Washington lived in a large white building two houses up the block during his first term as president.
2. *The Old Merchants of New York City* (New York, 1862), 1 ff.
3. Beaumont wrote this letter to his father, May 16, 1831, while Tocqueville and he were visiting the eastern United States. George W. Pierson, *Tocqueville in America* (1938; reprint, Baltimore: Johns Hopkins University Press, 1997), 64.
4. Tracy, 28, 39, 41.
5. Winchester 1963, 86.
6. *Dutchess County Doorways and Other Examples of Period-Work in Wood, 1730–1830* (New York: William Farquhar Payson, 1931), 62, see pls. 155–60.
7. William M. Bobo, *Glimpses of New York City by a South Carolinian (Who Had Nothing Else to Do)* (1852). The Kennedy house survived an 1845 fire and was leased in 1848 as a hotel. Described as "a relatively small and conservative concern kept on the European plan and sports fine punches" the "Washington Hotel," as it was called, was home to such dignitaries as the French diplomat Tallyrand and Henry Clay when they came to New York. Torn down in 1882, the Washington Hotel was replaced by the Washington Building, now known as the United States Maritime Building. When the hotel was torn down, the mantel was removed to a fifty-eight-room mansion in Greenwich, Connecticut, home of Dr. Victor C. Throne, a physician whose practice was located at 120 Broadway in New York City. When Throne's home was demolished in 1948, a local resident rescued the mantel from the dump and stored it in his basement until 1975, when he sold it to Dr. John Wholihan of Jackson, Michigan. Three years later Dr. Wholihan donated the mantel to the Diplomatic Reception Rooms.

Cat. 63 and 64

1. These andirons have previously been attributed to John Bailey of New York; see Conger and Rollins, *Treasures of State*, cat. no. 236. However, a recent survey of a more extensive body of similar andirons, including marked Bailey examples, indicates that the Collections's andirons do not have the combination of details found on marked Bailey pieces and are more in line with an attribution to the Whittinghams, as detailed in this entry.
2. I am indebted to Donald L. Fennimore and the extensive research files at the Winterthur Museum for providing photographs of comparable exam-

ples. See also Schiffer, Schiffer, and Schiffer, 70, figs. A, C.
3. This is a visual analysis that should be subject to a precise measurement of the urns.
4. See George H. Kernodle and Thomas M. Pitkin, "The Whittinghams: Brassfounders of New York," in James R. Mitchell, ed., *Antique Metalware* (New York: Universe Books, The Main Street Press, 1976), 65–68.

Cat. 70

1. Edward F. LaFond, Jr., first suggested this attribution. This piece was exhibited at the Girl Scouts Loan Exhibition, American Art Galleries, New York, 1929 (see Girl Scouts, no. 735); and published in "Long Text and Brief Sermon," *Antiques* 16, no. 5 (November 1929): 367.
2. Fales 1965, no. 59; and Benes, no. 58.
3. The Metropolitan Museum of Art's clock is illustrated in Heckscher 1985, no. 201. For clocks with pierced fretwork, see Rodriguez Roque, cat. no. 44, and an example at the Department of State (88.9; funds donated by Miss Louise Ines Doyle). See also Fitzgerald 1982, 84.

Cat. 71 and 72

1. Frémont, 95 (also quoted in Klapthor 1975, 52).
2. Klapthor 1975, 49, discusses circumstances leading to the directive contained in this Act.
3. Like all vases of this type, these were made in two parts, with the lower section of foot and pedestal bolted to the upper vase. The excessive wear on the gilding of the lower sections of this pair suggests that the bottoms were replaced at a later date, probably to preserve the paintings of the upper sections.
4. The diary of Gouverneur Morris (1752–1816), the wealthy American patriot, is quoted in de Guillebon, 300; see also 297–311 for more information on the export of Paris porcelain to the United States.

Cat. 73 and 74

1. Howard and Ayers 1978, 2: 500–501, classify this particular eagle as type 3g; they date the design 1800–1810.
2. Sharpe, 248.
3. See Sharpe, 250, for information on Baldwin and speculation about the marketing of the six pieces. See also Conger and Rollins, *Treasures of State*, cat. no. 169.
4. Sharpe, 250, relates that the second pair of flagons descended in the family of the New York resident Andrew Mount, but notes that no conclusive information has been found on the Collection's bowl. Jay family members and historians can find no record of the bowl having belonged to Jay or his descendants. See also Sharpe, 255, n. 18.

Cat. 75–81

1. This set is marked in the following manner: "I.LT" in block letters within a rectangular reserve, is struck twice on the bottom of the coffeepot and once on the sugar bowl, "I.LETELIER" once in the same manner on all other pieces except the cream pot, which is marked on the outside of the plinth "I.LT." Dimensions and weights for the other objects in the service are given in Conger and Rollins, *Treasures of State*, cat. no. 213.

Cat. 82

1. *New Encyclopaedia Britannica*, s.v. "John Adams."
2. Kane 1998, s.v. "Nathaniel Austin," and Flynt and Fales, 147.
3. Kane 1998, s.v. "Nathaniel Austin." The teapot,

teapot stand, and six surviving scalloped teaspoons are all engraved with the same cipher, "HC," for Hannah Carter. The teapot has the mark "J. Austin" overstriking "Revere"; while the matching stand is marked by Revere; and the six teaspoons bear the J. Austin mark only. Revere charged Nathaniel Austin for twelve scalloped teaspoons, twelve plain teaspoons, and a pair of silver tea tongs, and for engraving twenty-five ciphers in 1787. Nathaniel Austin billed William Smith, who married Hannah Carter in 1787, for these and other silver items. It is interesting to note that he passed along the costs charged to him by Revere directly and did not make a profit on Revere's work. The six surviving scalloped teaspoons are now at Yale (Buhler and Hood, 1: 191). The teapot and stand are in the Museum of Fine Arts, Boston (Buhler 1972, 2: 430–31).

4. See Buhler and Hood, 1: 197, and Garrett, 24.

5. The Museum of Fine Arts, Boston, recently acquired an unmarked coffeepot (2000.826) attributed to Revere and also owned originally by William and Hannah (Carter) Smith. It bears the acorn-and-leaf decoration and the buckled medallion also found on the Collection's coffeepot, and on several other objects marked by Revere. It is thought to have been made about 1798 for the Smiths and retailed by Austin, who was related to the Smiths and who served as middleman in other transactions between that family and Revere.

6. *Silver Supplement*, 15–16.

Cat. 83

1. *Benjamin Franklin and His Circle* (New York: Plantin Press, 1936), 40, cat. no. 32.

2. Ibid. See also Charles Coleman Sellers, *Benjamin Franklin in Portraiture* (New Haven and London: Yale University Press, 1962) and Louise Todd Ambler, *Benjamin Franklin: A Perspective* (Cambridge, Mass.: Fogg Art Museum, 1975).

3. Examples in terra-cotta are in the collections of the Metropolitan Museum of Art, New York, and the Walters Art Gallery, Baltimore. See Sellers, *Benjamin Franklin*, 373–74. A marble version attributed to Suzanne is at the Franklin Institute, Philadelphia. See *Antiques* 26, no. 3 (September 1934): 108.

4. See Christie's, New York, sale 1096, May 29, 2002, lot 187 and Sack Collection 1:31, no. 102. Jean-Baptiste Dubuc was another Parisian clockmaker who supplied mantel clocks to the American market. See Stuart P. Feld et al., *Neo-Classicism in America: Inspiration and Innovation, 1810–1840* (New York: Hirschl and Adler Galleries, 1991), 123.

5. *Benjamin Franklin and His Circle*, cat. no. 308.

6. See Wendy A. Cooper, *Classical Taste in America, 1800–1840* (New York: Abbeville Press, 1993), 45–47.

Cat. 84

1. Fulwar Skitwith to James Madison, September 3, 1806, in Klaptor 1999, 37.

2. For more information on Washington's social life in this era, see Barbara G. Carson, *Ambitious Appetites: Dining Behavior and Patterns of Consumption in Federal Washington* (Washington, D.C.: American Institute of Architects Press, 1990).

Cat. 85

1. Ehrenfried, 213–40.

2. Steblecki in *Paul Revere: Artisan*, 130–32; Ehrenfried, 223.

3. See Buhler 1972, 2: 408–9, 425.

Cat. 86

1. Barquist 2001, 129; Falino, 169–70.

2. Revere Daybook, 2:65, Massachusetts Historical Society, Boston (photostat in the possession of the Museum of Fine Arts, Boston).

3. Buhler 1972, 463–64.

4. Jane Bortman, "Moses Hays and His Revere Silver," *Antiques* 66, no. 4 (October 1954): 304–305.

5. The sugar basket was acquired through a partial purchase from a descendant of the original owner and through the gift of a one-third interest in the object from the Talley family.

Cat. 87

1. DAB, s.v. "Sylvanus Thayer."

2. Gordon 1977, pl. 20. The authors wish to thank Mrs. Gordon for confirming that the Nichols and Thayer services are separate.

3. The vases and a punch bowl are at Winterthur (see Palmer 1976, 136 and 141). The covered jug is in the Reeves Collection (see *Reeves Collection*, cover). A second punch bowl, also associated with Thayer, is owned by the Dietrich American Foundation, Philadelphia. A mug is in the New-York Historical Society (see Howard 1984, 115–16).

4. Howard 1984, 115, suggests that the War of 1812 was a time when the motif was particularly appropriate.

Cat. 88

1. Kane 1998, 837–40 (Deborah A. Federhen entry on Paul Revere, Jr.).

2. Revere to Geyer, January 19, 1784, in Deborah A. Federhen, "From Artisan to Entrepreneur: Paul Revere's Silver Shop Operation," in *Paul Revere—Artisan*, 85.

3. Buhler 1970, 430–31; Federhen, "From Artisan to Entrepreneur," 86; see also *Paul Revere—Artisan*, 156–57.

4. Federhen, "From Artisan to Entrepreneur," 75–82.

5. Barquist 2001, 238–39. The couple also inherited family silver that included Torah finials made by Myer Myers and later inscribed "Hays & Myers," perhaps for Samuel and Judith. Their granddaughter, Caroline Hays Cohen, donated the finials to the Touro Synagogue in 1892 (Barquist 2001, 198–200).

6. The objects were acquired through a partial purchase from direct descendants and through the gift of a one-third interest in them from the Talley family.

Cat. 89

1. For more on the Richardson family, see Fales *Joseph Richardson and Family*, 3–47, 153– 63.

2. A recent machine engraving on the foot records the family history: "James Smith & Jemima Russell, Married February 5 1787./ Mary Russell Smith, 1853. Emma Allen Merritt 1863/ Morris Hill Merritt 1913/ E.A./ 1863./ Sarah Ellen Richardson Married Nov. 10, 1928 Morris Hill Merritt."

3. By the 1790s the pineapple finial was supplanted with an urn-form finial, which echoed the body of the vessel in miniature and exaggerated the vertical thrust.

4. See Fales *Joseph Richardson and Family*.

Cat. 90

1. Willard, 46ff.

2. While some sources give 1822 as the patent date for the lighthouse clock, John Ware Willard cites and reproduces the patent for "an alarm clock" that

Simon Willard received in 1819 (Willard, 17). No known examples of these alarm clocks exist, but the lighthouse clocks, which were of the same general form, were probably made from about 1822.

3. Examples of lighthouse clocks can be seen in the White House, the Metropolitan Museum of Art, Winterthur, Old Sturbridge Village, and Deerfield Village.

4. Letter, Charles E. Buckley to Page Talbott, June 11, 1975, and letter, Mrs. Clifford Bellows to Page Talbott, April 13, 1989. The clock is one of many examples of high-style Boston classical furniture that belonged to this family.

5. The Collection is indebted to the following individuals for their parts in researching the clock and producing the dome: Joseph Twichell, Robert Cheney, Chris Bailey, Edward LaFond, David Colglazier, John Curtis, Eddy G. Nicholson, Philip Zea, and glass artist Josh Simpson and his team of glassblowers.

Cat. 91–93

1. Sir Algernon Tudor-Craig was the first to suggest that Fitzhugh may have been a corrupted pronunciation of Foochow (Fuzhoy), for the port, but J.B.S. Holmes pointed out that Foochow was not a Western port until the 1840s and was not associated with making or shipping china during the period of the Fitzhugh pattern's greatest popularity. See Howard 1974, 53, for a discussion of Tudor-Craig's first use of the term in 1927 and his 1929 explanation of origins; see Holmes, 130–31, for his explanation.

2. Holmes suggests that the name may have been used in America during the nineteenth century, and Jean McClure Mudge confirms his suggestion by citing references to the pattern in American manuscripts of the early 1800s (see Mudge 1981, 165).

Cat. 94 and 95

1. See Forbes for a discussion of the origins and uses of the rose palette and for a description of the two classifications. For additional examples in the Collection, see Conger and Rollins, *Treasures of State*, cat. no. 157.

2. Forbes, 26, discusses the resemblance to the annona's leaf.

3. Ibid., 25, identifies the phoenix and squirrel.

4. Mudge 1986, 161, speculates on textiles as a design source for tobacco-leaf patterns.

Cat. 96

1. Letter from Thomas Tucker, November 27, 1852, in the *Journal of the Franklin Institute* (January 1953): 43, quoted in Clement, 70. The information given in the entry on Tucker's enterprise is summarized in Clement, 70–82; *Tucker China*, passim; Curtis 1973, 339–74.

2. Curtis 1973, 358–61; see p. 366 for an illustration of "Vase pitcher," no. 7 from Thomas Tucker's notebooks.

3. For the monochrome pitcher, see Conger and Rollins, *Treasures of State*, cat. no. 181.

Cat. 97

1. See Sumpter Priddy III, J. Michael Flanigan, and Gregory R. Weidman, "The Genesis of Neoclassical Style in Baltimore Furniture," *American Furniture* 2000 (Milwaukee, Wis.: Chipstone Foundation, 2000), 59–99; the sideboard is illustrated as fig. 35. Unless otherwise noted, documentation for this entry is contained in this article.

2. Marilyn Johnson Bordes, *Baltimore Federal Furniture* (New York: Metropolitan Museum of Art, 1972), 7, and Weidman 1989, 256–71.

3. For a comparable urn with foliage, see a sideboard advertised by Joe Kindig, Jr., *Antiques* 58, no. 1 (July 1950): inside front cover.

4. For example, the duo was selected to lead the Baltimore cabinetmakers in the procession to celebrate the ratification of the Constitution.

Cat. 98

1. See Hipkiss, cat. nos. 28, 42, 43; Laura Fecych Sprague, ed., *Agreeable Situations: Society, Commerce, and Art in Southern Maine, 1780–1830* (Kennebunk, Me.: The Brick Store Museum, 1987), cat. no. 97; and Dean Thomas Lahikainen, "A Salem Cabinetmakers' Price Book," in Luke Beckerdite, ed., *American Furniture* 2001 (Milwaukee, Wis.: Chipstone Foundation, 2001), 168–69.

2. Hipkiss, cat. nos. 28 and 43.

3. Lahikainen, "Salem Cabinetmakers' Price Book," 169. The great Seymour commode at the Museum of Fine Arts, Boston, for example, was used in the chamber of Oak Hill.

Cat. 99

1. Liverpool, England, was the point of exportation and, possibly, decoration. See McCauley; see also Nelson.

2. Josiah Wedgwood considered pearlware a change rather than an improvement to the industry. See Noël-Hume, 235.

3. The "Drawing Books of the Leeds Pottery" refers to the type of coloring on the present jug as a "dip" because the white clay body was dipped into liquid colored clays (slips) to receive a solid color. See Towner, 53–54.

4. Pearlware printed with the Blue Willow pattern or painted with Chinese house patterns was not nearly as common as shell-edge decoration, but it certainly survives in America in higher proportion than wares with the hand-painted, gilded decoration shown here. Noël-Hume, 240 and 242, notes that while gilded, printed, and hand-painted decorations on creamware and pearlware are common enough in our museums today, no more than one percent of the ceramics archaeologically recovered at Williamsburg, for example, included such decorations.

Cat. 100

1. For comprehensive information on Shaw, see Elder and Bartlett, no. 18. The table is recorded in Hewitt et al., no. 372.

2. The engraved paper label on the swing leg reads "JOHN SHAW,/ CABINETMAKER,/ ANNAPOLIS./ 1790" (date in ink).

3. See Elder and Bartlett, 80ff. A virtually identical table (cat. no. 19) is at the Hammond-Harwood House, Annapolis.

Cat. 101

1. See Hewitt et al., no. 245, 181. The table is inscribed on the underside of the top: "This inlaid Table was/ given to Aunt Harmony/ Hamilton by her Step-Mother/ who was a native of/ East Haddam Conn-and/ went back there after/ Grandfather Emmons death/ in 1835- (Aunt Mary gives it to Charly)". "Aunt Mary" in the above inscription would seem to be Mary E. Church, and a later descendant's name, Caroline C. McElwain, is also included in a second inscription, torn and largely illegible. It descended in the Emmons-Hamilton-McElwain families, to the grandfather of

the donor. For additional information on provenance, see Conger and Rollins, *Treasures of State*, cat. no. 122.

2. The inlays are pictured in Hewitt et al., 75, 76, 78, and 80, and their frequency is charted there, 184–86.

3. Sheraton 1803, 2: 314.

4. Blackie, 22.

Cat. 102

1. For information on Crowninshield's career, see Gordon D. Ross, "The Crowninshield Family in Business and Politics, 1790-1830" (Ph.D. diss., Claremont Graduate School, 1964).

2. For a lengthy discussion of the Collection's large holdings of this type of chair, see Conger and Rollins, *Treasures of State*, cat. nos. 140–41.

3. Similar curved rear legs appear on many Salem shield-back chairs; see Randall 1965, cat. nos. 164–66, 168; Montgomery 1966, cat. nos. 19–20, 22.

4. Other examples of both versions survive. See Conger and Rollins, *Treasures of State*, cat. nos. 140–41 for documentation.

5. Salem craftsmen produced two types of chairs with Gothic-arched backs. On one, the tablet is ornamented with a swag of drapery similar to that shown in the Hepplewhite plate; on the other, a basket of fruit fills the tablet. See Randall 1965, cat. nos. 169–70.

6. Quoted in Swan 1934, 16.

7. Though more versatile than McIntire, Clarke performed many of the same tasks. In 1795 he charged the Sandersons £4.16.0 for "Making a set of H[ear]t open back Chairs[,] drafting carving and cutting the Paterns." Quoted in Swan 1934, 15. For more information on True, see Clunie 1977, 1006–13.

Cat. 103

1. Rice, 58; Smith 1976, fig. 3.

2. Montgomery 1966, 276.

3. Comstock 1968, 24.

4. Smith 1976, 350–59.

Cat. 104

1. Cornelius, pl. xxxvii.

2. Ibid., 53. Cornelius further states, p. 54, that "this acanthus . . . is very different from that found in design books, on Adam furniture or on . . .French earlier eighteenth-century furniture. . . . It partakes much more of the Directoire feeling which was no doubt affected by the flatness of the popular waterleaf ornament of Egyptian and Greek suggestion."

3. See Conger and Rollins, *Treasures of State*, cat. no. 143.

4. Cooper 1980, 261–63.

Cat. 105 and 106

1. An almost identical chair is in Sack *Collection*, 2: P4343 (ex-collection Israel Sack, Inc., New York, 1938, and ex-collection Charles K. Davis).

2. Twelve chairs from the larger of these two sets are owned by Winterthur and are described in Montgomery 1966, 120–21. An example that relates closely to the Collection's example is also owned by Winterthur (Ibid., 121–22). A side chair with a single-cross back and paw feet is illustrated in Cornelius, pl. I. Additional examples of related chair forms in the Department of State collection are discussed in Conger and Rollins, *Treasures of State*, cat. no.136.

Cat. 107

1. Tracy et al., no. 27.

2. Montgomery 1966, 126. For a similar chair owned by Winterthur, see Montgomery 1996, 127.

3. Cornelius, pl. xvii. Another sofa with curule base is at Boscobel; see Tracy, no. 10; Fitzgerald 1982, 116; and Sack Collection, no. 36.

4. Another almost identical sofa attributed to Phyfe was formerly in the collection of Dr. C. Ray Franklin. Except for minor differences in the choice of carved decoration, the sofa appears to be a near mate to the one in the Collection. This sofa was sold at Christie's, New York, sale 5736, October 13, 1984, lot 458. Other caned sofas attributed to Phyfe are at Yale (Kane 1976, cat. no. 230); Winterthur (Montgomery 1966, cat. no. 278); and in the Kaufman Collection (Flanigan, cat. no. 57). The caning on the Department of State's settee is a modern replacement.

5. Joy, 27. A sideboard with this motif was sold at Christie's, New York, sale 5410, October 13, 1983, lot 251, and a near mate was sold at Christie's, New York, sale 5370, June 2, 1983, lot 175.

Cat. 108

1. Diary entry of June 11, 1816; cited in Oliver, 57 and n. 1.

2. Oliver, 59 and nn. 6, 7.

3. Ibid., 62 and n. 8.

4. Reproduced in Kloss 1988, 24.

5. Adams 1918, 16–17.

Cat. 109

1. Oliver, 59.

2. Ibid., 62.

3. Oliver, 58 and n. 4.

4. Ibid., 8–9.

5. Oliver, 11.

6. Ibid., 62–63 and nn. 9–10. The portraits descended to Thomas Baker Johnson, brother of Louisa Catherine Johnson Adams; to Charles Francis Adams (d. 1886), the son of John Quincy Adams, in 1836; probably to his son, Charles Francis Adams (d. 1915); to his brother, Brooks Adams (d. 1927), by 1921; to his niece, Mrs. Robert Homans; to her son, Robert Homans, Jr.

The Nation Expands Westward: Discovery, Bounty, and Beauty

Introduction, p. 168

1. Ron Tyler, *American Canvas* (New York: Portland House, 1983).

2. Charles Coleman Sellers, *Mr. Peale's Museum*, a Barra Foundation Book (New York: W. W. Norton, 1980).

3. Earle E. Spamer, Edward Daeschler, and L. Gay Vostreys-Shapiro, *A Study of Fossil Vertebrate Types in the Academy of Natural Sciences of Philadelphia*, The Academy of Natural Sciences of Philadelphia, Special Publications 16 (1995).

4. Susan R. Stein, *The Worlds of Thomas Jefferson at Monticello* (New York: Harry N. Abrams, in association with the Thomas Jefferson Memorial Foundation, 1993), 63–68, 385–409.

5. Conger and Rollins, *Treasures of State*, cat. no. 180.

6. Klapthor 1999, 40–43.

7. The term is Walt Whitman's. See "By Blue Ontario's Shore," in *Leaves of Grass* (New York: Modern Library, 1921), 385 ("These States are the amplest poem, / Here is not merely a nation but a teeming / Nation of nations"). The title was bor-

rowed for a major bicentennial exhibition in Washington: See Peter C. Marzio, ed., *A Nation of Nations: The People Who Came to America as Seen Through Objects, Prints, and Photographs at the Smithsonian Institution* (New York: Harper & Row, 1976).

Cat. 110

1. Dunlap, 262.
2. On August 30, 1890, Congress appropriated $2,500 to purchase this portrait and one of John Quincy Adams (whom Clay served as secretary of state). The Adams portrait is no longer in the Collection.
3. *Secretaries of State* 1978, 21.

Cat. 111

1. Wilmerding et al. 1988, 99, no. 37.
2. Ronnberg, 64, 67.

Cat. 112

1. "John Watson Foster," in *Virtual American Biographies* (edited Appletons Encyclopedia, 2001), at www.famousamericans.net.

Cat. 113 and 114

1. For a discussion of these services, see Le Corbeiller 1977, 1124–29.
2. The other three plates in the Collection's group are 1985.43.2–4; see Conger and Rollins, *Treasures of State*, cat. no. 166. The Collection also includes eight dinner plates from another source. Forbes, 55, describes a large group of pieces from this service in the China Trade Museum (now part of the Peabody Essex Museum of Salem) given by the same donors. Two examples are in the collection of the Museum of Fine Arts, Boston (acc. nos. 69.390–91).
3. Although Le Corbeiller 1977, 1125, speculates that a bookplate of Winthrop Sargent, a relative of Ignatius, also may have provided the source for the Chinese painters, Forbes, 55, notes that the descent of the service is from Ignatius Sargent. For other objects from the Winthrop Sargent family in the Collection, see Conger and Rollins, *Treasures of State*, cat. nos. 207, 259, and 260). The Callender bookplate is illustrated in Le Corbeiller 1977, 1122.

Cat. 115

1. This linen press was exhibited at the Metropolitan Museum of Art's landmark exhibition *Nineteenth-Century America*, mounted in 1970.
2. Montgomery 1966, no. 452. A similar example is illustrated in an advertisement by H. & R. Sandor, New Hope, Pennsylvania, in *Antiques* 129, no. 6 (June 1986): 1127.
3. Elder and Stokes, 98.
4. Chippendale, pl. cxxx; Kirk 1982, nos. 639–42.

Cat. 116

1. This painting is signed and dated at the lower right, "J. Shaw. 1838. X." The large X is in red paint; it may be shorthand for "*pinxit*," Latin for "has painted it," though one would expect it to follow the artist's signature. If it represents a month or a numbering system, it has not been mentioned in the literature on Shaw. The painting was cleaned, relined, and mounted on a new stretcher in 1982 by Irwin Braun, Inc., New York. No inscriptions, labels, or other marks were observed on the original stretcher or the reverse of the original canvas.
2. Nygren et al., 46.
3. Quoted by Waterhouse, 232.
4. Nygren et al., 50, pl. 50. See Shaw's early *View in the Pennsylvania Countryside* (1823; High Museum of Art, Atlanta.

5. Jones 1970, 83.
6. It has been assumed that the Collection's painting is the View on the Kiskeminitas exhibited in 1838 at the Pennsylvania Academy of the Fine Arts (no. 32) and lent by its owner, James Reid Lambdin, a Pittsburgh native who had recently moved to Philadelphia to further himself as a portrait painter. It should be noted, however, that in the March 1841 exhibition of the Apollo Association, New York, Shaw showed *Landscape, View of the Salt Works on the Kiskiminitus* [sic] *River* (no. 81; "For sale"). The very specific title makes it an equally acceptable candidate for the Collection's picture, which has no provenance. Shaw's interest in the subject is seen in other paintings, for example, his *View near Saltsburg, Pa. (on the Conemaugh River)* exhibited at the Pennsylvania Academy of the Fine Arts in 1840 (no. 45; "For sale").
7. Rutledge, 201–2; and Cowdrey, 2: 325.

Cat. 117

1. The designation "hong" bowl for punch bowls decorated as this one is a modern collector's term. The 1785 invoice of one Captain Green for "4 Factory painted Bowles" brought back aboard the *Empress of China* may well be the only documentation for the name that was used at the time to refer to these bowls. See Mudge 1981, 95, 214.
2. For further descriptions of the hongs, see Jörg, 54–61; Le Corbeiller 1974, 115–17.
3. Le Corbeiller 1974 discusses a punch bowl in the collection of the Metropolitan Museum of Art that is nearly identical to the Department of State's punch bowl. For a review of the flags on hong bowls, see Le Corbeiller 1974, 117.
4. Howard and Ayers 1978, 1: 209, discuss the history of Canton scenes on punch bowls. For illustrations of the many varieties, see Hervouët et al., 23–29.
5. Howard and Ayers 1978, 1: 207.

Cat. 118 and 119

1. Another example of presentation silver in this style is the hot-water kettle made by John Chandler Moore for the firm of Ball, Tompkins and Black of New York in 1850 as a gift for Marshall Lefferts, president of the New York, New England, and New York State Telegraph Companies (*19th-Century America*, cat. nos. 141, 142).
2. For a brief history of the Wood and Hughes firm, see Rainwater, 191; Cramer, 28–32. These cups are marked "W&H" in block letters within a rectangular reserve, inside the bottom of each. For the partnership's early marks, see Belden 1980, 182, 454.

Cat. 120

1. The full inscription on the reverse reads: "President Madison/Copy from Wood by C King/Washington 1826."
2. Hall, 157–58. Painted in March 1817, just after Madison left office, the pair of portraits were given in June to the Madisons' close friends, Mr. and Mrs. Richard Bland Lee. They descended through the Lee family to Katherine W. Davidge (Mrs. John Washington Davidge) of Washington, D.C., who deeded them to the Virginia Historical Society in 1962 (received in 1967). See *Occasional Bulletin*, no. 15 (Richmond: Virginia Historical Society, 1967), 2–6.
3. The painting was owned by the marquis de Lafayette and descended in a family branch in Turin, Italy. It was consigned to Christie's, New York, Cecily sale, May 23, 1979, lot 3, where it was purchased by the Fine Arts Committee.

Cat. 121

1. Presumed to be the painting in Sully's list of paintings as published and enlarged upon by Biddle and Fielding, 233, no. 1260: "Head to right, white stock, high coat collar. The register states it was painted for the Military Academy at West Point, owned by Monroe's great-granddaughter, begun June 12th, 1829, finished June 17th, 1829. Head. Price, $50.00." This would mean that the head was a sketch for a full-length portrait for West Point. The date of this identification of the Department of State's head is more convincing than that of the later (1909) inscription on the reverse of the relined canvas: "President Monroe 1820."
2. Meschutt, 81 and n. 20.
3. A notable example from the same decade is Samuel F. B. Morse's second portrait of David Curtis DeForest, 1823, at Yale. DeForest desired "to have his portrait taken such as it would have been six or eight years ago." See Kloss 1988, 81–82. For Monroe's appearance in 1820, see Morse's portrait in the White House (Kloss, 1988, 58). It accords well with Sully's image. There is no record and no reason to believe that Sully painted Monroe in 1820. A second inscription is on the back of the Sully: "The above canvas with inscription formed/Part of [sic] the lining of the President Monroe/Portrait. This was removed when the painting/Was again relined in 1934. by A. J. Brooks/34 South 17th St./ Philadelphia."

Cat. 122

1. *In Memoriam: Benjamin Ogle Tayloe* (Washington: Published privately, 1872; printed by Sherman and Co., Philadelphia), 164
2. The Henry Clay Papers, Library of Congress, v. 14.
3. See Cornelius.
4. McClelland, pls. 83, 94.
5. Montgomery 1966, 337.
6. McClelland, pl. 187.

Cat. 123

1. This painting is not dated. See *Kennedy Quarterly* 8, no. 4 (January 1969): 241, for the date 1844, given as part of the title. Naylor, 203, states that the painting is dated 1844. Von Salzen repeats the date in the photo caption (p. 229) but omits any date in the catalogue entry (p. 180). If the painting was ever dated, it has disappeared (the edge of the canvas below the signature is cut and tattered and relined). I have retained the date as "ca. 1844" because it is reasonable to assume that MacLeod painted his *Glimpse* shortly before his (undocumented) move to New York. The painting is clearly signed, at lower right, "W McLEOD"; two later works of 1863 and 1873 (Corcoran Gallery of Art) are just as clearly signed "W MacLeod." Inconsistent spelling was common in the nineteenth century.
2. This is possibly the painting distributed by the American Art-Union in 1848. Von Salzen, 180: "In a letter to the Art Committee of the American Art-Union dated August, 1848, MacLeod submitted a 'small landscape representing a distant glimpse of the Capitol at Washington, D.C. from the Northeast. The piece is original and painted by myself—price $25.00.'" It was no. 130 in the Exhibition Records. A second, similar version of the painting was owned (1981) by Government Services Savings and Loan, Bethesda, Maryland. It could be the painting exhibited as no. 130. For early views of Washington, see Reed, 12.
3. Dickens, 114–15.

4. Truett, 35

Cat. 124

1. See Goldsborough 1983, 148, 151, and 153, for four similar water pitchers.

Cat. 125

1. Gerdts and Burke, 61, 66.

2. "Nature's Bounty," as the painting has been known, is not an inappropriate title, yet there is no certainty that Roesen used it. It has been attached to so many of his paintings that it is virtually useless in the identification of specific works.

3. Spassky, 108.

Cat. 126 and 127

1. Labels attached to the pine slats on the backs of the frames read: "Harrington & Mills,/140 Baltimore Street,/Manufacturers of/Looking Glasses,/Portrait and Picture Frames,/and all Descriptions of Gilt and Ornamental Work/Photographs, Drawings, and Engravings Framed and Mounted./Dealers in Plated Ware, Cutlery, House Keeping Articles, Gas, Fixtures, Chandeliers, &c. &c." Harrington & Mills operated their business at that address from 1864 to 1872, according to Baltimore city directories. The author wishes to thank Laura Cox of the Maryland Historical Society for the information on Harrington & Mills.

Cat. 128

1. *Literary World* 1, no. 18 (June 5, 1847): 419.

2. Ibid.

3. See Mount's diary entry, "Year 1847," in Alfred Frankenstein, *William Sidney Mount* (New York: Harry N. Abrams, 1975), 30.

4. Frederick C. Moffatt, "Barnburning and Hunkerism: William Sidney Mount's *Power of Music*," *Winterthur Portfolio* 29, no. 1 (spring 1994): 19–42, quotation 24. This is perhaps the most probing and thoroughly researched article written on the painting in its cultural/historical context, but it is not without unproven assumptions and errors of interpretation.

Cat. 129

1. Viola et al., 140. See also Tyler, 203; Julie Schimmel, "John Mix Stanley and the Imagery of the West in Nineteenth-Century American Art" (Ph.D. diss., New York University, 1983), 230–31. Truettner, 20 and 184.

2. Unlike Catlin who, of course, did not have access to the Daguerrean camera (the process was first published in 1839), Stanley did not paint his Indians directly but later, in the studio, from sketches and daguerreotype images. He was "one of the earliest photographers of the Indian" (Viola et al., 138).

3. Ibid., 142–43.

Cat. 132

1. Roosevelt l968, 64–65. First published in book form as *Ranch Life and the Hunting Trail* (New York: The Century Company, 1888).

2. "Remington and Kipling had been drinking companions at The Players and had become friends in the course of Remington's illustrating a Kipling story for *Cosmopolitan*. . . . The two were called 'well matched in audacity, frankness, and power of picturesque speech.'" See Samuels and Samuels, 231.

3. Shapiro 1988, 19.

Cat. 133

1. The painting is signed and dated at the lower right, "TYMORAN. 1900" ("TYM" in mono-

gram). Moran's monogram is better described as a cipher, since it combines western imagery—an arrowhead and perhaps a steer's horns—with the initials, one of which stands for a nickname: "Yellowstone." After the exhibition of his first paintings of the Grand Canyon of the Yellowstone, he appended the epithet to his cipher.

2. Tyler, 160 and 204, n. 100.

3. John Wesley Powell, "The Cañons of the Colorado," *Scribners Monthly* 9 (January 1875); quoted in Tyler, 160.

4. For further discussion of his paintings and a capsule biography of Moran, see Kloss 1985, 72, 200–202.

Cat. 134

1. For the basic study on Dallin, see Francis.

2. The original bronze version of the *Medicine Man* now stands in Philadelphia's Fairmount Park. It won a silver medal at the Paris Exposition in 1900. See *Sculpture of a City*, 210.

3. The best study of *Appeal to the Great Spirit* is in Greenthal et al., 268–78.

4. See *Report of Special Commissioners: J. W. Powell and G. W. Ingalls on the Condition of the Ute Indian in Utah* (Washington, D.C.: Government Printing Office, 1874). Dallin would have been twelve or thirteen years old at the time of Powell's expeditions, and his memories of Indian life in his native area are verified and illustrated in Powell's reports.

5. Caproni 1915, 8; Caproni 1894, 228.

6. Other versions of the twenty-inch-tall bronze statuettes, bearing the same inscription and date as the Collection's example, are in the Montclair Art Museum, Montclair, New Jersey; the Smith College Museum of Art, Northampton, Massachusetts; the Buffalo Bill Historical Center, Cody, Wyoming; and the Museum of Fine Arts, Boston.

JONATHAN L. FAIRBANKS Katharine Lane Weems Curator Emeritus of American Decorative Arts and Sculpture, Museum of Fine Arts, Boston

GAIL F. SERFATY Director, Diplomatic Reception Rooms, U.S. Department of State, and Curator, Blair House

DAVID L. BARQUIST Associate Curator of American Decorative Arts, Yale University Art Gallery

WENDY A. COOPER Lois F. and Henry S. McNeil Senior Curator of Furniture, Winterthur Museum

WAYNE CRAVEN Henry Francis du Pont Winterthur Professor of Art History Emeritus, University of Delaware

DONALD H. CRESSWELL Proprietor, The Philadelphia Print Shop

BERT R. DENKER Senior Librarian, Visual Resources, Winterthur Library

ELLEN PAUL DENKER Museum consultant, writer and lecturer on American decorative arts

BEATRICE B. GARVAN Curator Emeritus of Decorative Arts, Philadelphia Museum of Art

JENNIFER F. GOLDSBOROUGH Teacher on silver and ceramics, Masters Program in the History of Decorative Arts, Parsons School of Design and Cooper-Hewitt Museum

BROCK JOBE Professor of American Decorative Arts, Winterthur Museum

WILLIAM KLOSS Independent scholar and lecturer for seminars on European and American art from the Renaissance to the twentieth century

THOMAS S. MICHIE Curator of Decorative Arts, Museum of Art, Rhode Island School of Design

ROBERT D. MUSSEY, JR. Principal owner of Robert Mussey Associates, a Boston conservation firm

PAGE TALBOTT Independent curator and decorative and fine arts consultant

GILBERT T. VINCENT President, New York State Historical Association, Fenimore Art Museum and The Farmers' Museum

BARBARA McLEAN WARD Director/Curator, Moffatt-Ladd House and Garden, and lecturer, Museum Studies Program, Tufts University

GERALD W. R. WARD Katharine Lane Weems Senior Curator of Decorative Arts and Sculpture, Museum of Fine Arts, Boston

GREGORY R. WEIDMAN Furnishings Project Coordinator, Historic Hampton Inc., and consultant for Hampton National Historic Site

Many of the entries in the book originally appeared in *Treasures of State* (1991), edited by Clement E. Conger and Alexandra W. Rollins, and have been updated by these authors to reflect recent scholarship.

Bibliography

Note: Entries are arranged by the key-word and short-title citations used in the notes to the catalogue entries.

ADAMS 1918   Henry Adams. *The Education of Henry Adams*. Boston, 1918. Reprint. Boston: Houghton Mifflin, 1961.

ADAMSON   Jeremy Elwell Adamson. *Niagara: Two Centuries of Changing Attitudes, 1697–1701*. Exh. cat. Washington, D.C.: Corcoran Gallery of Art, 1985.

ANDREWS   William Loring Andrews. *Paul Revere and His Engraving*. New York: Charles Scribner's Sons, 1901.

BARQUIST   David L. Barquist. *American Tables and Looking Glasses in the Mabel Brady Garvan and Other Collections at Yale University*. New Haven: Yale University Art Gallery, 1992.

BARQUIST 2001   David L. Barquist et al. *Myer Myers: Jewish Silversmith in Colonial New York*. Exh. cat. New Haven: Yale University Art Gallery in association with Yale University Press, 2001.

BECKERDITE 1986   Luke Beckerdite. "A Problem of Identification: Philadelphia and Baltimore Furniture Styles in the Eighteenth Century." *Journal of Early Southern Decorative Arts* 12, no. 1 (May 1986): 21–64.

BELDEN 1980   Louise Conway Belden. *Marks of American Silversmiths in the Ineson-Bissell Collection*. Charlottesville: University Press of Virginia for the Henry Francis du Pont Winterthur Museum, 1980.

BELDEN 1983   Louise Conway Belden. *The Festive Tradition: Table Decoration and Desserts in America, 1650–1900*. New York and London: Norton, 1983.

BENES   Peter Benes. *Old-Town and the Waterside: Two Hundred Years of Tradition and Change in Newbury, Newburyport, and West Newbury, 1635–1835*. Newburyport, Mass.: Historical Society of Old Newbury, 1986.

BIALOSTOCKI   Jan Bialostocki. "The Firing Squad from Paul Revere to Goya: America, Russia, and Spain." In Jan Bialostocki, *The Message of Images: Studies in the History of Art*, 211–18. Vienna: IRSA, 1988.

BIDDLE 1963   James Biddle. *American Art from American Collections: Decorative Arts, Paintings, and Prints of the Colonial and Federal Periods*. Exh. cat. New York: Metropolitan Museum of Art, 1963.

BIDDLE AND FIELDING   Edward Biddle and Mantle Fielding. *The Life and Works of Thomas Sully (1783–1872)*. Philadelphia: privately printed, 1921.

BLACKIE   Blackie and Son. *The Victorian Cabinet-Maker's Assistant. 1853*. Reprint. New York: Dover, 1970.

BRIGHAM   Clarence S. Brigham. *Paul Revere's Engravings*. 1954. Reprint. New York: Atheneum, 1969.

BROWN 1978   Joan Sayers Brown. "Skippets." *Antiques* 114, no. 1 (July 1978): 140–41.

BUHLER 1972   Kathryn C. Buhler. *American Silver, 1655–1825, in the Museum of Fine Arts, Boston*. 2 vols. Boston: Museum of Fine Arts, 1972. Distributed by New York Graphic Society, Greenwich, Conn.

BUHLER AND HOOD   Kathryn C. Buhler and Graham Hood. *American Silver: Garvan and Other Collections in the Yale University Art Gallery*. 2 vols. New Haven and London: Yale University Press for the Yale University Art Gallery, 1970.

CAPRONI 1894   Pietro P. Caproni and Brother. *Catalogue of Plaster Cast Reproductions from Antique, Medieval, and Modern Sculptures*. Boston: Pietro P. Caproni and Brother, 1894.

CAPRONI 1915   Pietro P. Caproni and Brother. *Caproni Casts: American Indians and Other Sculptures by Cyrus E. Dallin*. Boston: Pietro P. Caproni and Brother, 1915.

CARPENTER 1954   Ralph E. Carpenter, Jr. *The Arts and Crafts of Newport, Rhode Island: 1640–1820*. Newport, R.I.: Preservation Society of Newport County, 1954.

CATALOGUE OF AMERICAN PORTRAITS   *Catalogue of American Portraits in The New-York Historical Society*. New Haven and London: Yale University Press for the New-York Historical Society, 1974.

CHIPPENDALE   Thomas Chippendale. *The Gentleman & Cabinet-Maker's Director*. London: self-published, 1754; London: J. Haberhorn, 1755; London, 1762. Reprint. New York: Dover, 1966.

CIKOVSKY   Nicolai Cikovsky, Jr., et al. *Raphaelle Peale Still Lifes*. Exh. cat. Washington, D.C.: National Gallery of Art; Philadelphia: Pennsylvania Academy of the Fine Arts, 1988. Distributed by Harry N. Abrams, New York.

CLEMENT   Arthur W. Clement. *Our Pioneer Potters*. New York: self-published, 1947.

CLUNIE 1977   Margaret Burke Clunie. "Joseph True and the Piecework System in Salem." *Antiques* 111, no. 5 (May 1977): 1006–13.

COMSTOCK 1968   Helen Comstock. *The Looking Glass in America, 1700–1825*. New York: Viking, 1968.

CONGER AND ROLLINS, TREASURES OF STATE   Clement E. Conger, Alexandra W. Rollins et al. *Treasures of State: Fine and Decorative Arts in the Diplomatic Reception Rooms of the U.S. Department of State*. New York: Harry N. Abrams, 1991.

COOPER 1980   Wendy A. Cooper. *In Praise of America: American Decorative Arts, 1650–1830: Fifty Years of Discovery Since the 1939 Girl Scouts Loan Exhibition*. Exh. cat. New York: Knopf, 1980.

CORNELIUS   Charles Over Cornelius. *Furniture Masterpieces of Duncan Phyfe*. Exh. cat. New York: Metropolitan Museum of Art, 1922. Reprint. New York: Dover, 1970.

COWDREY   Mary Bartlett Cowdrey. *American Academy of Fine Arts and American Art-Union, 1816–1852*. 2 vols. New York: New-York Historical Society, 1953.

CRAMER   Diana Cramer. "Wood and Hughes." *Silver* 22, no. 6 (November–December 1989): 28–32.

CROSSMAN AND STRICKLAND   Carl L. Crossman and Charles R. Strickland. "Early Depictions of the Landing of the Pilgrims." *Antiques* 98, no. 5 (November 1970): 777–81.

CUMMING 1958   William P. Cumming. *The Southeast in Early Maps*. Princeton, N.J.: Princeton University Press, 1958.

CUMMING 1966   William P. Cumming. *North Carolina in Maps*. Raleigh, N.C.: State Department of Archives and History, 1966.

CUMMINGS 1964   Abbott Lowell Cummings, ed. *Rural Household Inventories*. Boston: Society for the Preservation of New England Antiquities, 1964.

CURTIS 1973   Phillip H. Curtis. "The Production of Tucker Porcelain, 1826–1838: A Reevaluation." In Ian M. G. Quimby, ed. *Ceramics in America: Winterthur Conference Report*. Charlottesville: University Press of Virginia for the Henry Francis du Pont Winterthur Museum, 1973. 339–74.

DAB   *Dictionary of American Biography*. 20 vols. Allen Johnson and Dumas Malone, eds. New York: Charles Scribner's Sons, 1927; supplements, 1944, 1958.

DE GUILLEBON   Régine de Plinval de Guillebon. *Porcelain of Paris 1770–1850*. Trans. Robin R. Charleston. New York: Walker and Company, 1972.

DENKER   Ellen Paul Denker. *After the Chinese Taste: China's Influence in America, 1730–1930*. Exh. cat. Salem, Mass.: Peabody Museum of Salem, 1985.

DETWEILER 1982 Susan Gray Detweiler. *George Washington's Chinaware*. New York: Harry N. Abrams, 1982.

DICKENS Charles Dickens. *Pictures from Italy and American Notes*. London and New York: Harper, 1907.

DOWNS 1952 Joseph Downs. *American Furniture, Queen Anne and Chippendale Periods in the Henry Francis du Pont Winterthur Museum*. New York: Macmillan, 1952.

EHRENFRIED Albert Ehrenfried. *A Chronicle of Boston Jewry from the Colonial Settlement to 1900*. Boston: privately printed, 1963.

ELAM Charles H. Elam, ed. *The Peale Family*. Exh. cat. Detroit: Detroit Institute of Arts, 1967.

ELDER AND BARTLETT William Voss Elder III and Lu Bartlett. *John Shaw, Cabinetmaker of Annapolis*. Exh. cat. Baltimore: Baltimore Museum of Art, 1983.

ELDER AND STOKES William Voss Elder III and Jayne E. Stokes. *American Furniture, 1680–1880, from the Collection of the Baltimore Museum of Art*. Baltimore: Baltimore Museum of Art, 1987.

EVANS Dorinda Evans. *Benjamin West and His American Students*. Exh. cat. Washington, D.C.: Smithsonian Institution Press for the National Portrait Gallery, 1980.

FAIRBANKS Jonathan L. Fairbanks. "Queen Anne and Chippendale Furniture: Department of State Diplomatic Reception Rooms, Washington, D.C." *The Connoisseur* 191 (May 1976): 48–55.

FAIRBANKS AND BATES Jonathan L. Fairbanks and Elizabeth Bidwell Bates. *American Furniture: 1620 to the Present*. New York: Richard Marek, 1981.

FAIRMAN 1927 Charles E. Fairman. *Art and Artists of the Capitol of the United States of America*. Washington, D.C.: U.S. Government Printing Office, 1927.

FALES JOSEPH RICHARDSON AND FAMILY Martha Gandy Fales. *Joseph Richardson and Family: Philadelphia Silversmiths*. Middletown, Conn.: Wesleyan University Press for the Historical Society of Pennsylvania, 1972.

FALES 1965 Dean A. Fales, Jr. *Essex County Furniture: Documented Treasures from Local Collections, 1660–1860*. Salem, Mass.: Essex Institute, 1965.

FALES 1973 Martha Gandy Fales. *Early American Silver*. Rev. ed. New York: E. P. Dutton, 1973.

FALINO Jeannine Falino. "'The Pride Which Pervades thro every Class': The Customers of Paul Revere." In Jeannine Falino and Gerald W.R. Ward, eds., *New England Silver and Silversmithing, 1620–1815*. Boston: Colonial Society of Massachusetts, 2001. Distributed by University Press of Virginia, Charlottesville. 152–82.

FELLER John Quentin Feller. "China Trade Porcelain Decorated with the Emblem of the Society of the Cincinnati." *Antiques* 118, no. 4 (October 1980): 760–68.

FITZGERALD 1982 Oscar P. Fitzgerald. *Three Centuries of American Furniture*. Englewood Cliffs, N.J.: Prentice-Hall, 1982.

FLANIGAN J. Michael Flanigan. *American Furniture from the Kaufman Collection*. Washington, D.C.: National Gallery of Art, 1986. Distributed by Harry N. Abrams, New York.

FLYNT AND FALES Henry N. Flynt and Martha Gandy Fales. *The Heritage Foundation Collection of Silver, with Biographical Sketches of New England Silversmiths, 1625–1825*. Old Deerfield, Mass.: Heritage Foundation, 1968.

FORBES H. A. Crosby Forbes. *Yang ts'ai: The Foreign Colors*. Milton, Mass.: China Trade Museum, 1982.

FORMAN 1983 Benno M. Forman. "German Influences in Pennsylvania Furniture." In Scott T. Swank et al., *Arts of the Pennsylvania Germans*, 102–70. New York: Norton, 1983.

FOWLER AND CORNFORTH John Fowler and John Cornforth. *English Decoration in the 18th Century*. Princeton, N.J.: Pyne Press, 1974.

FRANCIS Rell G. Francis. *Cyrus E. Dallin: Let Justice Be Done*. Springville, Utah: Springville Museum of Art, 1976.

FREDERICKSON AND GIBB N. Jaye Frederickson and Sandra Gibb. *The Covenant Chain: Indian Ceremonial and Trade Silver*. Ottawa: National Museums of Canada, 1980.

FRÉMONT Jesse Benton Frémont. *Souvenirs of My Times*. Boston: D. Lathrop, 1887.

FRENCH Hollis French. *Jacob Hurd and His Sons, Nathaniel and Benjamin, Silversmiths, 1702–1781*. 1939. Reprint. New York: DaCapo, 1972.

GARRETT Elisabeth Donaghy Garrett. *The Arts of Independence: The DAR Museum Collection*. Washington, D.C.: National Society of the Daughters of the American Revolution, 1985.

GERDTS AND BURKE William H. Gerdts and Russell H. Burke. *American Still-Life Painting*. New York: Praeger, 1971.

GERSHENSON 1967 Doris Fisher Gershenson. "The Detroit Home of Mr. and Mrs. Charles H. Gershenson." *Antiques* 91, no. 5 (May 1967): 637–41.

GIRL SCOUTS *Loan Exhibition of Eighteenth and Nineteenth Century Furniture and Glass . . . for the Benefit of the National Council of Girl Scouts, Inc*. Exh. cat. New York: American Art Galleries, 1929.

GORDON 1977 Elinor Gordon. *Collecting Chinese Export Porcelain*. New York: Universe, 1977.

GOTTESMAN 1938 Rita Susswein Gottesman, comp. *The Arts and Crafts in New York, 1726–1776: Advertisements and News Items from New York City Newspapers*. New York: New-York Historical Society, 1938.

GREENE Benjamin Greene. *Benjamin Greene ledger, 1734–1758*. Massachusetts Historical Society, Boston.

GREENTHAL 1985 Kathryn Greenthal. *Augustus Saint-Gaudens, Master Sculptor*. New York: Metropolitan Museum of Art, 1985.

GREENTHAL ET AL. Kathryn Greenthal, Paula M. Kozol, Jan Seidler Ramirez, and Jonathan L. Fairbanks. *American Figurative Sculpture in the Museum of Fine Arts, Boston*. Boston: Museum of Fine Arts, 1986.

HALL Virginius Cornick Hall, Jr. *Portraits in the Collection of the Virginia Historical Society*. Charlottesville: Virginia Historical Society, 1981.

HAYWARD AND KIRKHAM Helena Hayward and Pat Kirkham. *William and John Linnell: Eighteenth-Century London Furniture Makers*. 2 vols. New York: Rizzoli International, 1980.

HECKSCHER 1973 Morrison H. Heckscher. "The New York Serpentine Card Table." *Antiques* 103, no. 5 (May 1973): 974–83.

HECKSCHER 1985 Morrison H. Heckscher. *American Furniture in the Metropolitan Museum of Art*. Vol. 2, *Late Colonial Period: The Queen Anne and Chippendale Styles*. New York: Metropolitan Museum of Art/Random House, 1985.

HECKSCHER AND BOWMAN Morrison H. Heckscher and Leslie Greene Bowman. *American Rococo, 1750–1775: A Taste for Luxury*. New York: Metropolitan Museum of Art; Los Angeles: Los Angeles County Museum of Art, 1992.

HERVOUËT ET AL. Francois Hervouët, Nicole Hervouët, and Yves Bruneau. *La Porcelaine des compagnies des Indes: À décor occidental*. Paris: Flammarion, 1986.

HEWITT ET AL. Benjamin A. Hewitt, Patricia E. Kane, and Gerald W.R. Ward. *The Work of Many Hands: Card Tables in Federal America, 1790–1820*. New Haven: Yale University Art Gallery, 1982.

HINCKLEY F. Lewis Hinckley. *A Directory of Queen Anne, Early Georgian and Chippendale Furniture: Establishing the Preeminence of the Dublin Craftsmen*. New York: Crown, 1953. Reprint. New York: Crown, 1971.

HINDES Ruthanna Hindes. "Delaware Silversmiths, 1700–1850." *Delaware History* 12, no. 4 (October 1967): 247–308.

HIPKISS Edwin J. Hipkiss. *Eighteenth-Century American Arts: The M. and M. Karolik Collection of Paintings, Drawings, Engravings, Furniture, Silver, Needlework, and Incidental Objects Gathered to Illustrate the Achievements of American Artists and Craftsmen of the Period from 1720 to 1820*. Cambridge, Mass.: Harvard University Press for the Museum of Fine Arts, Boston, 1941. Reprint. Cambridge, Mass.: Harvard University Press, 1950.

HOLMES J.B.S. Holmes. "Fitzhugh and Fitzhughs in the China Trade." *Antiques* 89, no. 1 (January 1966): 130–31.

HORNOR 1935 William Macpherson Hornor, Jr. *Blue Book, Philadelphia Furniture: William Penn to George Washington, with Special Reference to the Philadelphia–Chippendale School*. Philadelphia: privately printed, 1935. Reprint. Washington, D.C.: Highland House, 1977.

HOWARD 1974 David Sanctuary Howard. *Chinese Armorial Porcelain*. London: Faber & Faber, 1974.

HOWARD 1984 David Sanctuary Howard. *New York and the China Trade*. New York: New-York Historical Society, 1984.

HOWARD AND AYERS 1978 David Sanctuary Howard and John Ayers. *China for the West*. 2 vols. London: Sotheby Parke-Bernet, 1978.

HULTON AND QUINN Paul Hulton and David B. Quinn. *The American Drawings of John White, 1577–1590*. 2 vols. London: British Museum; Chapel Hill: University of North Carolina Press, 1964.

HUMMEL 1976 Charles F. Hummel. *A Winterthur Guide to American Chippendale Furniture: Middle Atlantic and Southern Colonies*. New York: Crown, 1976.

HUNNEWELL James F. Hunnewell. *A Century of Town Life: A History of Charlestown, Massachusetts, 1775–1887*. Boston: Little, Brown, 1887.

INCE AND MAYHEW William Ince and John Mayhew. *The Universal System of Household Furniture*. 1762. Reprint. London: Alec Tiranti, 1960.

JOBE AND KAYE Brock Jobe and Myrna Kaye, with the assistance of Philip Zea. *New England Furniture: The Colonial Era: Selections from the Society for the Preservation of New England Antiquities*. Boston: Houghton Mifflin, 1984.

JONES 1970 Samuel Jones. *Pittsburgh in the Year 1826*. Reprint. New York: Arno, 1970.

JÖRG C.F.A. Jörg. *Porcelain and the Dutch China Trade*. The Hague: Martinus Nijhoff, 1982.

JOY Edward T. Joy. *English Furniture, 1800–1851*. London: Sotheby Parke-Bernet/Ward Lock, 1977.

KANE 1976 Patricia E. Kane. *300 Years of American Seating Furniture: Chairs and Beds from the Mabel Brady Garvan and Other Collections at Yale University*. Boston: New York Graphic Society, 1976.

KANE 1998   Patricia E. Kane, ed., et al. *Colonial Massachusetts Silversmiths and Jewelers: A Biographical Dictionary Based on the Notes of Francis Hill Bigelow and John Marshall Phillips.* New Haven: Yale University Art Gallery, 1998. Distributed by University Press of New England, Hanover and London.

KIRK 1982   John T. Kirk. *American Furniture and the British Tradition to 1830.* New York: Knopf, 1982.

KLAPTHOR 1975   Margaret Brown Klapthor. *Official White House China: 1789 to the Present.* Washington, D.C.: Smithsonian Institution Press, 1975.

KLAPTHOR 1999   Margaret Brown Klapthor. *Official White House China: 1789 to the Present.* Rev. ed. New York: Barra Foundation in association with Harry N. Abrams, 1999.

KLOSS 1985   William Kloss. *Treasures from the National Museum of American Art.* Exh. cat. Washington, D.C.: National Museum of American Art; Baltimore: Smithsonian Institution Press, 1985.

KLOSS 1988   William Kloss. *Samuel F. B. Morse.* New York: Harry N. Abrams and the National Museum of American Art, Smithsonian Institution, 1988.

KOHN   Richard H. Kohn. *Eagle and Sword.* New York: Free Press, 1975.

LE CORBEILLER 1974   Claire Le Corbeiller. *China Trade Porcelain: Patterns of Exchange.* New York: Metropolitan Museum of Art, 1974.

LE CORBEILLER 1977   Claire Le Corbeiller. "China Trade Armorial Porcelain in America." *Antiques* 112, no. 6 (December 1977): 1124–29.

LITTLE   Nina Fletcher Little. *Michele Felice Corné, 1752–1845.* Exh. cat. Salem, Mass.: Peabody Museum of Salem, 1972.

LOCKWOOD   Luke Vincent Lockwood. *Colonial Furniture in America.* 3d ed. 2 vols. New York: Charles Scribner's Sons, 1926. Reprint. New York: Castle Books, 1951.

MACQUOID   Percy Macquoid. *A History of English Furniture.* 4 vols. London: Lawrence & Bullen, 1904–8.

MACQUOID AND EDWARDS   Percy Macquoid and Ralph Edwards. *The Dictionary of English Furniture from the Middle Ages to the Late Georgian Period.* 3 vols. London: Country Life, 1924–27.

McCAULEY   Robert H. McCauley. *Liverpool Transfer Designs on Anglo-American Pottery.* Portland, Me.: Southworth-Anthoenson Press, 1942.

McELROY 1970   Cathryn J. McElroy. "Furniture of the Philadelphia Area: Forms and Craftsmen Before 1730." Master's thesis, University of Delaware, 1970.

MESCHUTT   David Meschutt. "A Rediscovered Portrait of James Monroe by Chester Harding." *American Art Journal* 15, no. 4 (autumn 1983): 78–81.

MILLER 1957   V. Isabelle Miller. *Furniture by New York Cabinetmakers, 1650 to 1860.* Exh. cat. New York: Museum of the City of New York, 1957.

MONKHOUSE AND MICHIE   Christopher P. Monkhouse and Thomas S. Michie. *American Furniture in Pendleton House.* Providence: Museum of Art, Rhode Island School of Design, 1986.

MONTGOMERY "REGIONAL PREFERENCES"   Charles F. Montgomery. "Regional Preferences and Characteristics in American Decorative Arts: 1750–1800." In Charles F. Montgomery and Patricia E. Kane, eds., *American Art: 1750–1800, Towards Independence.* Boston: New York Graphic Society for the Yale University Art Gallery and the Victoria and Albert Museum, 1976. 50–65.

MONTGOMERY 1966   Charles F. Montgomery. *American Furniture: The Federal Period in the Henry Francis du Pont Winterthur Museum.* New York: Viking, 1966.

MONTGOMERY AND KANE   Charles F. Montgomery and Patricia E. Kane, eds. *American Art: 1750–1800, Towards Independence.* Boston: New York Graphic Society for the Yale University Art Gallery and the Victoria and Albert Museum, 1976.

MORISON   Samuel Eliot Morison. *The Oxford History of the American People.* New York: Oxford University Press, 1965.

MORRISON ET AL.   Russell Morrison et al. *On the Map: An Exhibit and Catalogue of Maps Relating to Maryland and the Chesapeake Bay.* Exh. cat. Chestertown, Md.: Washington College, 1983.

MORSE 1902   Frances Clary Morse. *Furniture of the Olden Time.* New York: Macmillan, 1902. 2d ed. New York: Macmillan, 1917.

MOSES   Michael Moses. *Master Craftsmen of Newport: The Townsends and Goddards.* Tenafly, N.J.: MMI Americana Press, 1984.

MUDGE 1981   Jean McClure Mudge. *Chinese Export Porcelain for the American Trade.* 2d ed. Newark: University of Delaware Press, 1981.

MUDGE 1986   Jean McClure Mudge. *Chinese Export Porcelain in North America.* New York: Clarkson N. Potter, 1986.

NAYLOR   Maria Naylor. "American Paintings in the Diplomatic Reception Rooms of the Department of State." *The Connoisseur* 192, no. 773 (July 1976): 198–207.

NELSON   Christina H. Nelson. "A Selected Catalogue of the Liverpool-Type Historical Creamwares and Pearlwares in the Henry Francis du Pont Winterthur Museum." Master's thesis, University of Delaware, 1974.

19TH-CENTURY FURNITURE   *19th-Century Furniture and Other Decorative Arts.* Exh. cat. New York: Metropolitan Museum of Art, 1970.

NOËL-HUME   Ivor Noël-Hume. "Creamware to Pearlware: A Williamsburg Perspective." In Ian M. G. Quimby, ed., *Ceramics in America: Winterthur Conference Report.* Charlottesville: University Press of Virginia for the Henry Francis du Pont Winterthur Museum, 1973. 217–54.

NYGREN ET AL.   Edward J. Nygren et al. *Views and Visions: American Landscape Before 1830.* Exh. cat. Washington, D.C.: Corcoran Gallery of Art, 1986.

OLIVER   Andrew Oliver. *Portraits of John Quincy Adams and His Wife.* Cambridge, Mass.: Belknap Press of Harvard University Press, 1970.

OTT   Joseph K. Ott. *The John Brown House Loan Exhibition of Rhode Island Furniture.* Exh. cat. Providence: Rhode Island Historical Society, 1965.

PALMER 1976   Arlene M. Palmer. *A Winterthur Guide to Chinese Export Porcelain.* New York: Crown, 1976.

PARK   Lawrence Park. *Gilbert Stuart: An Illustrated Descriptive List of His Works.* 4 vols. New York: W. E. Rudge, 1926.

PATTERSON   Jerry E. Patterson. *The City of New York: A History Illustrated from the Collections of the Museum of the City of New York.* New York: Harry N. Abrams, 1978.

PAUL REVERE: ARTISAN   *Paul Revere: Artisan, Businessman, and Patriot: The Man Behind the Myth.* Boston: Paul Revere Memorial Association, 1988.

PAUL REVERE'S BOSTON   Jonathan L. Fairbanks et al. *Paul Revere's Boston, 1735–1818.* Exh. cat. Boston: Museum of Fine Arts, 1975.

PENNY   Nicholas Penny, ed. *Reynolds.* Exh. cat. London: Royal Academy of Arts, 1986.

PHILADELPHIA: THREE CENTURIES   *Philadelphia: Three Centuries of American Art.* Exh. cat. Philadelphia: Philadelphia Museum of Art, 1976.

PORCELAINIERS   *Les Porcelainiers du XVIIIc siècle français.* Paris: Librarie Hachette, 1964.

PRIME 1929   Alfred Coxe Prime, comp. *The Arts and Crafts in Philadelphia, Maryland, and South Carolina, 1721–1785: Gleanings from Newspapers.* Topsfield, Mass.: Wayside Press for the Walpole Society, 1929.

PRIME 1932   Alfred Coxe Prime, comp. *The Arts and Crafts in Philadelphia, Maryland, and South Carolina, 1786–1800: Series 2, Gleanings from Newspapers.* Topsfield, Mass.: Wayside Press for the Walpole Society, 1932.

PROWN 1966   Jules David Prown. *John Singleton Copley.* 2 vols. Cambridge, Mass.: Harvard University Press, 1966.

PRUCHA   Francis P. Prucha. *Indian Peace Medals in American History.* Lincoln: University of Nebraska Press, 1971.

RAINWATER   Dorothy T. Rainwater. *Encyclopedia of American Silver Manufacturers.* New York: Crown, 1966.

RALSTON   Ruth Ralston. "Franklin and Louis XVI–A Niderviller Group." *Bulletin of the Metropolitan Museum of Art* 26 (November 1925): 271–73.

RANDALL 1965   *American Furniture in the Museum of Fine Arts, Boston.* Boston: Museum of Fine Arts, 1965.

RANDALL 1974   "Benjamin Frothingham." In Walter Muir Whitehill, Brock Jobe, and Jonathan L. Fairbanks, eds., *Boston Furniture of the Eighteenth Century.* Boston: Colonial Society of Massachusetts, 1974. 223–49.

REED   Robert Reed. *Old Washington, D.C., in Early Photographs, 1846–1932.* New York: Dover, 1980.

REEVES Collection   *Chinese Export Porcelain from the Reeves Collection at Washington and Lee University.* Lexington, Va.: Washington and Lee University, 1973.

RICE   Norman S. Rice. *New York Furniture Before 1840 in the Collection of the Albany Institute of History and Art.* Exh. cat. Albany, N.Y.: Albany Institute of History and Art, 1962.

RODRIGUEZ ROQUE   Oswaldo Rodriguez Roque. *American Furniture at Chipstone.* Madison: University of Wisconsin Press, 1984.

ROLLINS   Alexandra West Rollins. "Furniture in the Collection of the Dietrich American Foundation." *Antiques* 125, no. 5 (May 1984): 1100–19.

RONNBERG   Erik A. R. Ronnberg, Jr. "Imagery and Types of Vessels." In John Wilmerding et al., *Paintings by Fitz Hugh Lane.* New York: Harry N. Abrams, 1988. 61–104.

ROOSEVELT 1968   Theodore Roosevelt. *Ranch Life in the Far West. Reprint.* Flagstaff, Ariz.: Northland, 1968.

ROSENBAUM   Jeanette M. Rosenbaum. *Myer Myers, Goldsmith, 1723–1795.* Philadelphia: Jewish Publication Society of America, 1954.

RUTLEDGE   Anna Wells Rutledge. *Cumulative Record of Exhibition Catalogues: The Pennsylvania Academy of the Fine Arts, 1807–1870; the Society of Artists, 1800–1814; the Artists' Fund Society, 1835–1845.* Memoirs of the American Philosophical Society 38. Philadelphia: American Philosophical Society, 1955.

SACK COLLECTION   *American Antiques from the Israel Sack Collection.* 9 vols. Washington, D.C.: Highland House, 1969–89.

SACK 1950   Albert Sack. *Fine Points of Furniture: Early American.* New York: Crown, 1950.

SACK 1987   Harold Sack. "The Furniture [in the Diplomatic Reception Rooms]." *Antiques* 132, no. 1 (July 1987): 160–73.

SACK 1988   Harold Sack. "The Development of the American High Chest of Drawers." *Antiques* 133, no. 5 (May 1988): 1112–27.

SACK 1989   Harold Sack. "The Bombé Furniture of Boston and Salem, Massachusetts." *Antiques* 135, no. 5 (May 1989): 1178–89.

SAMUELS AND SAMUELS   Peggy Samuels and Harold Samuels. *Frederic Remington: A Biography*. Garden City, N.Y.: Doubleday, 1982.

SCHIFFER AND SCHIFFER   Herbert F. Schiffer and Peter B. Schiffer. *Miniature Antique Furniture*. Wynnewood, Pa.: Livingston Publishing, 1972.

SCHIFFER, SCHIFFER, AND SCHIFFER   Herbert F. Schiffer, Nancy Schiffer, and Peter B. Schiffer. *The Brass Book*. Exton, Pa.: Schiffer Publishing, 1978.

SCHWARTZ AND EHRENBERG   Seymour I. Schwartz and Ralph Ehrenberg. *The Mapping of America*. New York: Harry N. Abrams, 1980.

SCULPTURE OF A CITY   *Sculpture of a City: Philadelphia's Treasures in Bronze and Stone*. New York: Walker, 1974.

SECRETARIES OF STATE 1978   *The Secretaries of State: Portraits and Biographical Sketches*. Department of State Publication 8921. Washington, D.C.: U.S. Department of State, 1978.

SELLERS 1969   Charles Coleman Sellers. *Charles Willson Peale with Patron and Populace: A Supplement to Portraits and Miniatures by Charles Willson Peale*. Transactions of the American Philosophical Society 56. Philadelphia: American Philosophical Society, 1969.

SHAPIRO 1988   Michael Edward Shapiro et al. *Frederic Remington: The Masterworks*. Exh. cat. New York: Harry N. Abrams, 1988.

SHARPE   Elisabeth K. Sharpe. "Chinese Export Porcelain with Arms of Rhode Island." *Antiques* 139, no. 1 (January 1991): 246–55.

SHEPHERD   Raymond V. Shepherd, Jr. "Cliveden and Its Philadelphia–Chippendale Furniture: A Documented History." *American Art Journal* 8, no. 2 (November 1976): 2–16.

SHERATON 1803   Thomas Sheraton. *The Cabinet Dictionary*. 2 vols. London, 1803. Reprint. New York: Praeger, 1970.

SILVER SUPPLEMENT   [Kathryn C. Buhler.] *Silver Supplement to the Guidebook to the Diplomatic Reception Rooms*. Washington, D.C.: U.S. Department of State, 1973.

SMITH 1970   Robert C. Smith. "Masterpieces of Early American Furniture at the United States Department of State." *Antiques* 98, no. 5 (November 1970): 766–73.

SMITH 1972   Thomas E.V. Smith. *The City of New York in The Year of Washington's Inauguration, 1789*. 1889. Reprint. Riverside, Conn.: Chatham Press, 1972.

SMITH 1976   Robert C. Smith. "Architecture and Sculpture in Nineteenth-Century Mirror Frames." *Antiques* 109, no. 2 (February 1976): 350–59.

SPASSKY   Natalie Spassky. *American Paintings in the Metropolitan Museum of Art*. Vol. 2, *A Catalogue of Works by Artists Born Between 1816 and 1845*. Princeton, N.J.: Princeton University Press, 1984.

SWAN 1934   Mabel Munson Swan. *Samuel McIntire, Carver, and the Sandersons: Early Salem Cabinet Makers*. Salem, Mass.: Essex Institute, 1934.

TEMPLEMAN   Eleanor Lee Templeman. "The Lee Service of Cincinnati Porcelain." *Antiques* 118, no. 4 (October 1980): 758–59.

THORNTON 1987   Peter Thornton. "Upholstered Seat Furniture in Europe, 17th and 18th Centuries." In Edward S. Cooke, Jr., ed., *Upholstery in America and Europe from the Seventeenth Century to World War I*. New York: Norton, 1987. 29–38.

TILMANS   Emile Tilmans. *Porcelaines de France*. Paris: Éditions Hypérion, 1953.

TOWNER   Donald Towner. *The Leeds Pottery*. New York: Taplinger, 1965.

TRACY   Berry B. Tracy. *Federal Furniture and Decorative Arts at Boscobel*. New York: Boscobel Restoration, Inc., and Harry N. Abrams, 1981.

TRUETT   Randall Bond Truett, ed. Washington, D.C.: *A Guide to the Nation's Capital*. Rev. ed. New York: Hastings House, 1968.

TRUETTNER   William H. Truettner. *The Natural Man Observed: A Study of Catlin's Indian Gallery*. Exh. cat. Washington, D.C.: Smithsonian Institution Press, 1979.

TUCKER CHINA   *Tucker China, 1825–1838*. Exh. cat. Philadelphia: Philadelphia Museum of Art, 1957.

TYLER   Ron Tyler. *Visions of America: Pioneer Artists in a New Land*. New York: Thames and Hudson, 1983.

VERNER   Coolie Verner. *Smith's Virginia and Its Derivatives*. London: Map Collectors' Circle, no. 5, 1968.

VINCENT   Gilbert T. Vincent. "The Bombé Furniture of Boston." In Walter Muir Whitehill, Brock Jobe, and Jonathan L. Fairbanks, ed., *Boston Furniture of the Eighteenth Century*. Boston: Colonial Society of Massachusetts, 1974. 137–96

VIOLA ET AL.   Herman J. Viola, H. B. Crothers, and Maureen Harman. "The American Indian Genre Paintings of Catlin, Stanley, Wimar, Eastman, and Miller". In Peter H. Hassrick et al., *American Frontier Life: Early Western Paintings and Prints*, New York: Harry N. Abrams, 1987. 131–66.

VON ERFFA AND STALEY   Frederick von Erffa and Allen Staley. *The Paintings of Benjamin West*. New Haven and London: Yale University Press, 1986.

VON SALZEN   Candace Neilson von Salzen. "William Douglas MacLeod, His Life, Curatorship, and Art." Master's thesis, George Washington University, 1981.

WAINWRIGHT   Nicholas B. Wainwright. *Colonial Grandeur in Philadelphia: The House and Furniture of General John Cadwalader*. Philadelphia: Historical Society of Pennsylvania, 1964.

WARD 1983   Barbara McLean Ward. "The Craftsman in a Changing Society: Boston Goldsmiths, 1690–1730." Ph.D. dissertation, Boston University, 1983.

WARD 1988   Barbara McLean Ward. "'In a Feasting Posture': Communion Vessels and Community Values in Seventeenth- and Eighteenth-Century New England." *Winterthur Portfolio* 28, no. 1 (spring 1988): 1–24.

WARD 1988A   Gerald W.R. Ward. *American Case Furniture in the Mabel Brady Garvan and Other Collections at Yale University*. New Haven: Yale University Art Gallery, 1988.

WARD 1989   Barbara McLean Ward. "The Edwards Family and the Silversmithing Trade in Boston, 1692–1762." In Francis J. Puig and Michael Conforti, eds., *The American Craftsman and the European Tradition, 1620–1820*. Hanover, N.H.: University Press of New England for the Minneapolis Institute of Arts, 1989.

WARREN 1975   David B. Warren. *Bayou Bend: American Furniture, Paintings, and Silver from the Bayou Bend Collection*. Houston: Museum of Fine Arts, 1975.

WARREN 1976   David B. Warren. "Bancroft Woodcock: Silversmith, Friend, and Landholder." In *Bancroft Woodcock, Silversmith*. Wilmington: Historical Society of Delaware, 1976.

WATERHOUSE   Ellis Waterhouse. *Painting in Britain 1530 to 1790*. 4th ed. Pelican History of Art Series. New York: Penguin Books, 1978.

WEIDMAN 1984   Gregory R. Weidman. *Furniture in Maryland, 1740–1940: The Collection of the Maryland Historical Society*. Baltimore: Maryland Historical Society, 1984.

WEIDMAN 1989   Gregory R. Weidman. "Baltimore Federal Furniture: In the English Tradition." In Francis J. Puig and Michael Conforti, eds., *The American Craftsman and the European Tradition, 1620–1820*, 256–81. Hanover, N.H.: University Press of New England for the Minneapolis Institute of Arts, 1989.

WEIL   Martin Eli Weil. "A Cabinetmaker's Price Book." In Ian M. G. Quimby, ed., *American Furniture and Its Makers: Winterthur Portfolio* 13. Chicago: University of Chicago Press, 1979. 175–92.

WHITEHILL   Walter Muir Whitehill, Brock Jobe, and Jonathan L. Fairbanks, eds. *Boston Furniture of the Eighteenth Century*. Boston: Colonial Society of Massachusetts, 1974.

WILLARD   John Ware Willard. *Simon Willard and His Clocks*. 1911. Reprint. New York: Dover, 1968.

WILMERDING MARINE PAINTING   John Wilmerding. *American Marine Painting*. 2d rev. ed. New York: HARRY N. ABRAMS, 1987.

WILMERDING ET AL. 1988   John Wilmerding et al. *Paintings by Fitz Hugh Lane*. Exh. cat. Washington, D.C.: National Gallery of Art; New York: Harry N. Abrams, 1988.

WOODHOUSE   Samuel W. Woodhouse, Jr. "Thomas Tufft." *Antiques* 12, no. 4 (October 1927): 292–93.

Index

A

Acheson, Mrs. Dean, 204
Adam, Robert, 126
Adams, John, 104, 112, 125, 129–30, 141
Adams, John Quincy, 121, 138, 166, 173
    portraits of, 16, 30, 102, 130–31, 165, 167, 170–71
Adams, Louisa Catherine Johnson, 16, 30, 102, 130–31,
    164, 166
Adams, Samuel, 103, 104
Affleck, Thomas, 62, 87, 94
Allison, Michael, 31–32, 161, 169–70, 184–85, 192
Allston, Washington, 30, 166
andirons, 135
architectural features, 26, 28–33
Arnold, Benedict, 79
Arthur, Chester A., 182
Ash, Thomas and William, 129
Austin, Josiah, 141
Austin, Nathaniel, 129, 141

B

Backer family, 80
Balch, Daniel, 137
Baldwin, Jesse, 133, 139
Baltimore, 92, 132, 154, 172, 196
Bancroft, George, 176
Bankson, John, 154
Barrett, Walter, 134
Bate, John, 27
Bateman, Hester, 119
Bateman, Peter and William, 103, 119
Bayard family, 83
Beaumont, Gustave de, 134
Beckerdite, Luke, 67
Beekman, James W., 66
Beekman, William, 66
Beekman family, 31
Bellamy, John Haley, 53
Belle, Augustin-Louis, 114
Benjamin Franklin State Dining Room, 17, 26, 31, 32
Bernard, Nicholas, 62
Bialostocki, Jan, 104
Bingham, George Caleb, 174, 200–201
Bird, John N., 153
Blake, John Bradbury, 95
Blatteau, John, 32
Blaylock, Odolph, 31
Bodmer, Karl, 171
bombé form, 28–29, 54–55, 58, 61–62, 73
bookcase, 29, 38–41, 54–55
Bortman, Mark, 15–16
Boston, 60, 62, 73, 74, 129–30, 141, 144–45, 148
Boston Massacre, 100, 104–5
Boudinot, Elias, 183
Bours, John, 72
boxes, 35, 98, 102, 120, 121, 125
Boydell, John, 50
Boze, Joseph, 103, 122
Bryant, William Cullen, 170, 202
Buffon, comte de, 170
Buhler, Kathryn C., 75, 148
Bulfinch, Charles, 132, 174, 194
Burke, Edmund, 63, 126, 128, 173, 175
Burnett, Charles A., 120
Burr, Aaron, 115
Burt, Benjamin, 148
Byers, David, 31
Byrnes, Thomas, 84

C

Caffieri, Jean-Jacques, 142
Caldwell, James, 104
Callender, Joseph, 183
Callow, Stephen, 66
Cant, Thomas, 88
Caproni, P. P., 212
Carracci family, 40
Cartier, Jacques, 38
Cary, Alpheus, 133
case furniture
    bombé chest of drawers, 28–29, 58, 61–62, 73
    bombé desk and bookcase, 54–55
    bureau dressing tables, 29, 62, 70
    commode, 155
    high chest of draawers, 38–40, 90–91
    linen press, 31–32, 169–70, 184–85
    spice chest, 31, 64
Catlin, George, 204
Ceracchi, Giuseppe, 115
chairs
    arm, 31, 80–81, 86, 94, 126–28, 130–32, 162
    easy, 58–59, 77
    roundabout, 72
    side, 28–29, 30, 38–41, 64, 76, 85, 92–93, 133, 159, 175
Chapu, Henri-Michel, 212
Charles V, Holy Roman Emperor, 103
Charlton, Ann Phoebe, 92
Chase, Stephen, 71
Chase family, 183
Chesterfield, Lord, 130
Chippendale, Thomas, 26, 54, 71
Chippendale style, 31, 41, 61–62, 76, 80–81, 92–94
Chisholm, Archibald, 157
Choisy, Claude-Gabriel, marquis de, 114
Christie, Lansdell, 16
Cincinnatus, Lucius Quinctius, 102, 112–13
Claggett, William, 31, 69
Clark, William, 171
Clarke, Daniel, 159
Clarkson, Thomas, 50
Clay, Henry, 20, 173, 178–79, 192
Claypoole, Josiah, 88
Clement family, 183
Clinton, General Henry, 110
clocks, 31, 69, 132, 133, 137, 142, 150
Cody, Buffalo Bill, 212
coffeepots, 61, 84, 129–30, 140, 141
Cogswell, John, 73
Comegys, Cornelius and Catherine, 140
commode, 155
Comstock, Helen, 160
Conger, Clement E., 14, 22, 26–27, 28, 32–33
Connell, James, 62
Copley, John Singleton, 29, 62, 63, 72, 98, 109–11, 132
Corné, Michele Felice, 40, 46–47
Cornelius, Charles, 161
Courteney, Hercules, 62
Crèvecoeur, Hector St. Jean de, 35
Crowninshield, Benjamin Williams, 133, 159
Cumming, William P., 42
Currier & Ives, 175–76, 206–7
Curtis, Lemuel, 137

D

Dallin, Cyrus Edwin, 176, 177, 212–13
d'Angers, Pierre-Jean David, 30, 98–99
Deane, Silas, 108
DeBry, Theodore, 40, 42, 44

Delaveau, Joseph, 90
Delisle, Guillaume, 45
Desham, John, 70
desks, 29, 38–41, 54–55, 102, 121
Dickens, Charles, 194
Dickinson, John, 102
Dietrich, H. Richard, 16
Dolley Madison Powder Room, 31, 126–28
Dulles, John Foster, 182
Dunlap, William, 115, 178
Duval, Claude-Jean Autral, 112

E

eagle motif, 32, 41, 53, 98, 102–3, 112, 129,
    133, 146–47, 158, 160, 177, 184–85
earthenware jug, 156
Elevator Hall, 18–19, 29
Ellison, Thomas, 80
engravings, 42–45, 104–5, 114, 200–201
Entrance Hall, 29, 38–40
Eustis, William, 129
Evans, David, 62

F

Farnsworth, Oliver, 139
Federhen, Deborah A., 148
Fentham, Thomas, 160
Fitzhugh family, 151
Forman, Benno M., 64
Foster, John Watson, 182
Fox, Sarah Pleasants, 65
Francastel, Nicholas-Jean, 112
Franklin, Benjamin, 34, 53, 60, 82, 85, 100,
    101, 123, 128, 142
    depictions of, 29, 108, 138
Franklin, William Temple, 101
Fraprie, Stephen T., 189
Fraser, James Earle, 177
Frémont, Jesse Benton, 138
Frothingham, Benjamin, Jr., 29, 38–41, 54–55, 62

G

Gale, William, 189
Gallaher, William F., 102
Gallery, The, 14–15, 28–29, 58, 175
Gautier, Louis-Adolphe, 201
George C. Marshall Reception Room, 32
Geyer, Frederick William, 148
Giles, James H., 183
Gillingham, James, 62, 85
Ginsburg, Benjamin, 16, 28
goblets, 170, 174, 189
Goddard family, 31, 62, 68–70
gold, 170, 174, 189
Gordon, Elinor, 133
Gostelowe, Jonathan, 62
Goupil, Vibert & Co., 174
Goya, Francisco, 104
Grant, Anne, 66
Grant, Ulysses S., 182
Great Seal of the United States, 32, 41, 98,
    103, 112, 129, 139, 146, 177
Greenberg, Allan, 20–21, 29–30, 31, 32–33
Greenough, Horatio, 133
Grenville, Hester, 95

H

Hamilton, Alexander, 115
Hamilton, Dr. Alexander, 75
Harding, Samuel, 67
Hariot, John, 42
Harmar, General Josiah, 123
Harrison, Benjamin, 182
Harrold, Robert, 71
Hayes, Rutherford B., 182
Hays, Judith, 148
Hays, Moses Michael, 25, 130, 144–45, 148
Heckscher, Morrison H., 62, 79, 94
Heflin, Pat, 14
Hemphill, Alexander Wills, 153
Henry Clay Dining Room, 24–25
Hepplewhite, George, 126, 154, 159, 184
Hersey, George L., 32–33
Hill, Samuel, 46
Hogarth, William, 24, 62–63
Hoheb, Arthur Bruce, 30, 98–99
Hole, William, 44
Holmes, J. B. S., 151
Homans, Robert, 16
Hooper, Robert Chamblett, 109
Hope, Thomas, 163
Hopkins, Gerrard, 92
Hopkins, Stephen, 68
Hornor, William MacPherson, 90
Houdon, Jean-Antoine, 30, 101, 106, 142
Howe, General William, 110
Howell, James, 196
Howell, William, 60
Hughes, Jasper W., 189
Hull, John, 58
Hulme, John, 153
Humphreys, Richard, 84, 128
Hunnewell, Jonathan, 145
Hurd, Jacob, 30, 61, 74–75, 128

J

James, Edward, 62
James Madison State Dining Room, 28, 31, 133
James Monroe Reception Room, 13–15, 31–32,
    129, 169–70
Jarvis, John Wesley, 101, 116
Jay, John, 101, 116–17, 139
Jefferson, Martha, 103, 122
Jefferson, Thomas, 18, 63, 101, 125, 168, 170–72
    objects owned by, 103, 121, 122
    portraits of, 30, 31, 98–99, 102, 106–7
John Quincy Adams State Drawing Room, 22–24,
    30, 58–59, 101, 102, 130–31
Johnson, T. B., 166
Jones, Edward Vason, 14–19, 22–24, 28–31
Jones, John Paul, 30, 31
Jones, William, 160
Jugiez, Martin, 62
jugs, 133, 139, 156

K

Kennedy, Archibald, 134
Kettell, Jonathan, 137
Key, Francis Scott, 38–41, 92
Key, John Ross, 92
King, Charles Bird, 118, 170–71, 172, 190
Kirk, Samuel Child, 174, 196–97
Kissinger, Henry A., 17
knife box, 35, 102

Knight, William, 71
Knox, Henry J., 112–14

L

La Tour, Maurice Quentin de, 122
Lafayette, marquis de, 124, 172
Lane, Fitz Hugh, 172–73, 174, 180–81
Latrobe, Benjamin Henry, 172
Laurens, Henry, 101
Lawrence, Thomas, 166
Lawson, Richard, 154
Lee, Arthur, 108
Lee, Henry "Light-Horse Harry," 25, 113
L'Enfant, Pierre Charles, 112, 114, 129
Leonard, Benjamin, 192
Leonard, Jacob, 120
Leslie, Charles Robert, 30, 130–31, 164–67
LeTellier, John, 140
Leupp, Charles M., 202
Leveau, Jean Jacques, 114
Lewis, Meriwether, 171
Lewis, Samuel, 120
linen press, 31–32, 169–70, 184–85
lithographs, 174–76, 202–3, 206–7
Livingston, Robert, 171
Locke, John, 24
Logan, James, 34
Lomazzo, Giovanni Paolo, 27
Long, Stephen H., 171
Loockerman, Vincent, 31, 94
Louis XVI, King of France, 108
Louisiana Purchase, 168, 171

M

MacLeod, William Douglas, 172–73, 194–95
Macomber, Walter M., 13–15, 31
Madison, Dolley, 20, 143, 172
Madison, James, 20, 140, 143, 170–71, 172, 190
Mallet, Louis, 142
Manigault, Charles, 183
Mannings, David, 110
mantels, 100, 134
maps, 38, 40, 42–45, 214
Marchant, Adeline B., 178
Marchant, Edward Dalton, 173, 178–79
Martha Washington Ladies' Lounge, 16, 31, 60
Martineau, Harriet, 194
Masi, Seraphim, 120
Mather, Increase, 27
McClelland, Nancy, 192
McIntire, Samuel, 46, 53, 159
medals, 41, 98, 101–2, 118
Mengs, Anton Raphael, 40
Mickle, Samuel, 62
Mifflin, Thomas, 64
Millard, Herbert, 30
mirrors, 35, 58, 89, 160
Moll, Herman, 40, 45
Monroe, James, 171, 172–73, 191
Montgomery, Charles F., 160, 192
Montresor, John, 110
Montresor, Mrs. John, 29, 98, 110–11
Moore, John Chandler, 189
Moran, Thomas, 32, 176–77, 210–11
Mount, William Sidney, 174, 202–3
Mulliken, Samuel, 137
Myers, Myer, 78, 130
Myers, Samuel, 148

N

Nast, Jean Nepomucène Hermann, 143
Native Americans, 102, 118, 170, 177, 204–5, 212–13
neoclassicism, 126–33
New York, 60, 62, 66, 77–81, 134–35, 155,
    161–63, 188, 192
Newcomb, Lucinda, 192
Newport, 62, 68–70
Niderville factory, 29, 108
Nini, Jean-Baptiste, 142
Nixon, Richard, 28
Noël, Alphonse-Léon, 174, 202–3

P

paintings
    historical, 32, 40–41, 46–47, 50–51, 56–57
    landscape, 32, 33, 41, 52, 173–74, 176, 180–81,
        186–87, 194–95, 210–11
    portrait, 40–41, 49, 96–97, 101, 102, 106–7, 110–11,
        115–17, 124, 172–73, 178–79, 182, 190–91
    portrait miniatures, 103, 109, 122–23
    still life, 32, 174, 198–99
    Western subjects, 204–5, 208–11
Palladio, Andrea, 24
Palmer, Francis F., 170, 206–7
Parkman, Francis, 175
Parsons, Ella, 85
Parsons, William, 85
Paschall, Joseph, 88
Peale, Charles Willson, 31, 102, 106–7, 123, 170
Peale, Raphaelle, 123
Peale, Titian Ramsay, 171
pearlware, 156
Pelham, Henry, 100, 104
Pelletreau, Elias, 16
Pelletreau, Mr. and Mrs. Robert H., 16
Penn, John, 50, 87
Penn, William, 34, 50
Penn family, 93
Phalipon, Adolphe, 124, 172
Philadelphia, 34–35, 60, 62, 64–65, 67, 87–88, 90–94,
    128, 133, 140, 149, 153
Phyfe, Duncan, 20, 31, 126–28, 132, 161, 162–63, 192
Pickering, Timothy, 41, 48, 112, 128
Pitt, William, 95, 100
polygrams, 115
Poole, William, 84
porcelain
    American, 133, 153
    basket, 25
    Chinese export, 25, 133, 129
    covered tureen and stand, 152
    dinner services, 25, 129, 132, 151, 183
    English, 156
    French, 132, 139, 143
    garniture, 136
    jugs, 133, 139
    plates, 103, 113, 146–47, 177, 183
    punch bowl, 24, 25, 188
    statuette, 29, 108
Porter, William, 76
Poussin, Nicolas, 40
Powell, Colin, 18
Powell, John Wesley, 210, 212
Price, William, 60
Prime, Nathaniel, 134
Prown, Jules, 109

Quakers, 34–35
Queen Anne style, 31, 61, 64, 74–75

Raleigh, Sir Walter, 38, 42
Randolph, Benjamin, 62, 94, 102
Ransom, Carolyn Olson, 170–71
Raphael, 40
Regency style, 132
Remington, Frederic, 176, 177, 208–9
Revere, Paul, 25, 58, 62, 100, 104–5, 129–30,
    132, 141, 144–45, 148
Revolutionary War, 100–101
Reynolds, Helen Wilkinson, 134
Richardson, Francis, 149
Richardson, Joseph, Sr., 84, 118
Richardson, Joseph, Jr., 84, 102, 118, 128, 149
Richardson, Nathaniel, 84, 128, 149
Richardt, Ferdinand, 33, 41, 52
Robb, Sarah Carson, 133
Robinson, Thomas, 60
Rockwell, Norman, 174
Roesen, Severin, 32, 174, 198–99
Rogers, William P., 17
Rollins, Alexandra W., 14
Roosevelt, Theodore, 176, 177, 208–9
Rupp, Israel Daniel, 175
Rush, William, 53
Rusk, Dean, 16–17, 18
Ruskin, John, 186
Russell, Jemima, 128
Rust, Enoch, Jr., 121
Ryder, James F., 56

Sack, Harold, 16, 94
St. Clair, Arthur, 123
St. Memin, Charles de, 132
Salmon, Robert, 180
Sanderson, Robert, 58
Sanson, Nicolas, 45
Sargent, Ignatius, 183
Sargent family, 183
Sartain, John, 174, 200
Sauvage, Charles-Gabriel, 108
Savage, Edward, 116
Savery, William, 62, 65
Scheffer, Ary, 124
Schweizer, Paul D., 115
sculpture, 30, 98–99, 133, 176, 177, 212–13
settees. See sofas and settees
Seymour, Samuel, 171
Seymour, Thomas, 26
Shaw, John, 132, 157, 184
Shaw, Joshua, 173, 186–87
Shaw, Samuel, 113, 129
Sheraton, Thomas, 26, 126, 163
Shoemaker, Jonathan, 92
Shultz, George P., 17
sideboard, 130, 132, 154
silver, 61–62, 129–30, 174
    bowl, 144
    coffee and tea service, 140
    coffeepots, 61, 84, 129–30, 141
    consular seal, 98, 119
    covered sugar basin, 128, 149

    medals, 102, 118
    repoussé, 196
    salver, 82
    sauceboat, 75
    sugar basket, 145
    tankards, 30, 61, 74, 78
    teapots, 83, 130, 148
    water pitcher, 174, 196–97
skippet, 98, 120, 177
Skipwith, Fulwar, 143
Smith, George, 126, 163
Smith, James, 128
Smith, Captain John, 44
Smith, Robert C., 160
Smith, William, Jr., 60
Smither, James, 128
snuff box, 125
Society of the Cincinnati, 24, 25, 41, 101–3, 112–14, 129
sofas and settees, 60, 62–63, 66, 87, 126–28, 132, 163
Sparrow, Thomas, 157
Sprague, Dr., 54
Stanley, John Mix, 175, 204–5
Steuben, Frederick Wilhelm von, 112
Steward, Joseph, 72
Storer, Ebenezer, 15, 29, 61–62, 73
Stuart, Gilbert, 29, 40, 49, 101, 116, 132
Sully, Thomas, 173, 191
Suzanne, François-Marie, 142
Syng, John, 82
Syng, Philip, Jr., 82–83

tables
    card, 31, 79, 126–28, 129, 132, 157, 158,
        161, 172–73, 192–93
    china, 30, 71, 130–31
    tea, 31, 61, 67, 88
tankards, 74, 78
Tayloe, Benjamin Henry, 192
teapots, 83, 130, 140, 148
Thayer, Sylvanus, 146, 177
Thayer, William M., 176
Thomas Jefferson State Reception Room, 17,
    30–31, 62–63, 98, 100–101, 172–73
Thomson, Charles, 128
Tocqueville, Alexis de, 134
Townsend, Edmund, 70
Townsend family, 31, 62, 68–70
Townshend Acts, 100, 104
Treaty Room, 20–21, 33, 170–71
Trenchard, James, 149
True, Joseph, 159
Trumbull, John, 106, 115
Tucker, William Ellis, 133, 153
Tuckerman, Edward, 145
Tufft, Thomas, 62, 65, 85

Valois, Gabriel, 62
Van Rensselaer, Stephen, 96–97
Van Wagenen family, 77
Vanderlyn, John, 52
Varick, Abraham, 79
Varick, Richard, 79
Varick family, 31
vases, 136, 138
Verplanck, Samuel, 66
Vitruvius Pollio, Marcus, 27

Wady, James, 69
wall plaque, 53
wall sconces, 169–70
Wansey, Elijah, 84
Warner, Andrew Ellicott, 196
Warwick, Alice Harrison, 16
Washington, George, 27, 79, 87, 100–103, 112,
    114, 118, 126, 128, 134, 135
    objects owned by, 24, 25, 41, 48, 113
    portraits of, 29, 30, 40, 49, 101, 133, 138, 142
Washington, George Steptoe, 157
Washington, Lucy, 157
Washington, Samuel, 157
water pitchers, 133, 153, 174, 196–97
Weaver, William J., 115
Webb, Daniel, 63
Wedgwood, Josiah, 156
Wentworth, John, 71
West, Benjamin, 40, 50–51, 166
Whipple, William, 71
White, Hannah, 109
White, John, 40, 42–43, 44
Whittingham, Richard, Sr., 135
Whittingham, Richard, Jr., 135
Wied, Maximilian, Prince zu, 171
Wilkes, John, 100
Willard, Archibald, 32, 56–57
Willard, Simon, 133, 137, 150
Williams, Samuel, 88
Wilson, Richard, 186
wine cooler, 41, 48, 128
Wingate, Paine, 137
Wollett, William, 50
Wood, Charles, 189
Wood, David, 137
Wood, Jacob, 189
Wood, Joseph, 190
Woodcock, Bancroft, 61, 84
Woodcock, Isaac, 84
Wordsworth, William, 202
Wright, Joseph, 186
writing box, 102, 121
Wyllis, George, 72

Young, Moses and Stephen, 161